1993

Exploring the Midwestern Literary Imagination

David D. Anderson
Founder, Society for the Study of Midwestern Literature

Exploring the Midwestern Literary Imagination

Essays in Honor of David D. Anderson

edited by
Marcia Noe

The Whitston Publishing Company
Troy, New York
1993

Library of Congress Catalog Card Number 92-64472

ISBN 0-87875-430-X

Printed in the United States of America

Acknowledgements

Special thanks are due to Roger Bresnahan and Marc Van Wormer of Michigan State University for the hard work they have done on this project and for their patience and good counsel.

Contents

Dimensions of the Literary Midwest

Midwestern Literary Identities

Midwestern Discontinuities

Foreword

Dave Anderson as Audience: An Essay on Reception Aesthetics

Ronald Primeau

A "Festschrift for David D. Anderson," the announcement read. What a good idea, and the memories swarmed in: the significant books he's written, the enthusiasm he spreads around, the twenty years of instructive and enjoyable academic conferences he's organized. Others in this volume will celebrate Dave as an exemplary teacher-scholar, a sensitive and prolific author. Life-long friends will share memories. I haven't known Dave as well as many others have. I was never his student, at least not in any formal sense. I never taught with him, at least not in a classroom. We didn't sit on committees or write grant proposals together. But I, too, have my stories to tell, and they all somehow come back to seeing Dave, the author-editor-teacher-scholar-conference planner, as a solitary figure sitting in the audience *listening* to all he brought together.

The twenty years of the Society for the Study of Midwestern Literature roughly parallel my academic career. I left graduate school in 1971, went to teach at Central Michigan, and attended my first Society meeting down the road in East Lansing a year later. By that time I had been to eight or ten academic conferences, but none of them prepared me for what I would find at my first SSML. It's all been said before about the cooperation, the enthusiasm and the spirit of sharing at Society conferences. I listened a great deal and people welcomed me in. The atmosphere seemed rigorous enough but not really threatening: no one-upmanship, no name dropping, and credential building saved for elsewhere. The force behind these meetings was, as we know, David D. Anderson. But how exactly did he do it?

Back home in the classroom I am primarily a teacher of composition. I profess a belief in a process-oriented writing model with heavy emphasis on revision; a major element of that revising is audience awareness. I do a great deal of work with audience adaptation, anticipatory feedback and audience-building. Walter Ong was telling us back in 1975 how useful it was to understand that "The Writer's Audience Is Always a Fiction," and I was trying to make the composition class a laboratory for understanding how all that fictionalizing can work out with good results. At the same time, I didn't expect to find much connection between teaching composition and a scholarly conference on midwestern literature. I had been led to believe (no one to blame but myself) that fretting over whether the right hand knew what the left was doing would just increase professional anxiety. I started writing papers for these annual meetings, and I would mention to my students what I was up to. They were curious about who my audience was at these (and other) professional conferences. Again that solitary figure of Dave Anderson out in the crowd, listening and encouraging. Was Dave Anderson a prototype audience? Is that how he worked his magic for the Society?

For about 15 years I've also taught literary theory, and I have a special interest in reader-response criticism or what is now often called reception theory. Again Ong, but also Gerald Prince (1973) who says that every author develops his narrative as "a function of a certain type of reader whom he bestows with certain qualities, faculties, and inclinations according to his opinion of men in general (or in particular) and according to the obligations he feels should be respected." Composition and literary theory were thus intertwined, but would a midwestern literature conference be connected to either or both? At the Society meetings I saw one version of Prince's "particular," that solitary figure in the crowd again who not only listened but answered mail, sought manuscripts for publication, stimulated real discussion from the floor, and (with his seemingly indefatigable and indispensable wife Pat) gave an annual party aptly called a "convivium." Is Dave Anderson Riffaterre's "super reader" after all? Is he Poulet's "self on loan to another"? What can all this Society work be but Sartre's "generosity"? And as my composition students and I kept learning, anticipation of this "generosity" guides purpose, shapes the work, *energizes* a developing text. Prince says "writers frequently have a public they don't deserve." I felt that at Society meetings and it was all to the good.

For these twenty years Dave Anderson has been both real and fictionalized audience for me and for countless others. I think my stories are typical. I often wrote to Dave with suggestions for conference papers or research projects. It amazed me that this super-busy overachiever never failed to respond. Those short handwritten notes always got right to the point and managed to mix business and pleasure as if they should never be separated. What he said was always encouraging, sometimes provocative or surprising. He told me once that he knew people who were on the scene of what I was "covering," and it wasn't quite like what I'd proposed (get the facts, Ron). In response to one of my electronic projects, he stated, "I'm a book man myself, chalk and blackboard" (be careful of the McLuhan Staff, Ron). I noticed, though, that the "book man" encouraged and helped with films and videos by others before it was all that fashionable. Encouragement—something new—enthusiasm in the seasoned scholar. These handwritten notes answered questions patiently, even when they were opening right on an idea for me when for him the show had been running a while. These notes and phone calls would also set up opportunities, bring people together productively, and help me enjoy even more work I already liked. Dave has always been a masterful editor as well, great to be on panels with, and (a real test) seems even to enjoy his own parties. A wide-ranging and sympathetic reader, he is an insightful and understated and good-natured critic. Five years into my career, I remember fishing for gimmicks from a man who doesn't know the meaning of the word. I wanted to know how to "take off" or "make it big" or some such. "Just keep doing your work," he would say, admonishing yet knowing I needed a lift at the same time, confident that I'd find my way.

Dave Anderson as audience was contagious in the Society. The people who came to the meetings did their homework. They could blockbuster it with the best of them but brought along instead graciousness and good humor. These were not merely "competent" but close to "ideal" readers—readers and listeners who "co-created" the texts and presented with warmth and integrity. It was Bleich's community of interpreters, creating

Barthes's readerly texts, Eco's open texts, Rosenblatt's "exploration." Bloom's "strong readers" came regularly to the Kellogg Center. My paradigm of what constituted an academic conference had shifted. Dave's "misprision" was leading the way to a reexamination of midwestern culture, regional studies and the canon of American literature as a whole. Dave has been simply elegant at inviting people in on what Sullivan calls an "ongoing conversation about literature." He invites us in, makes us all comfortable and secure, then sits and listens to us listening to each other.

Dave is a multi-faceted audience. "Fit audience, though few" reminds me that I have a few more stories. Dave and I were on a MLA program together in New York the first morning of the convention at 8:00 a.m. Almost no one came. Nonetheless, I felt I had a good audience sitting next to me, and Dave acted as though he were speaking to hundreds. Humor has always been a big ingredient also. At one of the Society's annual meetings, I was on a panel with Dave, Gene Dent, Jerry Nemanic, and Clarence Andrews. Our topic was "Is there a Midwest? If so, how do we define it?" Gene got the bright idea that Dave would speak last, and the four of us would proclaim that after years of deliberation, we'd reluctantly concluded that it was doubtful that such a place existed. I think we managed the hoax well enough for 10-15 minutes, and a bewildered Dave gave us more than we had asked for in response. Calm, receptive, good on the uptake, he suggested we might be out of our minds.

Maybe this isn't complex theory I'm presenting here, but I think the connections Dave enacts are important in academic life today. Teacher-scholars ought to behave at professional conferences in ways at least consistent with what they expect of their students. Audience in composition classes ought to mean the same thing it does in literature classes or in classes in literary theory. In general our rhetorical and literary theories ought to match up with what we profess to be about in our own work. Dave Anderson is very good at making connections. When I worked in a restaurant, I saw a good manager who knew how to do (and would do himself) anything he expected anyone else to do. At the SSML annual meetings, I saw Dave handling correspondence, welcoming people, coordinating the schedule, editing publications, pouring water, introducing people, presenting papers. He was seasoned at all this (and of course didn't do it alone). Yet he would also sit out there in that audience and attend each conference like it was his first. A buoyant rookie out there—a humble figure sitting in the audience at the conferences he had planned and nursed along. A formidable yet unintimidating presence, he'd ask questions. I'm not sure how everyone reacted to this but I'd be refreshed, refueled. I'd forgive myself for being naive. I'd leave every one of the conferences encouraged I was probably doing all right, anxious to write to several people, ready to explore some new angles. With my students I'd keep on anticipating audience response. That letter writer, editor, author, solitary figure in the crowd would help me fictionalize readers. Dave's convivium was always a great reception; the mood was Whitman's "profound lesson of reception" ("Song of the Open Road"); this is reception aesthetics in practice. Dave Anderson as audience may be his most significant legacy for us all—so far.

In *The Cool Fire* Bob Shanks has defined the chief task of the television director as playing the role of the audience for the talent all along the way until they are actually on the air. Shanks directed the game show *Concentration* with great success for over ten years. Dave has been the director of SSML for two decades. He searches out, develops, teaches, encourages, and listens to the talent. All this might be what we like about him the most.

Good readers often write well because they know how readers behave, the research tells us. This is, of course, true about Dave's own writing. And he has also built an audience in SSML, not as an apologist for midwestern literature, but by bringing together people with different skills and interests, by bringing together the scholarly and the popular. Dave as audience is contagious. Has DeWar's featured him in a profile yet? "In the past twenty years David Anderson has read almost everything, written a dozen great books and shaped the SSML. He ranges back to the classics but has a special interest in the American Midwest. He enjoys books and buys many antiques, travels around the world, is known as a synthesizer." (I don't actually know his scotch.)

I haven't said anything new for people who know Dave. They know what kind of audience he is. This project is "a secret from Dave Anderson" read the Festschrift project announcement from the SSML Executive Board and officers. "Do not contact Dave with questions or comments about this project." They were right to worry. We might routinely have contacted

Dave. Of course. We often do. Though I heeded the warning, I couldn't help but look over my shoulder, fictionalize a bit, look out into that crowd, and imagine that ideal reader listening.

Introduction

Marcia Noe

In 1971, David D. Anderson founded the Society for the Study of Midwestern Literature to define and explore the midwestern literary imagination.

At its first annual meeting, members focused their discussions on three topics: "The Dimensions of the Midwest: Geographic and Literary," "The Durability of Midwestern Literary Identities," and "Identifiable Cultural Elements in Midwestern Life and Literature."

In his keynote address at the 20th annual meeting of the Society, Dave Anderson noted that these three topics have continued to be its guiding concerns, suggesting lines of inquiry that scholars of midwestern literature have pursued in their work over the past 20 years. Is there such a thing as the Midwest, in terms of geography as well as in terms of literature, and if there is, how do we define it? Is there a canon of midwestern literature and, if so, which authors are included? What elements of our culture make it uniquely midwestern?

The essays collected in this volume reaffirm Dave's assertion that these three questions still guide our work today. In the first section, Frederick Stern explores several ways of defining midwestern literature. Leland Krauth suggests an operational definition of midwestern literature as he discusses many writers of the region who have been nurtured and sustained by the work of Mark Twain. Douglas Wixson and Roger Bresnahan test the boundaries of midwestern literature as Wixson discusses the career of a proletarian novelist and Bresnahan makes a case for midwestern influence on the work of a Philippine writer.

In the second section, Philip Gerber and William Miller discuss two thoroughly midwestern writers now firmly ensconced in the canon of American literature while Scott Donaldson and John Hallwas write about authors who come less readily to mind when one thinks of midwestern literature, at the same time locating them within midwestern contexts.

In the third section, scholars examine those aspects of the region that Ronald Primeau has called our "inexhaustible midwestern contraries" (32). Jill Gidmark traces an image pattern in the fiction of a Minnesota writer that lends a sinister quality to rural settings often imagined as idyllic. Bernard Engel discusses T. S. Eliot's double regional identity and the resulting dualities in his poetry. Guy Szuberla focuses on the double-sided image of Babel in Chicago fiction. Ellen Uffen examines ethnic tensions in an urban midwestern context while Robert Narveson looks at religious conflict in the rural Midwest. Kenneth Robb shows how two midwestern writers give new dimensions to a well-known midwestern character type.

In the two essays that frame this collection, Ronald Primeau and James Seaton characterize the man this book honors largely through paradoxical statements. David D. Anderson is described as "a formidable yet unintimidating presence"; a prolific writer who is an ideal audience, a highly published scholar who has made helping younger members of the Society one of his highest priorities. Like the literature he has studied for over 20 years, Dave Anderson embodies paradoxes and dualities. And like the region of his birth, Dave exemplifies Primeau's "distinctively midwestern fusion of disparate elements" (33), elements which have enriched and strengthened the man, the literature, and the region.

Work Cited

Primeau, Ronald. "Slave Narrative Turning Midwestern: Deadwood Dick Rides into Difficulties." *MidAmerica* 1 (1974): 16-35.

Dimensions of the Literary Midwest

What is "Regionalism," and If You Know That, Where Does the Midwest Begin and End?

Frederick C. Stern

"Regionalism" as a concept has been an aspect of literary studies in the United States for a long time now. Though some of our earlier critics seemed not conscious of a literature outside of New England and New York, in time it became clear that there is indeed a literature outside these centers, that often it is important, and that it has to be considered. In the "Introduction" to volume 2 of *The American Tradition in Literature,* in a section entitled "Regionalism," Bradley, Beatty and Long write:

> Mark Twain, the earliest gigantic figure among the regionalists, was indebted, like Harte and Cable and other contemporaries, to progenitors among the humbler comic journalists. From the Age of Jackson onward, they had inundated the popular press with anecdotes and fiction drawn from sources deep in the common life of America. In this literature, most of it decidedly regional in character, the humorous anecdote mingled with white and Negro folklore, with frontier tall tales and hunting stories, and with folk song and balladry. The best of the regional literature, serious and comic, ultimately provided a better understanding of the United States as a whole . . . a movement that had begun in broad humor and in the wider horizons of the West and Southwest produced also, particularly among the women writers and the New Englanders, the accurate depiction of the domestic scene, the narrow life, the individual character, caught in some humble light that reminds the readers of the work of *genre* painters of the Flemish school, at once highly individuated and intensely national. In fiction thus motivated, the in-

> creasing consciousness of the influence of environment on character and fate prepared the way for the growing spirit of naturalistic and sociological determinism (7-8).

It is difficult to know quite where to begin, if one wanted to take issue with several of the assumptions about the nature of art and nation implicit in this statement, but fortunately, I need not do so here. I am more interested in noting the view of region implied in such a statement.

The source for such a conception of literary regionalism lay, it ought to be clear, in a conception of political and economic regionalism that gave literary regionalism at least the semblance of validity. In 1943, in a volume of massive importance for its day, the historian of ideas Merle Curti writes:

> The colonies not only differed from Europe in physical environment and social conditions, they differed from one another; and each colony was further divided into regions, some of which had much in common with similar regions in neighboring provinces. The differences between the settled districts along the seacoast and the less populated inland or frontier country were no less striking. He who swung an axe in the back country had a different outlook from the merchant, the artisan, or the planter in the coastal regions. The varied economies that developed as a result of differences in soil, climate and natural resources in New England, the Middles Colonies, the Southern Colonies and the back country in all these sections affected the number and character of schools, libraries, colleges, newspapers, and indirectly the most basic attitudes toward nature and society (27).

Even from this brief citation it is clear, I think, that the notion of "region" as a category by means of which one can understand the experience of the United States is deeply ingrained in our intellectual history as well as in our literary history. "Regionalism," then, was seen for many years a powerful source of explanation for much that was complex in the American experience.

But how significant, valid or useful—even, if I may be permitted a very old-fashioned term—how true is it? As we re-examine the canon of the literature of the United States, subjecting it to newer tests having to do with gender, class and ethnicity; as we apply fairly recent currents in "theory" to our study of this particular national literature, is "region" still a concept we can find useful? As we look at a United States—not to mention a world—to some degree at least homogenized by the incredible explosion in communications of the last several decades, from the television set to the computer to the jet plane, what use can we still make of the conception of regionalism, especially as a literary category?

One does not need to look very far to find serious questions raised about the concept of "region." In his recent very important work *Beyond Ethnicity*, Werner Sollors treats the issue of region as analogous to, at times facing the same problematics as, the major category the title of his work describes. In a chapter provocatively entitled "The Ethics of Wholesome Provincialism," Sollors writes that "Americans have adopted and continued to create complicated and unsystematically overlapping forms of particular regional, ethnic and religious identities." He goes on: "The Americans' unsystematic desire to identify with intermediary groups—larger than the family, smaller than the nation—may be based on real or imagined descent, on old or newly adopted religions, on geographic area of origin, socialization, or residence, on external categorization, on voluntary association, or on defiance" (175-6).

Sollors' point is telling. In an effort to understand the peculiarities of the culture of this large and complex nation, efforts at subdivision have been many. One might add to Sollors' list such recently important division terms as "generation," and, with special emphasis, "gender," or even "sexual preference." Sollors goes on to identify what seem to him to be the problematics of divisions like ethnicity and region: "What is prominent in ethnic and regional conceptualizations," he writes,

> is not the complex model that such an intricate situation would require but a surprisingly resilient pattern that includes the following recurring elements:
>
> 1. Dualistic procedures which juxtapose regions and ethnic groups with something elusive one may call the "un-region" and the "un-ethnic group."
>
> 2. Dichotomizations of regionalisms and ethnicities into "good" and "bad" forms, usually on the understanding that good and organic group identities are located in the *juste milieu* between two bad ones.

> 3. Interpretations of regions and ethnic groups that are at once analogous to the nation and to the individual, with the result that even the *scholarly* rhetoric of regionalism and ethnicity reflects the redemptive rhetoric of American civil religion and that the search for "good" group identity permeates American culture (176).

Sollors then discusses examples of such "divisions" from a remarkably wide variety of writers, ranging from Josiah Royce and Randolph Bourne to W. E. B. DuBois. In all cases, it seems to me, he indicates the logical and rhetorical problems such divisions entail. It is not my intent here to follow Sollors' discussion of ethnicity—itself a matter of serious and important dispute—but to take the issue of region, which he uses merely as one example of "divisions," and to examine it in more detail. My method here will diverge from Sollors' as well. I am not so much interested in focusing on *texts* that deal with this issue as I am in asking how the matter has been used in literary and cultural studies.

What *use* has been made of the concept of region? In some instances, region has been merely an organizational means—the Midwest Modern Language Association, the South Atlantic Modern Language Association—which has not staked any claims for some uniqueness, for more than merely useful separation from "un-region." But that has certainly not been true in all cases. A society which states in its very name that it will *study* midwestern literature is also making a claim that the category is a *subject*, with borders and limitations, and that the geographic portion of the title gives some special hallmark to literature which can be called "midwestern."

I. "Region" is a Myth

The questions *this* raises are many. Does such a title suggest some value judgment about the literature it purports to study—or, in other words, is midwestern literature *better* than other regional literatures—southern say, or New England, Atlantic Seaboard or Far Western? If it is not better, then does not the title at the very least suggest that a literature which can be called "midwestern" is, by the very nature of that geographic designation, *different from* literature from other such regions—and, of course, if we accept "midwestern" we must also accept these other regional designations as having some validity. If, then, midwestern literature is different from other literatures—different enough to make a valid basis for its study *qua* midwestern literature, in what do such differences lie? Do they lie in the locale in which the literature takes place? Do they lie in the place of birth of the writer, or the place of residence, or both or either? If one is talking about theatre, which involves not only writing but also production, is the study of midwestern theatre limited to work written by writers "from" the Midwest, or can it also include the *production* of plays in the Midwest—or only plays which are set in the Midwest? And of course, to make the problem here even more difficult, if we talk about film, do we mean film produced in the Midwest, or only film about the Midwest? Is there something else—some flavor, some way of using language, some stylistic or conceptual structure, that can identify a "midwestern" text, regardless of its locale, or the origin or domicile of its author? If "Midwest" literature is a significant category, how does it relate to other divisions of the literature of the United States which we might well study? Ethnicity and gender rank first in such divisions, because each of them has about it concerns of oppression and therefore require the most careful consideration, but there are other possible divisions. Can we consider "popular culture of the Midwest?" Can we consider a proper topic for study "African-American writers of the Midwest" or "Jewish women writers of the Midwest" or "working-class writers of the Midwest?" The question in all these cases is the same, of course—what does "Midwest" add to the delineation of the topic of study which is of value and not merely geographically adventitious?

The problem is even more complicated when one considers just what "the Midwest" is. One journal, *The Old Northwest,* has resolved the issue by stating that it takes its title and its interests from the states that were originally part of the old "Northwest Territory." But this historic designation, while perhaps useful for the journal, doesn't in any way demonstrate that these states *in the present* constitute any sort of entity which one can contrast with "non-Old Northwest Territory," or that literature from "the Territory" has any special qualities. For another instance of the difficulty involved in deciding where the Midwest begins and ends, I will take the liberty of quoting myself.

Writing about the North Dakota-born poet Thomas McGrath, I described his "particular agrarian 'midwesternism,'" and then added, "I do not want to make of McGrath a 'midwestern poet' by any means." Describing the variety of locales which play a role in his long poem *Letter to an Imaginary Friend*, I end my discussion by writing: "Moreover, *midwestern* is a term of peculiar application to the North Dakota farm country west of the Minnesota border where he was raised, since in some designations this portion of the nation can also be seen as the beginning of 'the West.' Indeed, what Frederick Manfred describes as 'Siouxland' . . . was described in a collection of essays by [the collection's] title *Where The West Begins*. Among localities discussed in this volume are western Minnesota, North Dakota, and some contiguous areas" (12). "The Midwest" then, is a geographic locale a little uncertain, in Sollors' term certainly an "unsystematic" locale, which, though perhaps its center is clear, has borders that waver, east, west and south (though the Canadian border limits it at the north, if we want to remain within the political boundaries of the United States of America). Other regions are more clearly defined, perhaps by a common and readily identifiable history, as are the New England states and as is the South, but that is not true of such regional designations as "Midwest," or "South Atlantic," or even "the West."

What I have suggested to this point is fairly simple: The notion of a regional literature has about it several problems having to do with definition—what *is* the Midwest; and with limitation—what constitutes a "midwestern" literature, and how can we delineate and define it? These are not new problems, I think. We have known about their existence and have by and large ignored them. I will turn to possible reasons for ignoring them before long.

There are, it seems to me, newer problems, deriving from theoretical concerns which have become important. I only have space to raise a few of them, and, at that, I only have space to *raise* some of these issues, without any effort to address them fully. These can well stand as exemplary and suggestive for many more that could be raised.

One concern has to do with language. If anything has happened to our study of literature in recent years it has been a return to a careful examination of the language of literary production. Rhetoric and syntax, figure—metonymy, synecdoche, metaphor in general—have been the subject of study with intensity greater than was the case for many years. Yet, I have seen no evidence in such language studies which can offer a basis for the designation "region"—midwestern or any other. No one, as far as I know, has found that midwestern writers use or are attracted to one or another form of figurative language which can distinguish "region" from "un-region." While some efforts have been made, and they are sometimes quite challenging, to demonstrate that women's writing or African-American writing does share some language forms which distinguish such texts from, say, male writing or non-African-American writing, no such claim has been made for "region." Even our most easily recognizable literary region, that is, the South, cannot be shown to share for all or even most of its writers any such unifying linguistic materials—or to say this another way, it would be difficult to demonstrate that Lillian Smith and Faulkner and Welty and Percy all write "the same way," though they certainly share some historic concerns which have to do with race and with southern history. Perhaps more extensive such work is now in someone's computer. If so, it would indeed prove important for the concept I am discussing here.

Another problem has to do with the notion of "canon." By and large, it seems to me, criticism interested in regional literature has often kicked quite hard at the limitations of a particular canon, but on the other hand, there has been no general attack on the very *idea of* a canon from regional sources, at least not to my knowledge. That is, regionalism has not challenged the existence of any canon at all and has not even challenged the existence of the long-established canonical figures in the literature of the United States. Rather, regionalists have tended to argue, there are writers in *their* particular bailiwick who *also* ought to be part of the canon, ought not to be excluded, or that the writers from "their" region have not been sufficiently acknowledged as major canonical figures. The usual argument made for such figures—I deliberately eschew examples here to avoid hurting particular feelings—is that *this* writer is "as good as" the big names the rest of the critical world has been celebrating and has only been excluded or not sufficiently celebrated because of some bias by the "un-region" against the region or as the result of some blindness, some lack of insight which comes from the peculiar limitations of the "un-region," which "the region" is fortunate to have avoided. Such arguments (and I have attempted to make one myself in the work on

Thomas McGrath mentioned) are sometimes telling, but they do not, in any fundamental way, challenge the very conception of canon as it is now being challenged by feminists, by African-American and other ethnic theorists, and by those who raise the challenge of "cultural," as opposed to literary, studies. To put this another way, regionalism seems to me not to be distinguishable from "un-regionalism" by its challenge to the idea of a canon, but only by its desire to add to the canon one or another putatively "neglected" figure.

Still another issue having to do with our theoretical concerns I will call, for the sake of simplicity, the issue of "mimesis." The very concept that region influences writing in some significant way suggests, it seems to me, that literature is essentially and centrally *reflexive* of a reality which we can discern—and discern in ways we can trust to be, whatever that may mean, "truthful." For if there is a distinction between region and "un-region" which does not lie in language, that distinction can only be tested by an "outside the text"—the region. That is, we must assume that the reality which is region is reflected in the writing that the region produces, or that the region describes, and that we can find a relationship between the text and the reality which we can describe.

A crude analogy will make my point clearer, perhaps. If we call a work of literature *French*, we mean by that term two things—that it is produced by a person who is by birth or legally or by self-definition a member of the nation, the political, historical and legal entity called France. But we *also* mean that it is written in the *language* called French, which is clearly distinguishable from all other languages. I am aware that the problem is not that simple, that writers from various parts of the Francophone world, from Haiti or parts of the African or Asian continents or from French-speaking Canada also write in the language called French, though they do not identify with the political entity called France. But the problem for "region" in the United States is even more complicated. A writer who might well identify her or himself with the region called "the Midwest," *has* no language to write in other than that in which writers from any other region, or from the un-region, write. Thus, while we can test the notion of "French literature" in comparison to English, Italian, German or Chinese literature by the language in which it is written, which is certainly reflexive of a reality of life in several parts of the world, as complicated as that reality may be in the aftermath of colonialism, we cannot so test regional literature. We may well want—should we be impelled to do so—to test the "Frenchness" of a work of literature by asking in what language it is written, and we may then well have to develop subsets of "French" which change national identity. French-speaking Canadians or Haitians will require a separate category and separate for each of them of course. But at least we will have the over-all general term "French" to apply to the language of the text.

The regional literature of the United States is all written in English. But unlike the instance of Francophone literature I have offered above, we do not have national identities to add to the name of the language. French-Canadian, French-Haitian make self-evident sense. English-Midwestern, or English-South Atlantic, or even English-Southern do not, I suggest, make the same sort of sense, since the essential *national* history for all regions is the same as that of the "un-region," even though its local particulars may vary. That is, the category of language only separates regional or any other literature in that language from other, non-English literatures. It does not provide a separation from "un-region," but only a separation from "un-nation," and even there, the complexity of English-writing speakers in other parts of the world besides the continental United States must be kept in mind, as in the case of French-writing speakers I have cited above.

I can summarize the various ideas I have suggested above, I think: "region" is not a demonstrable entity based on a language which separates it from "un-region"; "region" is not a demonstrable entity based on a common language-use, style, rhetoric or other such aspects of writing which separate it from "un-region"; region is not a demonstrable entity based on a sense of canon which is outside of or opposed to the canon—if there is still such—of the generality "the literature of the United States"; region begs the question of mimesis, of a reflexive view of literature which is much under attack from current theoretical constructs; and, finally, the geographic delimitation of some "regions"—the Midwest as instance—is not very clearly or easily defined, though some regions are more readily defined by some common aspects of history.

It seems clear to me, then, that the separation of region from "un-region" is no simple matter, either in theoretical terms or even in terms of such simple matters as to what constitutes the geographic locus of a region. Region, however, is argued for on quite another basis than any of these. The argument is essentially the argument of some common *culture* which separates a region from all other sections of the nation, from "unregion." What is meant by this concept—which is rarely, if ever, delineated precisely in discussions of region—is in itself enormously complex.

First, it seems to me, the concept of region is an oppositional one—as, Sollors suggests, are all of the divisions he discusses. That is, literature, book publishing, all of the attributes which go to make a national literature have, in the 20th century and especially since World War II, been so dominated by New York and, to a lesser degree, by the West Coast, that critics and others who find literary value in the production of writers from other parts of the country have felt it necessary to argue for the validity of writing from these areas. In some cases, I suppose, it can be argued that this is a form of special pleading because the writer in question has not won the acclaim of a sufficient number of critics. Those who oppose such regional arguments will say that if there is such an establishment, it has had no difficulty in appreciating Faulkner or Eudora Welty, despite their obvious and indisputable "southerness." Of course, many suggestions have been made to explain why the South had a particular appeal for the entire United States at a particular moment in our literary history. It is difficult, however, to make such arguments for all "regions," and in particular to make them for the Midwest. In any case, it seems to me that those who argue in favor of the validity of regionalism as a critical construct do so in part out of a sense of "opposition" to the "hegemonic rule" of a putative Eastern (with a far Western branch) "establishment."

Secondly, and perhaps more important, the argument for region suggests that somehow regional history *must* give some special characteristics to writers who have shared it in their biographical lives or who have studied it or used it as "locale," and that it must be reflected in the psychologies of the characters they create. The influence of Chicago on Carl Sandburg, Nelson Algren, Theodore Dreiser, Richard Wright, Sherwood Anderson or Gwendolyn Brooks is seen not only as the influence of a particular big city in which much of their work is located, but also as the influence of a region—the Midwest—of which Chicago is a hub of some sort. Willa Cather or Hamlin Garland, who often wrote about characters who live in a midwestern farmland, it is said, wrote about them differently than would have been the case had they written about such characters from other regions of the country. Some regional *culture* is here alleged—though rarely spelled out—which is different from the culture of other regions. How one validates such a concept from biographies as different as those of the writers I have mentioned I don't know, but it seems to me that the central conception here is that somehow this "region" of which Chicago is a major hub and perhaps the spiritual center is distinguishable from other regions and from "un-region," and that this distinction weighs to the advantage of the region.

The point I have been trying to make is in the main an application of Sollors' comment, cited above, that there is some desire in the United States to provide for "dichotomization," which can be found to be "good" and located somehow in the "*juste milieu* between two bad ones," that is, in some form of opposition to other regions, or to "un-region," or simply to a recognition by others of the importance of a partially separable *culture* for the region. I will say here simply that such a concept seems to be as unprovable as any of the others I have discussed.

II. And Yet . . . and Yet and Still . . .

Though it seems to me that any effort at systematic examination of the concept "region," and in particular of the concept "midwestern region" must fail and indeed does fail, we are, somehow, persuaded that the concept has some validity, expresses some sort of "truth." Living our lives, we feel that those vast prairies which extend from central Pennsylvania to the eastern part of Montana must have *some* influence on the minds of those who live there—whether that is reflected in their psychology or not—and hence in the substance of their literary texts or in the psychology of the characters they create. The country folk of Cather and Garland ARE, we feel, different from the country folk of New England or the Northeast. The prairie shapes perception, conception, psychology in ways different than the mountains or the seacoast do. Chicago IS different, we feel, from New York or Boston or Atlanta or, most surely, from San Francisco or Los Angeles, and the psychology of characters living in it is different from those living in other cities and different not only because of the city itself but because of the city's place within the region we call "the Midwest." We have not as yet, and perhaps we cannot ever, spell out with any degree of systematic accuracy just wherein that difference lies, nor can we make hard-and-fast rules about the degree to which, *whatever* these differences may be, they affect the writer or ought to affect his/her characters.

Werner Sollors is absolutely right, then. The division into "region" and "regionalism" is certainly "unsystematic." It is not the "complex model that . . . such a situation would require," and, to the extent that a preference for some particular region is expressed, it does have about it something of that search for "civil religion" Sollors cites. Yet and still, it is difficult to live any length of time in a region, to be sensitive to its landscape, urban or bucolic, and not to be convinced of the effect that such a landscape has on the individual, whether that individual is the writer her/himself, or whether that individual is the writer's characters.

Wherein, then, even acknowledging the "unsystematic" nature of any such designation, can we find the sources of regionalism to lie, and to what degree, or to what extent, can we use the construct in our efforts to understand the literature of the United States? Is "regionalism" of any use at all—given the contradiction that, at least in my discussion here, I find in the *logic* of any regional concept we develop on the one hand and in the *feeling* we seem to have that the concept does have some "real life" validity? In such an effort to find out if there is validity to "region," can we find anything that validates the idea of "region"?

Again, the best I can do in the limited space available is to suggest a few ideas:

1. Though "oppression" is surely an inappropriate term as we think of the relationship between the literary "power centers" in the history of the United States, it does seem that writers who come from "the boonies," from the Midwest or even the South through most of our history must somehow break through the community of Eastern-establishment writers in order to achieve critical attention. It is difficult—though not, I believe, impossible—to establish the existence of such an "Eastern establishment." However, ties we have come to think of sometimes as "networking," group allegiances which are sometimes centered around journals, publishing houses, politi-

cal associations, or universities do make it easier for writers from the East to break into print. Though the issue here is less oppression than it is in matters of race or gender, there is a sense in which writers from the regions outside the East feel themselves faced by a network to which they must gain admission before they can be properly treated. This is another "unsystematic," perhaps in any ultimate sense unprovable notion, but I have yet to meet or to read about a writer not from the East who has not felt it. To say this another way, writers feel the need to go to New York (as painters once felt the need to go to Paris and now feel the need to go to New York) before they can make their mark, and they feel an "oppositional" force—hard to define and perhaps mythic but nonetheless real-seeming—which they must join or overcome before they can receive the recognition they feel their due.

2. Experience suggests that landscape, urban or agrarian, *does* have an influence on the way the mind and feelings work. Though the mechanism is not clear to me, Chicago *feels* different from New York or San Francisco; the mountains of the Yellowstone area *feel* different from the prairie flatland or the river bottoms of the Midwest, or of New England; the very climate of the Southwest *feels* and makes one feel different than the cold and heat of the midwestern winter or the heat of the seacoast South. Landscape and geography do, in some way difficult to detail here, have some effect on the mindset of the artist and hence, one can suppose, on the content and approach of his/her work. I can make this point by analogy. Any moment in time does have about it a feel somewhat different from any other moment in time. Indeed, it is possible to argue that the mindset of an individual is determined to a large extent by the time when (s)he comes of intellectual age, that such a moment is the hallmark against which all previous and subsequent moments are measured; or, to say this another way, that the *norms* one thinks "natural" are established at a particular point in one's historical experience, and that all previous and subsequent moments are measured against that sense of "the natural," "the normal." Even if one makes a strong effort to change one's sense of that "natural," it requires an *effort*, and an on-going conscious determination to do so. Chekhov gives us an example of this phenomenon in *The Cherry Orchard*: "I'm a man of the eighties," says Gaev. "They run down that period, but still I can say I have had to suffer not a little from my convictions in my

life" (97). The process I describe here, which is, I think, familiar to everyone who has lived long enough to experience several major changes in "the way the world is," has its counterpart in the sense of "the natural" which derives from locale, I believe, and in that sense from region. If one has first sensed "the natural world" to look like the Indiana farmland and expects cities in such a setting to look like Indianapolis, it takes much experience to find a different sense of what is "natural." If, then, art is influenced by the artist's psychology, region must have some influence on writing, on the art created by the individual, or at the least, is *likely* to have such an influence. Region, in that sense, plays a role in the artist's work of art and perhaps also—an issue in reception theory far too complicated to do more than broach here—in the psychology of the audience which reads his/her writing.

3. Even if the limits of a particular region are a little fuzzy—where, indeed, *does* the Midwest begin and end?—there is something of a common history and even a common economics to particular areas of the nation, such that this commonality is reflected in politics and therefore, perhaps, in psychology. It may be that "rustbelt," for example, is a better designation than "Midwest" for the central part of the United States. Though these two terms are not coterminous, they do describe that central portion of the nation which has historically developed a good deal of heavy industry, certain kinds of mining (coal mining in particular) and certain kinds of farming, especially in corn, and other similarities of economic life. These similarities have helped to produce some similarities of history. I will only mention two or three. Immigrants of particular European origins have migrated to these areas in large numbers. Thus, while Jews for the most part (though by no means exclusively so) came to New York, non-Jewish Poles were more likely to come to Pennsylvania or Illinois or the northwest corner of Indiana where the steel mills were thriving. That the milieu, then, in which writers in Chicago or Pittsburgh or Gary grew up was different from that in which writers in New York grew up seems clear. Another example can be drawn from the historical experience of African-American migration from the South. For many, Chicago was a first waystation, and New York was an eventual destination, a fact which gives some shape to Richard Wright's fiction. My point is simply that as differences in history shape the individual to some extent—something we presume to be so

when we talk about gender or ethnicity—similar shaping holds for region. To say this another way: if gender and/or ethnicity are in part the shapers of individual psychology and therefore of writing, so is region, perhaps in a somewhat less insistent fashion. Social history, I believe, is in most cases, to some degree an important shaper of individual history. Though the work of art is not necessarily reflexive of any particular place or time, the psychology of the artist is surely influenced by place and time.

What I have attempted to say here and to demonstrate at least by a few examples is that though it is impossible to make of "region" a very definitive and definable category, it is nevertheless a category which—yet, and still—does seem to have some force in forming the psychology of individual writers as well as of audiences, though the particular shape that such forming will take is quite another matter, far beyond my scope here.

III. But What *Use* Is It?

The question remaining for me—again one I can only briefly adumbrate—is what use we can make of this rather nebulous but nonetheless, for me, convincing sense of "region." It seems to be most important to say, first of all, that not too much ought to be made of it.

The problem here is obvious enough. It is inevitable, I have suggested, that the minds of the writer and of the audience are shaped to some degree by region. It will be difficult, however, if not impossible, to say anything very specific about *how* the writer's mind is shaped, even if we agree on the characteristics of a region which might shape that mind. One writer—Theodore Dreiser, to stick to the Midwest—pretty much rejected his Terre Haute (and other Indiana towns') experience, though he took greatly to Chicago—but left Chicago soon enough. Carl Sandburg, on the other hand, born and raised in a small town like Dreiser, but in Illinois rather than Indiana, seems to have taken not only to Chicago, but also to the midwestern landscape, as both his verse and his biography amply attest. We can make something of this difference, but how much we can make of it is debatable given the enormous number of other differences between the style, the thought and even the genre involved. Thus, though we can discuss region as an influence on the writer we cannot easily and clearly show how this influence manifests itself, since it combines with everything else that makes the writer the person (s)he is. We certainly cannot use "region" as a category which will in any sense *predict* what a writer from a particular part of the country will do with his/her materials, nor can we make such predictions about audience. We must be very careful not to assign too high a level of importance to the notion of "region" in our efforts at literary understanding.

But we can do a few things. We can find that which is common, in subject matter, metaphor or other language and stylistic devices, or in philosophical or emotional outlook, to writers who come from or write about a particular region. Thus we can identify the force of region in particular works of art. We can examine the degree to which audience in one region of the nation "takes to" one or another work of art—when we can find differences in audience reaction between one region and another—and thus come to some conclusions about regional audiences, always doing so very carefully, however, so that it is in fact *regional* characteristics we are identifying and not others—ethnic, urban vs. rural, etc. We can speculate—and that, it seems to me, is all we can do—about the characteristics of region that impart some similarity to the work of particular writers and to the reactions of particular audiences and make the effort to suggest from such speculation some aspects of the characteristics of a region. I posit here a kind of backward formation which may tell us little about writers and writing but can be a useful tool for sociological, political, or broadly cultural studies.

If anything is demonstrated here, it seems to me, it is justification for Sollors' term that there is nothing very "systematic" about many of the dichotomies that we make, including region. I am not sure that the kinds of ideas we can justify on grounds of region add more than a mere descriptive rather than analytic quality to our effort to understand and interpret our literature or to deal with the way literature is produced or received.

And yet, and yet and still . . . I don't think we will give up the notion of region easily, nor do I think we need to do so. It helps us to organize our thoughts about literature by giving us a category, unsystematic, not particularly accurate though it may be, which makes us feel more comfortable in our decision as to what we wish to study. It gives us a comfortable place to look for influence on writer and audience—unsystematic though it may be. It helps us to arrive at understanding, unsystematic though it may be, of the shape of the nation that produces the art we study. We must be very careful not to let region confuse us about such major divisions as gender, ethnicity and class, and we must not attribute too much to region. But I guess we can keep the concept, if we keep the *caveats* I have suggested in mind. Let the idea of region thrive then.

Works Cited

Bradley, Sculley, Richard C. Beatty and E. Hudson Long. *The American Tradition in Literature*, 3d ed. v. 2. New York: W. W. Norton—Grosset & Dunlap, 1967.

Chekhov, Anton. *The Cherry Orchard*. Trans. Constance Garnett. In Samuel A. Weiss, ed. *Drama in the Modern World*. Lexington, MA: D. C. Heath, 1964.

Curti, Merle. *The Growth of American Thought*. New York: Harper & Brothers, 1943.

Sollors, Werner. *Beyond Ethnicity: Consent and Descent in American Culture*. New York: Oxford UP, 1986.

Stern, Frederick C., ed. *The Revolutionary Poet in the United States: The Poetry of Thomas McGrath*. Columbia, MO: U of Missouri P, 1988.

Mark Twain in Midwestern Eyes

Leland Krauth

"Give us back our origins, for I am out of season in any other land. . . . " —Edward Dahlberg

In his autobiography, *A Child of the Century*, Ben Hecht tells us that as a boy growing up in Wisconsin he had only penny-dreadfuls to read until this memorable day: "But on my thirteenth birthday a tremendous event took place. Four large boxes filled with books arrived in my room. They were gifts from my parents, but personally selected by my father under the advice of a scholar who was one of his brother Elks." Quickly opened, the boxes reveal first a fifteen-volume set of Shakespeare, then thirty volumes of Charles Dickens, followed by a fifty-two volume *History of the World*, and finally "thirty brick-red colored volumes of Mark Twain" (64-66). Hecht's situation is all too representative of the lot of midwestern writers. The literary impoverishment, the aspiration to learning, the reliance upon scholarly guidance, the general hunger for something beyond the material, the excitement over books: all this is typical enough. From Hamlin Garland, who complained that while Hawthorne sat in his study surrounded by books, he had only a moss-crusted woodshed (*Diaries* 23) to Wright Morris, who notes that Will's boy grew up reading *A Journey to the Moon* (35), the midwestern writer has felt the absence of culture. And while not every midwestern writer was blessed with four large boxes of books to fill the void, most, like Hecht, eventually discovered Mark Twain in abundance.

Twain is the seminal figure in midwestern writing, for as

David D. Anderson has argued, Twain, the "first and greatest of midwestern writers," is the one who shaped "the language and the substance of midwestern prose" ("Three Generations" 7).

Twain's accomplishment was largely unexpected by him. Although he courted success in all its conventional forms—wealth, prominence, power—he did not bank on achieving lasting fame—literary immortality. He joked in his autobiography about the short lifespan of humor and insisted that even when it was buttressed by didacticism, humor could not live "forever." "By forever," he added, "I mean thirty years" (273). Yet in his own lifetime and for thirty years after his death in 1910 he was very much on the mind of midwestern writers.

For the writers of the heartland Twain looms as a symbolic figure. He is not only an empowering predecessor but also the emblem of the problems and potentialities of the Midwest itself. He is paradoxically a figure who occupies either side of the region's dialogue with itself: the homeland as deprivation versus the homeland as enablement. Which place Twain assumes in this ongoing cultural dialectic depends on the writer who assesses him. For more often than not, what each midwestern writer finds in Mark Twain is an arresting mirror image. To see Mark Twain in midwestern eyes, then, is to see some of Twain himself, a lot of the writers who cite him, and something of the region's own self-definition.

In many ways the first midwestern writer to fix his eyes long and hard on Twain is still the most important. Through his book reviews, critical essays, and personal reminiscences, William Dean Howells not only evaluated Twain, he helped invent him. Howells's commentary on Twain, at first on the writer and at last on the friend, spanned Twain's creative life. Having, as he put it years later, "the luck, if not the sense" (5), to review favorably *The Innocents Abroad* (1869), the book that made Twain famous, Howells proceeded to promote Twain's career in review after review, as well as in periodic general assessments, until he published in the year of Twain's death his full-scale recollection and celebration, *My Mark Twain* (1910). In behalf of his friend, Howells carefully exerted his formidable authority, and he made no bones about his partisanship. His judgments, insightful and even prescient in some regards, are skewed by his effort to describe Twain in ways that would satisfy what he took to be the genteel standards of the Victorian-American ethos.

Generally Howells emphasizes the serious man behind the humor, the moralist beneath the buffoonery, the philosopher inside the raconteur. He recognized from the first the formative experience of their common midwestern past:

> We were natives of the same vast Mississippi Valley; and Missouri was not so far from Ohio but that we were akin in our first knowledges of woods and fields as we were in our early parlance. (15)

Howells was profoundly ambivalent about that "parlance." On the one hand, as everyone knows, he found himself embarrassed by Twain's crudity, apologizing for it as "Lincolnian" or "Elizabethan" (5), but at the same time he marveled at the raw vitality of Twain's language: "He used English in all its alien derivations as if it were native to his own air, as if it had come up out of American, out of Missourian ground" (17). Howells hears in Twain's work both the voice of rancor, of anger at injustice that explodes in "humanizing satire" (152), and the voice of drollery, of delight in incongruity that issues in "generous humor" (147). Trimming him to fit what he took to be the proper taste of the time, however, he repeatedly calls attention to the streak of tenderness in Twain's work. He highlights his "right feeling" and "clear thinking" (128), proclaiming his friend "the most serious, the most humane, and the most conscientious of men" (29). Significantly, Howells sees Twain's compassion as the direct outgrowth of his midwestern past. "Being always in the presence of the underdog," in his "early environment," he says, "he came to feel for him" (157).

While Howells often genteelizes Twain—his reviews are laced with such telltale adjectives as "delightful," "charming," "delicious"—he nonetheless perceptively roots him in a Midwest far distant from the refined East. In defining Twain's origins, Howells actually creates an analysis of the regional mind that is still compelling today. He argues to begin with that "the fundamental tone" of midwestern life is "the profoundly serious, the almost tragical strain." He accounts for this darkness by maintaining that in the face of "the mystery" of existence, the Midwest "trusts and hopes and laughs" only up to a "certain point," then "doubts and fears," and finally transcending its own anxiety, it "laughs again." For Howells this second laugh is both a sign of disillusioned "resentment," the "grim second-mind" of the Midwest, and the tactic which enables the region to endure its losses. To this stoicism Howells adds skepticism—a drive to question the received truths "of equality, of humanity, of representative government, and revealed religion." When answers are not forthcoming—or not adequate—the region responds, Howells says, "not mockingly, but patiently, compassionately." Whether or not the Midwest is a dark place of tragedy where living engenders doubt, anxiety, skepticism, stoic endurance, and compassionate acceptance, all this is for Howells the "genesis and evolution of Mark Twain" (148-49). For Howells, as he says at the end of *My Mark Twain,* the essential Twain is the writer "whose tragical seriousness broke in the laughter which the unwise took for the whole of him" (84).

Other midwestern writers of Howells's time unboxed a somewhat different Mark Twain. Hamlin Garland recalls first reading Twain aloud with his family "in a pioneer cabin in Mitchell County, Iowa" (Appreciation XI), and then writing a school essay on *Roughing It* when he attended the Cedar Valley Seminary—an essay that was criticized by his teacher as "too laudatory" (*Diaries* 192). Although he later wrote at least three "tributes" and one "appreciation" of Twain, Garland was never again excessive in his praise, partly because he, like Howells, was always bothered by Twain's profanity. Garland sees in Twain's writing a significant fulfillment of realism, or veritism, as he liked to call it, and he values him as a social historian. In his appreciative introduction to volume three of the Wells Definitive Edition of Twain's works, he describes *Roughing It* as "a social document of great value," a "perfectly sincere, vivid, and competent" account of an era, to which "the Historians of the Present and the Future" can turn "for a revealing record" (Appreciation XII-XIII). Garland affirms Twain's egalitarian principles and finds his politics as well as his realism rooted in the region of his birth: "He remained the Mid-Western American and literary democrat to the last" (Tribute 833).

The sense of Twain as a great democrat becomes the keynote for midwestern writers who came of age before the turn of the century. Three of them, Robert Herrick, Finley Peter Dunne, and George Ade, insist not only upon the democratic Twain but also upon the importance of Twain in transregional, transnational contexts.

Robert Herrick's Mark Twain is a writer shaped by "the pioneer lands," educated in "the printing office, the Mississippi River, and the newspaper," and made strong by "the strength of 'limitations'" (9). The "limitations" Herrick has in mind are the cultural vacancies of the Midwest, but for Herrick the region is the bedrock of the truly "indigenous" tradition in American writing, a tradition that Twain embodies in his "deeply American spirit" (9). Herrick defines that spirit as "a passionate individualism, a love of freedom, of self-expression, a religious faith in the power of individuality to conquer, to triumph, to achieve" (11). For Herrick this "real American tradition" is important first in contrast to what he terms the "imported" school of writing associated with New England, but ultimately its significance lies in its power to give the American abroad a distinct identity (9). Herrick sees Twain as a representative American, a committed democrat—"he believed in the ultimate saving virtue of the mass" (24)—who was able to maintain "his American standards" in the face of European politics, art, and social organization (10). Twain is in Herrick's eyes the greatest of the writers who express "the national culture, the national spirit" (9).

Finley Peter Dunne, Herrick's fellow Chicagoan, also sees Twain as a figure of international importance. Like Howells before him he underscores Twain's earnestness: "Mark Twain was in truth an extremely serious-minded man, subject to long fits of melancholy and disposed to violent opinions on political and religious questions" (258). Interestingly, Dunne defines his Mark Twain by distinguishing him from Howells. While he sees Howells as unable to conceive of anything "that he couldn't imagine happening in the little Ohio town where he was born," Dunne describes Twain as free of such "inveterate parochialism" (253). His Twain, like Herrick's, is a cosmopolitan who exerted his homegrown principles quite visibly in "foreign politics" (253). George Ade celebrates the same Twain even more stridently. For Ade Twain is an "inlander" (205), a member of "the shirt-sleeve contingent" (204), who possessed "real human qualities" (205). His Twain is the writer of "cheering volumes" (204), the man "big enough to be different" (205). Above all, Ade's Mark Twain is "the best" of America's "emissaries" to the Old World: "Any American who can invade Europe and command respectful attention is entitled to triumphal arches when he arrives home" (205-6). The arch Ade erects in tribute to his Twain is the bridge between common people: "'Why, certainly,'" he imagines everyone saying, "'he's one of us'" (206).

Midwestern writers for whom Twain was a contemporary

are all keenly aware of his roots. For them he is indeed "one of us." And for these writers their shared Midwest is the seedbed of his greatness. They see Twain's homeland as the source of his genius, whether that brilliance arises from his broad humanity, special social concerns, and deep seriousness, as it does for Howells, or springs from his authority as realistic social historian, as it does for Garland, or wells up from his democratic principles, as it does for Herrick, Dunne, and Ade. Their Twains differ somewhat, but they all believe that the Midwest Twain came from was a strengthening environment that empowered its inhabitants.

The next generation saw things differently. The writers from the Midwest who emerged in the first decades of the twentieth century, writers for whom Twain was a part of the more distant past, saw both a different Twain and, through him, a different Midwest.

The most public sighting of the new Mark Twain occurred on December 12, 1930. Although his subject was "The American Feat of Literature" in general and though his range of reference was wide indeed (it took in over seventy different writers), Sinclair Lewis's Nobel Prize acceptance speech told the world that Twain, "perhaps the greatest of our writers," was a "fiery old savage" who had been forced "into an intellectual frock coat and top hat" (15). For Lewis, Twain's fate was part of a large "American tragedy," a tragedy built of this paradox: that in a liberal society the writers "who first blast the roads to freedom become themselves the most bound" (16). Lewis, of course, seized the podium of world fame to excoriate America for failing to create "a civilization good enough to satisfy the deepest wants of human creatures" (6), for separating the intellectual life from all that is "new and vital and experimental," all that is "authentic" in America (12-13), and for making the writer feel "that what he creates does not matter"—that he or she is "only a decorator or a clown" (10).

For Lewis, Twain was at first one of the notable exceptions to this pathological avoidance of reality. Like Whitman before him and Dreiser after, he was "a great free Western wind" (8), and he helped to dispel the myths of a complacent American ideality. Identifying with the savage Twain, the early social critic, rather than the later frock-coated gentleman, Lewis himself felt free to challenge the cultural fiction "that all of us in Midwestern villages were altogether noble and happy" (16).

But while the radical Twain thus loomed for Lewis as a liberating predecessor, his Twain was in the end altogether too "tame" (15).

The new Twain that emerges here is, of course, the constrained, conventional one. Lewis comes down harder on the forces—gentility, respectability, and wealth—that quieted him and the people, notably Howells, who misguided him than he does on Twain himself. But the indictment is there. What Lewis plays out through Twain is, in fact, his own ambivalence about his midwestern past. For while he suffered from the disease he termed "The Village Virus" (216), he also felt the gentle, guiding embrace of what he called "The Long Arm of the Small Town" (273). Leave it, as he did, and criticize it, as he would, Lewis's own midwestern home was finally his measure of all things, for as he said, "it is extraordinary how deep is the impression made by the place of one's birth and rearing, and how lasting are its memories" (273). The impression of Mark Twain on Lewis was as deep—and as divided—as that of Sauk Centre. There is a kind of truth, then, as well as whimsy in his mock obituary in which he says he spent his last ten or fifteen years "devoting himself . . . only to his cats, his gardens, and his brief essays on such little-read novelists as Mark Twain" (105).

While Lewis's complaints against Twain are softened by his fondness for him, Edgar Lee Masters draws a starkly critical picture in his full-length study, *Mark Twain: A Portrait*. A rough outline for Masters's 1938 portrait was penciled three years earlier in "Mark Twain: Son of the Frontier," an essay he wrote for *The American Mercury* on the centenary of Twain's birth. In that piece he sees Twain as a writer "out of the uncontaminated American soil of the West," a figure shaped by the same mold that stamped Boone, Jackson, and Lincoln. This Twain is both a humorist who '"loved and satirized" the world and a realist who reported "the immediate scene." He is a man driven by a "lust of wandering" to pursue wealth and fame wherever he could find them, and in the end this Twain in Masters's eyes "rose higher than any American prose writer of his time" (67).

While limning the same Twain three years later in his book, however, Masters reverses his estimations of him. What was in the essay cause for praise becomes in the critical study grounds for condemnation. Twain is still a product of the hinterlands, still a comedian, still a would-be social critic, still devoted to money and notoriety, and still in the end a placeless person; but now he is seen as a failure. He fails *because of* his materialism and his rootlessness. Masters sees Twain as "the most tragic victim of the Gilded Age" (238). He is emphatic to the edge of violence over what he now sees as Twain's intolerable nihilism:

> The cause of Twain's spiritual collapse was that he had no genuine convictions about any important thing. He had no philosophy of life, no compelling ideas, no political principles, no theory of the literary art and faith, no belief in man, in liberty, in institutions, in possible progress for the race, in the potential influence of civilizing processes. (169)

Twain becomes a buffoon who only "laughed" and "guffawed" (113). Masters's portrait of a man, a gifted writer, without any "real political principles" stands in stunning contrast to the picture of Twain as a great democrat created by the nineteenth-century writers from the Midwest. For Masters Twain's career is a cautionary tale. In a parodic critical summary of Twain's life Masters elaborates on Lewis's frock-coated Mark Twain, insisting the while on his sad role as the representative type of his country:

> There is something strangely American about the ambitions of its enterprising men to want to marry a heiress, to get away from the native village, to find culture in Boston, to dress in a swallow-tailed coat and sit in a box with a banker, and to be gazed on with envy and admiration. (85)

Theodore Dreiser takes a more tolerant view of the writer he sees as both a "literary enigma" and a "Middle West American" (615). In his spirited polemic, "Mark the Double Twain," Dreiser posits, to begin with, two Mark Twains: one, "the hoaxing biographer of Tom Sawyer and Huckleberry Finn," a "wholesomely humorous" writer who exposed "little more than the minor or more forgivable flaws of American character"; the other, "the powerful and original and amazingly pessimistic thinker" whose cast of mind was "gloomy and wholly mechanistic" (615-16). Needless to say, Dreiser prefers the second of the two Twains. Like Masters and Lewis before him, he attributes the relative silence of the dark, serious Twain to the repressive and ignorant forces of American society as it was constituted in the Middle West as well as the East. For Dreiser Twain was the victim of convention—"convention, the dross of a worthless and meaningless current opinion" (626). He was restrained by a "dogmatic religion," by conservative "social and moral convictions on every hand," and by "the never ending benightedness of the mass" (620). He was further repressed, once he was established as a writer and buoyed up by "fame, love, and money," by "the companionship and applause of the acknowledged cognoscenti and literati of the ultra snobbish literary East" (624). In Dreiser's eyes Twain's "hobbledehoy genius" (624) was misdirected from the first, however, by the midwesterners of his day who were "semi-lunatic with bonanza religious as well as financial and 'moral' dreams" (623). For Dreiser, the "small-town world" of Twain's youth offered only "crudities and nonsensicalities" (624); his homeland failed him.

But Twain himself finally succeeded. Dreiser argues that the sense of two Mark Twains is an illusion. Twain was, he believes, not really double but only *playing* double, letting on, as Huck might say, to be genial and conventional while bitterly taking in "the cruelties, as well as the sufferings, of the individual and the world" (621). Dreiser celebrates this critical, dark-minded Twain. Ironically he values Twain for precisely the trait that Masters finds so objectionable: his nihilism (or near nihilism). No doubt seeing something of himself in the dark Twain, Dreiser revels in the idea that he conceives of life "from the depths of a giant despair" (619). Dreiser's approved Mark Twain is finally the writer who had a "gift as well as mood for dark and devastating, and at the same time quite tender and sorrowing, meditation on the meaning or absence of it in life" (616).

To one degree or another, the twentieth-century midwestern critics of Twain were all influenced by two books, one written by a displaced midwesterner, the other by a severe critic of the region. Ironically Albert Bigelow Paine, a native of Indiana, wrote an authorized biography of Twain that was so protective and so essentially laudatory that it all but demanded that others lodge criticism against Twain in the name of honest balance, if nothing else. And of course Lewis, Masters, and Dreiser did. They took many of their cues from Van Wyck Brooks's *The Ordeal of Mark Twain* (1920). Brooks argued that Twain was "a balked personality, an arrested development" who had suffered "a certain miscarriage in his creative life" (26-27), and he attributed much of this damage to an injurious environment. Interestingly, the core of Brook's argument appears in a series of letters to him from the midwestern writer who above all others felt a strong kinship with Twain, Sherwood Anderson.

For Anderson, Mark Twain was a lifelong obsession. He had a love-complaint relationship with him that emanated from the very core of his emotional and imaginative being. Before Brooks called it an "ordeal" Anderson saw Twain's life as a lost struggle. "He was," he wrote to Brooks, "maimed, hurt, broken" (*Letters* 34). In Anderson's eyes the thwarted Twain was blocked by his environment—or rather his two environments. To understand Twain, he told Brooks, "we have to remember the influences about him" (*Letters* 32). Those influences were first the "dreadful cheap smartness" and "shrillness" of the Midwest (*Letters* 34); and then the "tired, thin New England atmosphere" of the East with its "feminine force" (*Letters* 43). Making his argument of intellectual and artistic impoverishment as strongly as possible, Anderson indicted the whole of America as "broken off from the culture of the world" (*Letters* 34). Ironically, however, it is precisely Twain's putative failure that makes him so significant to Anderson. Again to Brooks he put the case: "In facing Twain's life you face a tragedy. How could the man mean what he does to us if it were not a tragedy? Had the man succeeded in breaking through, he would not have been a part of us" (*Letters* 34). Anderson speaks here as a fellow midwesterner (his "us" hardly includes the quite different Brooks), as one who has lived in and tried to create out of the same vacant world he believed Twain experienced. He confesses as much to Brooks, saying he understands Twain "because I have lived in such a barren place, felt myself so futile, because I have really always felt a lack of strength to continue struggling in a vacuum" (*Letters* 37). Anderson claims kinship with Twain through the bloodline of struggle and defeat: "For his very failure I love him" (*Letters* 34).

Yet like Dreiser (and unlike Masters and Lewis) Anderson believes that Twain came out all right in the end. His terms of praise are more diffuse, less precise, than his criticisms, but they are nonetheless strong. If Twain was in his view "a boy whipped and blown about by the winds of his times" (*Letters* 47), he was also "among the two or three really great American artists" (*Letters* 3). He was a powerful writer, an honest man, a person of "tenderness and subtlety" (*Letters* 32). Anderson believes Twain entered "deeply into the complex matter of living" (*Letters* 41). He finds Twain's writing "moving and valuable" because he sees in it a suggestion of the time when "mystery whispered in the grass, played in the branches of trees overhead, was caught up and blown across the horizon line in clouds of dust at evening on the prairies" (*Letters* 23). Surely, when he envisions Twain as a writer probing the "complex matters of living" and registering the "mystery whispered in the grass," Anderson is seeing in Twain chiefly himself.

Anderson not only reevaluates Twain in his letters, he also tries to rewrite Twain's works in his fictions. From "I Want to Know Why" with its vernacular-voiced innocent, to *Poor White* with its Huck-like son of town drunkard, Hugh McVey, to *Dark Laughter* with its Mississippi (and Ohio) river life and its explicit invocation of "Mark Twain, learning to be a river pilot. . . . What things he must have seen, felt, heard, thought!" (16), Anderson creates variation after variation of essential Twain material. He believed that in Twain's works, brilliant as they often are, "'there is too much of life left out'" (*Memoirs* 334). Anderson rewrites his Mark Twain by putting in some of what he senses Twain "left out." To Twain's essentially agrarian landscapes he adds the factories of industrialization; to Twain's celebrations of childhood innocence he adds the perplexities of adulthood; and to Twain's insistent attention to the pre- and asexual he adds the spectacle of a powerful sexuality. Thus he revisions Mark Twain.

Personally, in his own life, Anderson seems almost to have gone out of his way to create himself as other than Twain, his fellow countryman and literary kinsman. If Twain "paid the price of caving in" (*Letters* 60) to gentility and respectability, Anderson resisted them to the end, cultivating his own kind of bohemianism. If Twain faced "the complex and intricate world" (*Letters* 40) only to grow pessimistic, Anderson preserved his own enthusiasm, insisting, as if in reminder to himself, that "a man cannot be a pessimist who lives near a brook or a cornfield" (*Letters* 33). And if Twain was finally caught in the snare of American materialism, Anderson, as David D. Anderson has shown (*Sherwood Anderson* 163), mythologizes himself as a rebel who not only escaped that trap but in doing so set an example for his age. Yet as he repudiated Twain's life in his own, making himself an instructive symbol for his time, Anderson ironically repeated the fate of Mark Twain. For Twain was nothing if not a symbol for his own and succeeding generations.

As if there is a decorous proportion to be maintained between praise and brevity, some of the midwestern writers who laud Twain the most do so in the shortest of testimonies. Hemingway and Fitzgerald both pay high tribute in brief statements. In the case of Hemingway the concision accords with his cultivated economy of style: "All modern American literature comes from one book by Mark Twain called *Huckleberry Finn* (22). There is a deliberate flamboyance about the "all" and "one book" here. The power of the statement may arise from this extravagant absolutism or from the fact that, as with Hemingway's famous iceberg, seven-eights of its heft is concealed, in this case the whys and wherefores, the explanations of just *how* it all comes from Twain. Fitzgerald's less well known affirmation of Twain's significance is almost as terse as Hemingway's and equally cryptic: "Huckleberry Finn took the first journey *back*. He was the first to look *back* at the republic from the perspective of the West. His eyes were the first eyes that ever looked at us objectively that were not eyes from overseas" (qtd. in Piper). Huck does look back on his own experience, but how those adventures constitute the republic is unclear; and the idea that Huck's seeing is objective is dubious, to say the least. Nonetheless, for Fitzgerald no less than Hemingway Twain is an original and seminal writer.

Of all the midwestern writers who responded to Twain in the first thirty years after his death, the most influential are not the giants but two distinctly minor writers, Carl and Mark Van Doren. Today Carl is almost completely forgotten as a novelist and Mark is scarcely more remembered as a poet. Yet these brothers from the tiny village of Hope, Illinois—"Hope was a church, a school, a blacksmith shop, one store at first and two after a while, and ten houses" (Carl Van Doren, *Three Worlds* 2)—established Mark Twain not only in midwestern eyes but the eyes of the world. What they had to say about him was important because of the forums in which they said it. Both Van Dorens became professors at Columbia. Carl assessed Twain in such scholarly works as *American Literature: An Introduction, The American Novel, 1789-1939,* and the *Dictionary of American Biography,* while Mark evaluated his "almost . . . favorite author" (*Letters* 20) in reviews and articles in *The Nation* written while he was its editor; and they both passed judgment on him in their co-authored *American and British Literature Since 1890.*

Writing separately and together, they institutionalized Mark Twain.

The Van Doren's commentaries recapitulate the issues raised about Mark Twain by the earlier midwestern writers. Both see him, as Howells and virtually every other midwestern writer did, as an essentially American type. Like Herrick, Dunne, and Ade, they find his significance partly in his display of that American character abroad. As Carl puts it, Twain "made himself cheerfully at home in the world, yielding to it little of his original American self" (*American Literature* 59). Both Van Dorens see in Twain's works the realism that Garland prized, and Carl echoes Garland in pointing to Twain's "documentary value" (*American Novel* 155). Both acknowledge the social critic Lewis was drawn to, and Mark even suggests that "irony" is the very "grammar" of Twain's language ("A Century of Mark Twain" 473). The recurrent complaints against Twain's materialism, made most forcefully by Masters and Anderson, are both repeated and to a degree explained away as what Carl calls a commitment to "the victorious progress of an average democracy" (*American Novel* 138). And in a similar vein the tensions in Twain's life between western and eastern values noted by so many of the midwestern writers are laid to rest in Carl's synthesizing view: "He was a frontiersman who, having had his fill of the wilds, adapted himself gratefully to the comforts of civilization" ("Samuel Langhorne Clemens" 194). While both Van Dorens see the darker Twain condemned by Masters and admired by Dreiser, they are inclined to devalue the importance of this Twain, for as Mark observes, the cynical Twain did "not think far" ("A Century of Mark Twain" 473). Finally, both Van Dorens celebrate their brilliance of Twain's prose, his "art," as Mark puts it, "of writing without art" (Rev. of Mark Twain's *Autobiography* 524).

Although the Van Dorens see a Mark Twain who is at his best when, in Carl's phrase, he "turned back to his Middle Western recollections" (*American Novel,* 145), they do not make an issue of his midwestern origins. Perhaps because they are writing authoritatively for a national and even an international audience. Perhaps because their own Midwest, though a place of villages, farms, rural folk, and traditional values, was in at least one way special. Ben Hecht knew cultural scarcity in his Midwest (a scarcity broken so memorably by the surprising arrival of four boxes of books), and his experience is representative of that of most midwestern writers. But Carl and Mark Van Doren grew up in a different world; they inhabited a home, as Carl explained, in which there were "always books" and endless "reading" for its own sake:

> None of us knew or cared about literary chronology. Books for us were like stars, all apparently the same distance away, yet some brighter than others. Reading was simply experience otherwise denied us. We traveled without leaving Hope. When later we did leave, life was not so strange as we expected. Books had enlarged the village. (*Three Worlds* 49-50)

Books function here for the Van Dorens as windows on the wider world, just as they do for other midwestern writers, but there is a difference in degree so vast as to constitute a difference in kind. This underscores the fact that there is not one Midwest; there are many. Yet there is also a continuity within the differences between the privileged literary world of the Van Dorens and the culturally barren one experienced by so many midwestern writers in their youth. For while Carl and Mark had a library of books, they, like the other writers of the region, ended up, Carl says, liking "Mark Twain best" (*Three Worlds* 49).

Mark Twain once argued that the key to the creation of an authentic American literature was "*absorption*: years and years of unconscious absorption; years and years of intercourse with the life concerned" ("What Paul Bourget Thinks of Us" 131). He absorbed the region of his birth and youth, converting it into the subculture of his own best writing. In turn, the Midwest absorbed that writing and Mark Twain himself. He lived his first "forever," thirty years, as he had defined it, as the pole star in midwestern eyes.

Works Cited

Ade, George. "Mark Twain As Our Emissary." *Century Magazine* 1 (1910): 204-6.

Anderson, David D. *Sherwood Anderson: An Introduction and Interpretation.* New York: Holt, 1967.

—. "Three Generations of Missouri Fiction." *Midwestern Miscellany* 9 (1981): 7-20.

Anderson, Sherwood. *Dark Laughter.* 1925. New York: Liveright, 1970.

—. *Letters of Sherwood Anderson.* Ed. Howard Mumford Jones. Boston: Little, 1953.

—. *Poor White*. 1920. New York: Viking, 1966.
—. *Sherwood Anderson's Memoirs*. 1942. Ed. Ray Lewis White. Chapel Hill: U of North Carolina P, 1969.
—. *Sherwood Anderson: Short Stories*. Ed. Maxwell Geismer. New York: Hill and Wang, 1962.
Brooks, Van Wyck. *The Ordeal of Mark Twain*. 1920. New York: Dutton, 1970.
Dreiser, Theodore. "Mark the Double Twain." *The English Journal* 24 (1935): 615-27.
Dunne, Finley Peter. "On Mark Twain." *Mr. Dooley Remembers*. Boston: Little, 1963 239-68.
Garland, Hamlin. Appreciation. *Roughing It*. By Mark Twain. Vol. 3 of *The Writings of Mark Twain*. 37 vols. New York: Gabriel Wells, 1923-45.
—. *Hamlin Garland's Diaries*. Ed. Donald Pizer. San Marino: Huntington, 1968.
—. Tribute. *North American Review*. June 1910: 833.
Hecht, Ben. *A Child of the Century*. New York: Simon, 1954.
Hemingway, Ernest. *Green Hills of Africa*. New York: Scribner's, 1935.
Herrick, Robert. "Mark Twain and the American Tradition." *Mark Twain Quarterly* 2.2 (1937-38): 8-11, 24.
Howells, William Dean. *My Mark Twain: Reminiscences and Criticisms*. 1910. Baton Rouge: Louisiana State UP, 1967.
Lewis, Sinclair. *The Man from Main Street: Selected Essays and Other Writings: 1904-1950*. Ed. Harry E. Maule and Melville H. Cane. New York: Pocket, 1963.
Masters, Edgar Lee. *Mark Twain: A Portrait*. 1938. New York: Biblo and Tannen, 1966.
—. "Mark Twain: Son of the Frontier." *The American Mercury* Sept. 1935: 67-74.
Morris, Wright. *Will's Boy: A Memoir*. New York: Harper, 1981.
Paine, Albert Bigelow. *Mark Twain: A Biography*. New York: Harper, 1912. 2 vols.
Piper, Henry Dan. "Fitzgerald, Mark Twain and Thomas Hardy." *Fitzgerald Newsletter* 8 (1960): 31.
Twain, Mark. *The Autobiography of Mark Twain*. Ed. Charles Neider. New York: Harper, 1959.
—. "What Paul Bourget Thinks of Us." *Mark Twain on the Damned Human Race*. Ed. Janet Smith. New York: Hill and Wang, 1962. 125-42.
Van Doren, Carl. *American Literature: An Introduction*. Los Angeles: U. S. Library, 1933.
—. *The American Novel, 1789-1939*. 1921. New York: Macmillan, 1966.
—. "Samuel Langhorne Clemens." *Dictionary of American Biography*. New York: Scribner's, 1930.
—. *Three Worlds*. New York: Harper, 1936.
Van Doren, Mark and Carl Van Doren. *American and British Literature Since 1890*. New York: Century, 1925.
—. "A Century of Mark Twain." *The Nation* 23 Oct. 1935: 472-74.
—. Rev. of *Mark Twain's Autobiography*. *The Nation*. 12 Nov. 1924: 524.
—. *The Selected Letters of Mark Van Doren*. Ed. George Hendrick. Baton Rouge: Louisiana State UP, 1987.

"Through Me Many Long Dumb Voices": Jack Conroy and The Illinois Writers Project, 1938-1942

Douglas Wixson

"I have struck a city,—a real city,—and they call it Chicago. The other places do not count."
—Rudyard Kipling

On a grey, blustery day in early March 1938, Jack Conroy stepped from a bus at the Chicago terminal, weary from a long ride from Moberly, Missouri by way of St. Louis. He headed directly by trolley to Cottage Row, near where the Columbian Exposition had taken place years earlier. Nelson Algren lived at 3569 Cottage Row in an area known as Rat Alley among the artists who lived there. Formerly an arcade for the Columbian Exposition, Rat Alley offered cheap quarters for impecunious writers and artists like Algren, Michael Siporin and others, joined by Conroy who was utterly broke. Algren had arranged that Jack would write a review for the *Midwest Daily Record*, for which Jack was advanced ten dollars, enough to pay the bus fare (interview, Conroy, 26 Dec. 1978). Submitting pieces to Louis Budenz, editor of the *Record* (the Midwest version of the Community *Daily Worker*), Conroy was able to share Algren's rent and pay for whiskey, an expenditure that had begun to figure heavily in Conroy's slender budget since the end of Prohibition.

During the two years since Conroy and other talented writers were removed from their positions with the Missouri Writers Project in St. Louis, owing to ineptitude and political discrimination on the part of the Project's director, Geraldine Parker, a minion of the Pendergast machine, Jack had lived in near poverty in Moberly with his family, supported by slender returns from his writings and the meager salary of his wife, Gladys, who worked in the Brown shoe factory there. More than once, Conroy called upon his St. Louis friends to lend him money in humorously worded appeals such as "League for the Rehabilitation of Conroy" and the "Conroy Liberty Loan" (Conroy to Fallon, 17 Jan. 1938).

The new agenda of the Popular Front, already making itself known at the American Writers Congress of 1935 and in full swing by the Congress of 1937, had effectively sidetracked the Proletarian literary movement in which Conroy figured prominently on the basis of his first novel, *The Disinherited* (1933) and his work as editor of *The Anvil* (1933-1935). Now the cultural doyens, Party organs, and orthodox critics of the Left called for reconciliation with middle-class writers and artists in a United Front against fascism. Old hierarchies re-appeared, centered in New York radical intellectual circles like the Philip Rahv-William Phillips axis whose magazine, *Partisan Review*, had done a heist job on Conroy's *Anvil*. With Party approval, *Partisan Review* absorbed Conroy's subscription list without accepting Conroy's dedication to realistic fiction forged on the anvil of depression experience and divorced from the gloom and doom of literary naturalism.

Like Theodore Dreiser before him Conroy gravitated to Chicago to further his literary career. Chicago still attracted young midwestern writers long after the Renaissance of the 'teens and twenties. Dreiser, Sandburg, and others had made their names there; in Chicago in the 1930s new literary fortunes were being made, many of them tied to the work of the Illinois Writers Project on Erie Street in Chicago's Loop, only a stone's throw from the rooming house where Sherwood Anderson wrote *Winesburg, Ohio*, the mansion where Ernest Poole had grown up, and the office where Harriet Monroe edited *Poetry* magazine. Perhaps Jack saw something of himself in Dreiser: both had come from impoverished circumstances, struggling for recognition and acceptance which came slowly.

Conroy had grown up in a coal-mining camp outside Moberly, quit school at thirteen after his father's death in a mining accident, and begun an apprenticeship in the Wabash Railroad shops in Moberly. Later, after the Great Railroad Strike of 1922, he had wandered from street mill to auto factory to support his family, writing at night after the fatigue of assembly lines.

Jack had gathered more experience in his early years as a worker than most people do in a lifetime. Celebrated as a genuine worker-writer after the publication of *The Disinherited* and revered by writers like Algren and Richard Wright, whose early careers he had helped, Jack nonetheless was forced to begin anew in Chicago as shifting readers' tastes and the Nazi-Soviet pact (in 1939) shut out many young, promising writers like himself who had begun so propitiously to create a new humanitarian realism in literature, grounded in social practice and affirmative in its belief in constructive change. This new literature appeared in the little magazines of the early 1930s whose dedicated editors, like Conroy, hoped to provide an alternative to the growing appeal of escapist popular fiction among workers and the unemployed. Algren's first novel, *Somebody in Boots,* appeared in part in *The Anvil,* as did Meridel LeSueur's work and that of Richard Wright, Erskine Caldwell, Langston Hughes and James T. Farrell. Algren and Conroy had in mind reviving *The Anvil* in 1938, but to do so Conroy needed work and a great deal of support from his many literary friends.

Algren, who was already on the Illinois Writers Project, introduced Conroy to its state director, John T. Frederick. Familiar with his work as author and editor, Frederick invited Conroy to join the Project, remembering, too, Jack's generous offer to help out financially when Frederick's own little magazine was failing in 1933.[1] Frederick, Illinois state supervisor of the Federal Project, taught journalism and English at Northwestern University. Mild-mannered, serious and conservative, Frederick admired Conroy's literary work but looked disapprovingly on what he considered to be Conroy's and Algren's radical tendencies. By June of 1938, Frederick had received Conroy's application, yet problems arose since technically only writers on relief were hired. Fortunately Jack was not put through the humiliating means test, which included an assessment of one's personal belongings, but was hired in the special administrator category based upon his considerable experience as a writer and editor. Moreover, Jack had served on the Missouri Writers Project, indeed was considered for the position of state supervisor but was denied the post by the powerful Democratic party's Pendergast machine and its state WPA chief, Matthew Murray. The fact that Jack had walked the picket line of a writers' strike protesting the unjust dismissal of one of the Project members was enough to disqualify him in the eyes of the Party bosses who thought little enough of the Project anyway.[2]

Frederick put Conroy to work gathering tales from industrial workplaces. The idea came from the WPA's national folklore editor, Benjamin A. Botkin. Botkin was the former editor of the *Folk-Say* volumes which appeared in the early 1930s with their potpourri of folkloric miscellany. One of Botkin's early projects while folklore editor of the WPA was a collection entitled *American Stuff* (1937), an anthology of prose and verse submitted by Federal Writers Project members.[3] The materials gathered for *American Stuff* were an odd collection of Americana, including a short story by Vardis Fisher, a poem by Charlotte Wilder, Richard Wright's brilliant "The Ethics of Living Jim Crow," Negro spirituals, square-dance calls and a critical essay by Gertrude Stein! Sensitive to the lack of focus of the first volume, Botkin prepared an outline of a subsequent collection to be entitled *American Folk Stuff* and sent it to regional editors. Frederick sent the outline of the proposed volume's contents to his staff members, soliciting contributions. Frederick circulated Botkin's description of the proposed contents in December of 1938, hoping to elicit submissions by members of his staff. Since Jack had joined the Project the previous summer, Frederick's enthusiasm for the possibilities of industrial folklore had mounted. In an early memo to Jack, Frederick wrote: "This is good stuff on the bridge plant—just the sort of thing we want for that phase of our subject" (letter, Frederick to Conroy, 14 July 1938).[4]

Botkin's inspiration, Frederick's reception, and Conroy's "fieldwork" were the three principal factors in shifting the Project's focus from the study of folklore relics to the exploration of living lore created in the workplace. The scope of earlier Project inquiry included Morris dancing, cornhusking, apple cutting and other superannuated recreations, valued more for their quaintness than for their authenticity.[5] It is fair to say that the boost that these three men gave the study of that field was largely responsible for the production of industrial folklore on the Project.

Jack brought formidable credentials to the study of industrial folklore. First of all, he had spent years as a worker in railroad shops, steel mills, coal mines, auto plants and rubber heel factories. That experience alone was scarcely enough, of course, to qualify him as a folklore researcher. As a boy he had hung around the hitching lot behind the Merchants Hotel in Moberly, Missouri, hearing farmers swap tales on Saturdays. Later, in the

Wabash shops he had been submitted to the traditional hazing of the newcomer and observed attentively the various pranks the workers liked to play upon one another. Wherever he had worked, even during the brief periods of rest on automobile assembly lines, Jack participated in the storytelling of workers, hungry for diversion and appreciative of an entertaining tale or joke. Thus when Frederick assigned him to field work, gathering the lore of industrial workers in Chicago, Jack had to go no further than his own remarkable memory carried him.

Jack's special talent lay in recognizing the folkloric and linguistic interest in workers' lore and turning it to literary use. H. L. Mencken, who published six of Jack's stories in the *American Mercury* in the 1930s, was drawn to Jack's ear for workers' speech. And critics had praied *The Disinherited* for its authentic use of workers' idioms. John Dos Passos reviewed the book, calling it "an absolutely solid, unfaked piece of narrative. . . ." (qtd. in Aaron 25), and Erskine Caldwell praised Conroy's novel glowingly (letter, Caldwell to Conroy, NL 20). One reviewer wrote of Conroy: "He speaks for a people who are inarticulate as a rule; whose voice is only heard in times of desperation" (Rodriguez). Recapturing the words of workers by recreating their tales was another means of giving voice to people who as a class seldom leave written record of their lives. Jack had made generous use of workers' lore in his literary work; but it was years later, under Frederick's supervision on the FWP, that his systematic folklore collecting began. "It was Dr. Frederick," Conroy later wrote, "who set me to work on the Industrial folklore tales which really sent me on the folklore trail I've been pursuing ever since" (unpubl. ms.n.d.).

George Korson's studies of Pennsylvania coal miners in the 1920s were probably the earliest instance of the systematic investigation of occupational folklore applied to industrial work. Archie Green attributes Botkin, however, with the first use of the term "as a discrete term of categorization" (Green 213-44). Korson and Botkin were instrumental in planting the seeds, but Frederick's suggestion to his staff members in Chicago during the late fall of 1938 gave the term currency. Finally, it was Jack Conroy who made the first important contributions to the new area of study when he joined the FWP in the summer of 1938.

Conroy's first industrial folklore contribution to the FWP actually appeared under Nelson Algren's name. Recasting a traditional joke about an overtaxed worker who uses every moving part of his body to keep up with the pace of the job, Jack wrote a short tale called "True Blue Highpockets" which Algren, eager to show Frederick that he was producing and not fooling around, submitted under the title "Highpockets" (it appears in Ann Banks' *First-Person America* 90-92). Conroy was not one to feel possessive about his collection of tales, and besides, he owed Nelson a favor for helping him get on the Project. In addition, Conroy furnished Algren with another industrial folktale entitled "Hank the Freewheeler," later published in Botkin's *A Treasury of American Folklore* under Algren's name. Algren had probably never set foot inside an auto factory and the language is entirely Conroy's.

Algren felt chagrined when Frederick complimented him on the Highpockets tale. To spare further embarrassment Algren suggested that Frederick give the industrial folklore assignments to Conroy.[6] Algren did his "fieldwork" at the racetracks and in Chicago's *bas fond* from which he drew the material of *A Walk on the Wild Side, The Man with the Golden Arm*, and other novels.[7] During 1938 and 1939, Conroy submitted ten industrial folk narratives, as well as a number of personal narratives, gathered in North Clark Street bars and elsewhere. One of these, "A Miner's Apprentice," was an oral transcription Jack made of conversations with his nephew, Fred Harrison, the "Ed" of *The Disinherited*. It appears in Banks's *First-Person America* with the title "Fred Harrison." Conroy's industrial folk narratives appear in his *The Weed King & Other Stories* (Lawrence Hill, 1985). Frederick received the tales warmly and sought to find a commercial publisher to print them, along with other manuscripts collected on the Project.

In the meantime, Botkin asked to see Conroy's industrial tales, planning to publish them as part of a sequel to *American Stuff* (1937). The new volume, which never appeared, was to be called *American Folk Stuff*. Since *American Stuff*, Botkin had narrowed his subject matter to "a collection of readable tales from oral and traditional sources" (ms. "Amer. Folk Stuff"). Yet his aim was explicitly pluralistic; all ethnic, regional and occupational groups were eligible for inclusion, provided the material was sufficiently interesting, giving evidence of oral storytelling as an art. Much of the material later appeared in Botkin's *A Treasury of American Folklore* (1944), including six of Jack's tales. For some reason, Frederick did not include Conroy's tales in the manuscripts he submitted to Botkin for *American Folk*

Stuff. Botkin wrote Jack directly, expressing his disappointment and soliciting submission of his folk tales. "These are the very ones which I need for the book," Botkin wrote Conroy, "and I am asking Frederick again to see that I get them" (letter, 31 Jan. 1939). Perhaps Frederick was still toying with the idea of a commercial publisher for Conroy's tales. In any case, Jack did finally send his industrial narratives to Botkin which Botkin then forwarded to Henry G. Alsberg, Director of the FWP.

Alsberg, a cosmopolitan Easterner more at home with European literature than with Conroy's creative transcriptions of factory workers' idioms, criticized the "synthetic" style of the narratives written "in the tradition of the 'literary comedians' rather than folk humor" (Alsberg, Edit. Report). Alsberg, like many other romantics, was convinced that the "folk" were quite capable of producing copy for anthologies spontaneously, ignoring the fact that folk humor and storytelling are arts that, like folk musicianship, require skill and a thorough knowledge of tradition, both of which Conroy possessed in abundance. Alsberg's reactions to the earlier volume, *American Stuff*, showed his ambivalence concerning the publication of Project material, apart from the state guides. Alsberg was compelled to walk a highwire with his Writers Project in the face of political critics like Congressman Martin Dies who were quick to jump on the Project as an example of New Deal pork barrel.

By May of 1939, Botkin was calling his projected anthology *Nobody With Sense* (letter, Botkin to Frederick, 11 May 1939). Frederick had organized a folklore unit and was holding staff meetings. Frederick was still anxious to public Jack's folktales, even without Botkin (letter, Frederick to Conroy, 16 June 1939). In the meantime, however, new conceptions of folklore were being shaped on the various Projects, principally in New York and Chicago.

A July 13th meeting of Chicago staff members included Algren, Conroy, Margaret Walker (later celebrated author of *Jubilee*, poet, and Richard Wright memoirist), Stuart Engstrand (novelist), Hilda Polachek (field worker), Sam Ross (novelist and later Hollywood screenwriter), a field worker named Ben Gershman, and Abe Aaron who had contributed to Conroy's *Anvil* and encouraged his fellow Post Office worker, Richard Wright, to submit poems to *The Anvil*, Wright's first literary publication. Two general tendencies appeared as a result of these staff meetings and Botkin's principles. Botkin's manuscript, "The

Folk and the Writer," was the subject of much discussion in the meetings. In his essay Botkin grounds literature in folklore and folk experience; it "is the mold of literature . . . the greatest national flowerings of art are the product of the union of folk and individual art traditions" (2). Drawing upon the example of Steinbeck's *Grapes of Wrath,* Botkin underscores the creative elements of transcribing folk material into literature. It is not enough, Botkin argues, to imitate; the writer must re-create what he hears as a listener. Finally, the writer should give his material social significance (as Steinbeck does in *Grapes*). Of all the state projects, I believe, the Illinois Project best realized this aim, principally through its black history and industrial folklore work.

The New York Project, on the other hand, leaned toward documentary realism; folklore had come to be associated with the moribund and arcane "survivals" from the past, idealized by romantics, incapable of treating "the contemporary factors responsible for the feeling of social disintegration" (ms., Silver, NY FWP). New attempts to discover folk material in urban settings must begin with the cries of street vendors, the rhymes of children's games, and the stories of construction workers. Industrial lore, then, would entail recording these manifestations of the folk imagination in literal documentary manner.

Conroy's own approach, in contrast, involved the listener in a dialogic fashion with the informant. Favoring the folk process, such an approach, however, required a skilled interviewer. Sam Ross added that listening skills meant memorizing, not entire conversations verbatim, but the "punch images" ("Staff Conference"). The prospects for fashioning a new approach to folklore and folk storytelling seemed bright indeed in 1939. Documentary writing itself had created brilliant expressions in the work of Agee, Caldwell and in the productions of the Federal Theatre Project. Steinbeck, Algren and Conroy were working both folklore and documentary veins. The literary possibilities seemed as rich as the material itself which poured into Project offices every day from field workers who included Margaret Walker and Hilda Polachek.

Conroy and Algren found their materials close at hand. From memory and experience Jack provided material for Frederick's industrial folklore project. Near the Project offices was the tavern district of North Clark Street where Conroy and Algren "repaired," as Jack liked to say. Frederick gave free rein to the two novelists as long as they turned their submissions in on time. Free from constraining office work, and earning their $125 monthly salaries, Jack and Nelson did their "field work" in bars like the King's Palace, a watering hole for itinerant actors, bums, and workers. Here Jack heard the High Diver tale, told by a circus clown named Charlie De Melo, and Slappy Hooper, told him by Harold Sullivan (also a Project member) who had heard it from his father-in-law. Jack was able to reconstitute entire conversations overheard in taverns, submitting this as material to Frederick after deleting the "commonplace" from the manuscript. On the Madison Avenue skidroad Jack listened to railroad tales from a retired railroader named George Walton. From itinerant workers Jack gathered work narratives of the Montana copper mines ("That Burg Called Butte"; "A Job in the Couer d'Alene" [sic]). A couple of ex-typesetters named Harold Gunn and Floyd Nims gave Jack the basis of a story he would entitle, "The Type Louse." From his own experiences as factory worker, road worker, shop "car toad," Conroy produced "The Demon Bricksetter," "The Boomer Fireman's Fast Sooner Hound," "The Sissy from the Hardscrabble County Rock Quarries," and several others, some of which he subsequently developed into children's stories, in collaboration with Arna Bontemps, a point I shall return to presently.

Conroy and Algren may have made too frequent use of Frederick's dispensation allowing them to do their fieldwork during Project hours on North Creek Street and in a black tavern near Cottage Road (dubbed "Jolly John's" by Conroy), for Frederick ceased to allow both to be gone at one time from the Erie Street office. Frederick's desire to see a saleable book of industrial stories into print was not realized during his tenure as director, nor during that of the Project's succeeding director, Curtis MacDougall, who took over early in the fall of 1939. Nor did such a volume appear from the Federal Writers Project in Washington, D.C., despite Conroy's and others' submissions to a projected book to be called *Men at Work* (see *Illinois Writers' Newsletter* 9). Other areas of interest were receiving greater attention than industrial folklore, such as the black history project and the radio drama project. New social realities intruded by 1940, pushing aside folklore, which must have appeared whimsical to hardheaded critics of the Project. The Project was now under the State of Illinois; MacDougall was forced to scramble to find sponsors for the individual projects. Moreover, the state projects had come under a great deal of scrutiny from certain congressmen anxious to remove federal subvention. It was alleged that Communists were working on the Projects. Even Frederick, who respected their individual abilities as writers, refused to promote Conroy and Algren to supervisor positions. Frederick was sensitive to the increasing political scrutiny directed toward the Project and the accusations of red-baiters in Congress, appearing in the Chicago *Tribune* (MacDougall, ms.).[8] MacDougall, on the other hand, had no such qualms, making the two novelists supervisors on the basis of competitive examinations administered soon after MacDougall became director.

Assigned to the Illinois WPA Project 30068, initiated by Horace Cayton, whose purpose was to assemble the Chicago Afro-American Union Analytic Catalog, Jack ended his folklore researches for the Illinois WP and began to devote himself to an entirely new project for which, curiously, his earlier experience had well prepared him: black social history (Jack had grown up with black miners in Monkey Nest, worked alongside black workers in the auto factories, and received a Guggenheim in 1935 to study black migration from the South to northern factory cities).[9]

Early in 1938, Illinois WP workers had begun to investigate Negro religious cults and unorthodox churches in Chicago, such as the Moorish-American and Nation of Islam groups. The Project supervisor at the time was Katherine Dunham, who would later make her fame as a dancer. At the desk next to Jack was Arna Bontemps, who had figured prominently in the Harlem Renaissance. It was a fortuitous meeting, for both were novelists interested in folklore and social history; moreover, their writing styles were similar and each was willing to accept stylistic changes suggested by the other, a rare collegiality indeed among writers, who prefer autonomy as a rule. Their subsequent literary collaboration was the first such between black and white writers in American literature. Drawing upon Illinois WP material, the two writers produced two books on black social history (*They Seek a City* [1944] and *Anyplace But Here* [1966]). In addition, the two collaborated in co-authoring a number of successful children's books based upon Conroy's industrial folktales.

The Illinois Writers Project was disbanded in 1942, a victim of underfunding and war-time exigencies. Spinoff programs of the Project appeared, including civil defense and venereal disease control. Leaving the Writers Project in 1941, Jack and Nelson Algren worked for a time on the Venereal Disease Control unit. Their assignment was to survey prostitutes and servicemen on leave frequenting Chicago's redlight districts. The fieldwork covered ground familiar to Algren, but Conroy drew little from it to nourish his writing; similarly, editing a civil defense newsletter subsidized Jack's writing without making use of his creative talent.

During his subsequent years in Chicago Jack worked as an encyclopedia editor, grinding out copy in order to support his family. There were accomplishments, such as *They Seek a City* (1944), his anthology entitled *Midland Humor* (1947), best-selling juveniles such as *The Fast Sooner Hound*, yet Jack watched from the sidelines as his friend Nelson Algren achieved fame with *The Man with the Golden Arm* (1948). Moreover, younger writers, like Richard Wright, Willard Motley and Frank Yerby (all formerly with the Writers Project), whom he had published in *The Anvil* and *The New Anvil*, and to whom he had given encouragement during their early, difficult literary careers, were able to live and write, free of economic worry, while their former mentor labored, as Meridel LeSueur said, "in the encyclopedia mills." New social realities and prosperity fueled by the war fostered a new readership; the Cold War threw a cloth over much of the cultural achievement of the 1930s; the literary establishment, reconstituted following World War II, turned increasingly to European models such as modernism, which spoke of the human condition rather than human *conditions*. Part of the bitter legacy of the Cold War era in literature, from Conroy's perspective, was the preeminence of *Partisan Review*, originally an organ of the New York John Reed Club, later Trotskyist, then Cold Warrior-ish in inclination, whose editors had absorbed Conroy's *Anvil*, as mentioned earlier, and its considerable (by little magazine standards) subscription list.

Jack returned to Moberly in 1966, turning his hand once again to narratives of working-class people in autobiographical sketches of his childhood in the Monkey Nest mining camp. What he had labored to achieve in American letters—a literature representing truthfully the inherent worth and dignity of ordinary people, in their own idiom and drawing upon their traditional ore—came to fruition among black writers like Alice Walker, Zora Neale Hurston, Toni Morison, Ishmael Reed. In retrospect, Conroy's work seems cast in the same mold as that of these black artists. Conroy's work has never won the attention it deserves, yet it has continued to attract a small but dedicated readership over these many years. Nonetheless, Jack felt during his later years great satisfaction in knowing that the direction that his own writing and editing pursued—social history, folk narrative, sketches of working-class life, idiomatic language—pointed toward developments now hailed in black writing.

In the Depression decade of the 1930s, the various cultural programs of the Left were often heavy-handed propaganda efforts yielding little literary produce of lasting value. Yet certain writers, sympathetic with the values of the Left at the time, nonetheless evaded the narrow prescriptions of cultural doyens and orthodox theorists. Among those who made significant contributions to American letters was Jack Conroy, whose genius lay in giving authentic voice (in contrast to the tin ear of many a proletarian writer) to workers who seldom leave any written record of themselves.

Conroy's narratives reveal the verbal creativity of inarticulate people through the folklore they (re-)create and the richness of their idiomatic speech. A participant himself in the folklore processes of factory, mine and mill, Conroy later documented folk expression and turned it to humorous advantage in the folklore collections with the Writers Project. The populist impulses that animate Conroy's folk narratives express the grief, joy, and human dignity of working people. These narratives and his literary sketches tell us about workers' attitudes towards their occupations, the conditions of industrialization, and workers' resistance to degrading circumstances, manifest in both their play and their subversion.[10] From his own experience, he concluded that folklore reflects the way in which people compensate for adversity, humiliation, and isolation—the conditions of factory work for most people until the labor victories of the 1930s brought some relief. Despite the often dehumanizing conditions of mass production assembly lines and chronic unemployment, workers hold on to memories, actual or primordial, of *communitas*, of festivity, binding folk custom, and community values. Such values underlie their traditional lore, sustaining them and giving their lives worth and dignity.

Conroy's contributions to the Illinois Writers Project were only part of the rich legacy of literary work he leaves. Workers' idiom, folklore in industrial settings, expressions of resistance among oppressed people were the material of his writing long before he came to Chicago in 1938 and joined the Writers Project. In a sense, his work continues the tradition of creative activity that has existed marginally in American life, for instance, in the folk culture of the I.W.W., the workers' correspondence of union journals, the publications of the old Socialist press, and in the vast repertory of oral literature, fragments of which the project attempted to record. Conroy's work derives from this material, yet he extended it, giving it literary shape in his novel *The Disinherited* and numerous short stories anthologized in *The Weed King and Other Stories*. This is a remarkable achievement for one who, in America, belonged to a class of people who leave little or no written record. Conroy was privileged in that he was there to hear and record in his memory their voices. Through the "voice" of his texts, then, we are able to overhear these "many long dumb voices."

Notes

[1] Frederick wrote Conroy: "I shall hope to keep in touch with you, and trust that we can co-operate in some way in the future" (letter, 12 May 1933).

[2] See Jack Conroy, "Writers Disturbing the Peace," *New Masses* 21 (17 Nov. 1936): 13; George Lipsitz, "Striking Prose: The St. Louis Writers' Strike of 1936," *St. Louis Magazine* (March 1983): 4-46.

[3] See Stephen Vincent Benet's review in the *New York Herald Tribune*. Book Section (5 Sept. 1937).

[4] Also, see letters, Frederick to Conroy, 12 Aug. 1938; 9 Sept. 1938.

[5] See, for instance, Illinois Writers Project ms., Viola Edwards, Troy, IL, 28 Aug. 1936. Illinois Historical Society Library, Box 40.

[6] Conroy remembers that Algren "confessed" finally to Frederick that he didn't have experience in industrial settings to write industrial folklore. Interview, Conroy, 21 June 1987; 22 October 1978.

[7] Conroy recalls that Algren liked to give the impression that he didn't do anything for the Writers Project. In truth, however, he wrote the *Galena* guidebook and submitted occupational narratives like "When You've Lived Like I Done."

[8] Frederick later told MacDougall that he thought Algren and Conroy were Communists and hence was reluctant to promote them. Interview, Conroy, 21 June 1987.

[9] In a letter to Howard Wolf, 28 April 1938, Conroy writes that he is spending two days a week in the Newberry Library, working on a study of black migration, to be entitled *Any Place But Here* (sic). It is clear then that Conroy had intended to write such a book even before he was linked up with Arna Bontemps on the Project. The title was later used when Bontemps and Conroy revised *They Seek a City* in the 1960s.

[10] Time-motion studies, monotony, speed-up, were some of the conditions

characterizing assembly line work, in addition to the constant threat of layoffs among workers who were generally unskilled despite the sophistication of the factory processes.

Works Cited

Articles, Books:

Aaron, Daniel. Intro., *The Disinherited*. By Jack Conroy. NY: Hill and Wang, 1963.

Banks, Ann, ed. *First-Person America*. NY: Knopf, 1980.

Bloxom, Marguerite D. ed. *Pickaxe and Pencil: References for the Study of the WPA*. Washington, D.C.: Library of Congress, 1982.

Botkin, Benjamin A. *Folk-Say, a Regional Miscellany 1930*. Norman: U of Oklahoma P, 1930.

—. "The Folk and the Writer," unpubl. ms. Conroy Archives.

—. "*A Treasury of American Anecdotes*. NY: Crown, 1944.

—. "We Called it 'Living Lore,'" *New York Folklore Quarterly* 14 (Fall 1958): 189-201.

—. "WPA and Folklore Research: 'Bread and Song,'" *Southern Folklore Quarterly* 3 (March 1939): 7-14.

Conroy, Jack. "Days of The Anvil," *American Book Collector* 21 (Summer 1971): 15-19.

—. *The Disinherited*. NY: Lawrence Hill, 1982.

—. "Home to Moberly," *MLA Quarterly* (March 1968): 41-50.

—. "Memories of Arna Bontemps: Friend and Collaborator," *American Libraries* (Dec. 1974): 602-606.

—. *Midland Humor*. NY: A. A. Wyn, 1947.

—. "Radicals Sold Out So Cheap." Rev. of *Radical Visions and American Dreams*, by Richard H. Pells, and *The New Deal for Artists*, by Richard D. McKinzie. *Kansas City Star* (5 Aug. 1973): 3D.

—. *The Weed King and Other Stories*. Ed. Douglas Wixson. NY: Lawrence Hill, 1985.

—. "Writers Disturbing the Peace," *New Masses* 21 (17 Nov. 1936): 13.

Conroy, Jack and Arna Bontemps. *Anyplace But Here*. NY: Hill & Wang, 1966.

—. *They Seek a City*. Garden City, NY: Doubleday, Doran, 1945.

Green, Archie. "Industrial Lore: A Bibliographic-Semantic Query," *Western Folklore* 37 (July 1978): 213-244.

Hirsch, Jerrold. "Folklore in the Making: B. A. Botkin," *Journal of American Folklore* 100 (Jan.-March 1987): 3-38.

Illinois Writers' Project Newsletter 1 (28 Dec. 1940).

Kisor, Henry. "At Home with the Sage of Moberly," *Panorama, Chicago Daily News* (18-19 Aug. 1973): 2-3.

Mangione, Jerre. *The Dream and the Deal: The Federal Writers' Project, 1935-1943*. NY: Avon Books, 1972.

Penkower, Monty Noam. *The Federal Writers' Project, A Study in Government Patronage of the Arts*. Urbana: U of Illinois P, 1977.

Interviews:
Aaron, Abe. 14 Jan. 1990.
Conroy, 22 Oct. 1978.
Conroy, 26 Dec. 1978.
Conroy, 21 June 1987.
In addition, interviews with Sam Ross, Marion Knoblauch-Franc, Jerre Mangione, Margaret Walker, Meridel Le Sueur, Joseph Vogel, Paul Corey, Nathan Morris, Harold Sullivan, Studs Terkel.

Letters
Conroy to Fallon, 17 Jan. 1938.
Frederick to Conroy, 12 May 1933.
Frederick to Conroy, 12 Aug. 1938.
Frederick to Conroy, 16 June 1939.
Frederick to Conroy, 9 Sept. 1938.
Botkin to Conroy, 31 Jan. 1939.
Botkin to Frederick, 11 May 1939. Courtesy of the Illinois State Historical Society Library.
Caldwell to Conroy, in *New Letters* (Fall 1972): 20.

Manuscripts in Illinois Writer's Project Collection, Illinois State Historical Society Library, Springfield
Algren, Nelson. "When You've Lived Like I Done."
Alsberg, Henry. "Editorial Report on State Copy," 29 March 1939.
Conroy, Jack. "Fred Harrison."
—. "Slappy Hooper."
—. "The Boomer Fireman's Fast Sooner Hound."
—. "The Demon Bricksetter."
—. "The Type Louse."
—. "High Divers."
—. "North Clark St. Conversation."
—. "The Sissy from Hardscrabble County Rock Quarries."
Edwards, Viola. Troy, IL, 28 Aug. 1936, Box 40.
MacDougall, Curtis. "The Illinois Writers Project," 30 Oct. 1983.
Outline, "American Folk Stuff"
Silver, David. "Folklore of Urban Communities," New York Writer's Project.

José Garcia Villa and Sherwood Anderson: A Study in Influence

Roger J. Bresnahan

Expelled from the University of the Philippines in 1929 for publishing poems too erotic for the prudish sensibilities of the faculty, José Garcia Villa left for his self-imposed exile in the United States. Villa was introduced to American readers by Edward J. O'Brien in *The Best Short Stories of 1932* and again in *The Best Short Stories of 1933*. In the introduction to Villa's only short story collection, published in 1933, O'Brien referred to Villa as "among the half-dozen short story writers in America who count" (Villa 4). There he also made his now famous comment that Villa had been influenced by Sherwood Anderson. A careful reading of O'Brien's introduction to that volume of twenty-one stories will reveal, however, that the supposed influence of Sherwood Anderson is to be seen in the three autobiographical stories, "Wings and Blue Flame: A Trilogy." Furthermore, O'Brien almost immediately disavows the comparison when he adds that "Villa can in no wise be regarded as a mere disciple of Sherwood Anderson" for his work contains "a lyrical quality which is foreign to Sherwood Anderson's work" (Villa 4). By this time Villa had turned his energies exclusively to poetry. Knowing that, O'Brien was merely attempting to establish continuity between the fiction which Villa had already forsworn and the poetry he had commenced to write.

O'Brien's suggestion of Sherwood Anderson's influence on Villa cannot be wholly dismissed, for other perceptive critics have seen in Villa's work what O'Brien did not. Leopoldo Y. Yabes, in the introduction to the first volume of his multivolume anthology of Philippine short stories in English, understood that Villa, ever the experimenter with literary form, was indeed following Anderson in developing the modern American short story (Yabes xix-xxxvii). Following the defeat of Filipino forces in the Philippine-American War, English had become the language of instruction in Philippine public schools. Villa, who was born in 1906, is considered to be in the first generation of Filipino writers in English, the generation that experimented with new forms of the short story. In their hands it became a very different medium from the Maupassant-Poe tale as they continued to experiment with the forms just then being developed by Anderson, Hemingway, Wilbur Daniel Steele, William Saroyan, and Dorothy Parker. The way Filipino writers in English took hold of the short story form is nothing less than phenomenal. Today such Filipino writers as N. V. M. Gonzalez, Bienvenido N. Santos, Linda Ty-Casper, Gregorio C. Brillantes, Renato Madrid, Ninotchka Rosca, and others continue to experiment with their own forms of the short story.[1]

For O'Brien, Anderson's influence was merely in the subject-matter of the autobiographical stories. As such, the influence was superficial. Yabes goes deeper when he shows that Villa's stories were like Anderson's in that they do not adhere to the unities of the Poe-Maupassant type of story and that plot "is secondary to the portrayal of mood and character" (Yabes xxiv). Yabes delineates the Anderson model of the short story that Villa followed: "The general theme-statement of these tales concerns a certain mood caused by internal or external influences. . . . There is . . . no piling up of incident upon incident to lead up to an inevitable denouement, no deliberative attempt at straight narrative, no signs of mechanized-ness in structure. Nevertheless, the end leaves the reader with a sense of completeness" (Yabes xxiv).

To corroborate what Yabes has discovered in the short story form as practiced by Sherwood Anderson, we might turn to a number of perceptive readers. Not surprisingly, one such reader might be David D. Anderson, whose entry on Sherwood Anderson in the *Dictionary of Literary Biography* represents his most mature reflections on a writer to whom he has devoted many years of study. In this work, David Anderson tells us that Sherwood Anderson's "A New Note," published in Margaret Anderson's *Little Review* in 1914, was "an affirmation of the work he had begun and a statement of the sense of craft that was to dominate his work" (Anderson 5). By 1916, then, Sherwood

Anderson "had found, for the subject matter of his best work, those people who are deformed psychologically, people ne was to call grotesques. He had found, too, his language, the easy rhythms of the American heartland, and his form, the seemingly artless but carefully controlled meandering of an ancient oral tradition" (6-7).

David Anderson finds that "The Rabbit-Pen," Sherwood Anderson's first published story (*Harper's*, July 1914), forecasts his "later use of vivid harsh incidents" and his "future concern with love and the ironies of appearance" (Anderson 5). In "Sister" (*Little Review*, December 1915), David Anderson finds a story that is "impressionistic rather than realistic in technique," one in which "the prose is straightforward and natural, in the first-person manner of an oral storyteller" (5). Similarly, "a moment of horror" is central to "Hands," but it remains "low-keyed, not exploited but integral to the plot structure and intensely real. It provides a momentary insight into what makes Wing Biddlebaum a grotesque" (9).

Winesburg, Ohio, taken as a whole, is intensely evocative of a time and place—a backwater town in the hiatus between the Civil War and the period of industrial development whose material values Sherwood Anderson so much despised. Yet, as David Anderson observes, the individual stories are less about that time and that place than about the people themselves. "Each of them becomes the focal point and the substance of the story, as the nature of each is laid bare in a moment of Anderson's insight into what makes his people grotesques" (13). Villa's stories in *A Footnote to Youth* similarly focus on the psychic nature of individuals. But there is no unifying factor, no George Willard, no moment of hiatus between a cataclysmic historical event and a momentous conflict of values. It is not just Villa's flight to America and his resolute desire to remain there that have made him "the most outstanding alienated Filipino poet of all time" (Lopez 11-12).

Though supported by a sinecure at the office of the Philippine Commonwealth government in Washington and later at the Philippine Mission to the United Nations, Villa has written poetry so divorced from the Philippine situation as to be remarkable. Even in *Footnote to Youth*, Villa's local color evokes little sense of the Philippines. That may make his stories intensely human, but it also makes them as ethereal as his poetry.

Like Sherwood Anderson's stories, Villa's are "character-plotted," each containing "a revealing moment" in which the author "penetrates suddenly and sometimes shockingly to the character's psychological reality" (Anderson 13). But where Sherwood Anderson's intent was to examine "the place of the central character in the life of the community" (Anderson 13), Villa's attitude toward his characters is as distant and alienated as himself. Because "Anderson insisted that all his people . . . were worthy of love and compassion, not in spite of but because of their very grotesqueness" (Anderson 13), we can feel sympathy for the likes of Wing Biddlebaum. For Villa's characters we seldom feel such sympathy, for their frailties cannot be our own.

David Anderson shows that in each of the first three stories of *Winesburg, Ohio*—"Hands," "Paper Pills," and "Mother" —"the central character has an inner vision" (Anderson 14), that he or she is unable to communicate to others. Out of this misunderstanding, "what is beautiful becomes, instead, a perversion" so that *Winesburg, Ohio* "is a work in which Anderson not only defines the problem of human isolation, but asserts that it can be overcome, if only in moments, if we learn to transcend the walls that society and biology have erected among us" (Anderson 14).

The twenty-one stories in *Footnote to Youth* may be divided into five groupings: love stories, Christ-like stories, Rizal stories, lost-youth stories, and experimental pieces. This is not the order in which they are found in the book, and it is not clear whether it was Villa himself who devised the original ordering, or his editor at Scribner's, or even Edward O'Brien, who clearly had something to do with the volume being published. In any case, the ordering as they appear in the volume makes no sense, as other readers have noted (Arcellana 603-617).

The love stories all turn on a moment of cruelty to the beloved which also involves denial of the self. In the introductory and concluding sections of "Malakas," this point is made explicit: " . . . a love that is not cruel is dead. It is not love, what is alive, hurts" (Villa 57). This is the moral to Villa's version. Malakas resists marriage until he's twenty-two so he can marry Maganda. But she marries the youth Bayani instead and promises Malakas her first-born daughter if he will wait. The daughter, also named Maganda, is about to marry Malakas, who by then is thirty-seven, but she elopes with a youth. Like her mother, she promises Malakas her first-born daughter. The third-generation Maganda does love Malakas, despite the love of the youth Isagani for her. But as this latest Maganda waits on her wedding day, Malakas, now fifty, sends Isagani in his place. Wisdom being love and love wisdom, Malakas proves his love for Maganda by denying himself at last, though Villa makes this point at the expense of the Tagalog race, whose progenitors will never come together in his story, unless Villa is subtly inviting the reader to assume a fourth-general Maganda.

Similar to the tale of Malakas, is "Kamya," a story with a grotesque ending that approaches the notion of a moment of horror seen in Anderson's "Rabbit-Pen." Kamya is a beautiful girl of the tribe of Rajah Soliman, the local headman in the area of Manila at the time of the Spanish invasion. She is beloved of two young men, Mabi the hunter and warrior, and Isagani the poet and metal smith. Though Kamya is enthralled with Mabi, whose exploits are visible and whose strength is palpable, Isagani makes a beautiful gold knife as his gift to her, though he is ridiculed by others who know a gold knife would be useless. Of course, that's the point. It is an object of art, an end in itself. But because Isagani cannot take his eyes off the beauty of the knife, Kamya rejects him, believing the beauty of the gift could not be greater than her own beauty. On the day she is to be married to Mabi, Isagani stabs her with the gold knife. Kamya dies happy knowing that Isagani loved her best since he had chosen his most beautiful knife for her.

In "Valse Triste" Pepe attends midnight mass on Christmas Eve with his uncle Berting. There Berting points out Tinang, the love of his youth. When she had become pregnant his father had exiled him to Manila. On Christmas Eve he returned in secret, found Tinang in church, and asked to see their baby. But she had aborted the baby. Kissing her tenderly, Berting told her, "Good-bye, Tinang. For you are not a woman—you have not the heart of a woman, Tinang—you could kill your baby" (Villa 186). Wiser now, he wants Pepe to convey his sorrow for what he said and did. But Tinang tells Pepe no apology was necessary. When Berting had first abandoned her, she "dared to think he was not a man." But that final "slow cruel kiss . . . sealed my eyes with the great beauty of his manhood. . . . For the boy I loved was a man" (189-190).

Like the moments of horror that are the impetus for many of Sherwood Anderson's stories, these acts of simultaneous cruelty and self-denial cannot be rationally explained. In all of them, the woman is wronged, yet we are made to feel the male character thinks he has done it for her best interests. This is especially so in "Given Woman." Ponso asks the ugly Flora to live with him without marriage. Though she is offended, she agrees so she won't have to live as a servant. Ponso builds Flora a house with his own hands and in many other ways demonstrates his love for her. Though both want to express their love for each other, both remain silent. Ponso, deeply depressed when their child dies, announces he is leaving but will find Flora a better man. He gives her to a widower with three small children. The hurt and pain at the end of this story are palpable, as is the love. And that's the mystery.

The final story in the group of love stories is "The Fence," the story that Edward J. O'Brien published in *The Best Short Stories of 1933*. Here two women, Aling Biang and Aling Sebia, live in adjacent houses separated by a tall fence that was erected by Aling Biang out of spite ("Aling" is a title of familiar respect). Aling Biang's son and Aling Sebia's daughter grow into their teen years on opposite sides of the fence, only catching glimpses of each other. The sickly boy's only happiness is hearing the girl play the clangy notes of an off-tune guitar each night, breaking off her playing before the piece is done. She had played that guitar for three years when he whispered through the fence, speaking to the girl for the first time, "Play for me tonight." That night he waited in vain, finally dying at two a.m. The girl played at 3 a.m., and she played the whole piece. Aling Biang, mourning her dead son, "approached the window, stared accusingly outside and said in a low resentful voice: 'They are mocking. Who would play at such a time of morn as this? Because my son is dead.' But she saw only the fence she had built and strengthened, stately white in the matutinal moonlight" (Villa 37-38).

The intense moments of the group I would term the Christ-like stories are not harsh or cruel, as in the love stories, but sudden revelations to the reader. In "Yet Do They Strife" a small boy runs out of the house when his drunken father begins to beat his mother. Wandering outside, deeply troubled by his parents' arguing, he finds a weary stranger lying in a field of flowers, arms outstretched. The stranger has been watching but is weary and wants to go home. The boy loves the stranger immediately and accompanies him to a stream where the water is exceedingly sweet. Though still weary, the stranger returns to the field to watch again "because the earth needs me" (Villa 323).

The boy feels at peace as he returns home and knows he will meet the stranger again.

In other stories in this group the revelation is in the reader rather than the character. In "The Woman Who Looked Like Christ," for example, Aurora misses the point entirely when her boyfriend says she has the face of Christ. She is outraged that he has said she looks like a man. "Resurrection" is set on Easter morn. Here a man gets progressively more drunk, ignoring his wife's request that he get the midwife. He repeatedly knocks his head against a tree because the three previous babies have been born dead. A gentle stranger intervenes and looks deeply into the man's eyes. The missed revelation on the part of the characters lends a comic air to "Like My boy" in which a widow is assisted in labor by a woman accompanied by an infant. As the woman leaves she says, "Call him, woman—like my boy." When the widow brings the baby to town to be baptized, the priest wants to name him Jesus because he was born on Christmas Eve. The widow, suffering a failure of insight that the reader can hardly miss, adamantly refuses because she has promised the woman who helped that she would name the baby after the boy. As she never asked the woman what her boy's name was, her own son has no given name.

Several stories turn on a relationship of resemblance to the Philippine national hero, José Rizal. In the simplest of these, "Son of Rizal," the narrator meets a man on a train who is from Calamba, the home town of José Rizal, who claims to have been born of Josephine Bracken, the Irish woman to whom Rizal is said to have been married on the eve of his execution by the Spanish for treason. Later the narrator brings this illiterate local character a bust of Rizal, but the story falls flat. "The Daughter of Rizal" is more interesting for the way in which the girl considers herself to be the offspring of the national hero. Her mother had done the young José Rizal a favor and in return he did a crayon portrait of her. Years later the woman, though heavy with child, insisted on witnessing the execution of the man she had always loved from afar. As the shots rang out, she fainted. Because of the fall, her baby daughter was born blind, and thus the girl calls herself the daughter of Rizal.

"The Man Who Looked Like Rizal" tells of "an insignificant person but for his face that resembled Rizal's" (Villa 266). Though he was an ugly, illiterate workman, when his daughter came home from school and told him that he looked like Rizal, this "weak puny man . . . imagined he was really Rizal and forgot his ugly reality" (271). But becoming a national hero carried with it not only glory, but responsibilities as well. When his wife ran away with another man he acted magnanimously. And when the other man knocked him down in the street, he walked away from a fight because the national hero doesn't engage in brawls.

Related to the three stories of the Rizal-sequence is "Story for My Country." Here the narrator recalls the day his older brother, José, left home, the last day he saw him. José had been severely beaten by their father for letting a rabbit escape. As the two boys lay on the sleeping mat together, José ran his fingers through the younger boy's hair. Now, years later, the younger brother wishes he had told José how much he loved him, wished he had brought José and their father together so perhaps José might not have left. But like the feelings between Ponso and Flora, they were never uttered. Now grown up with a son of his own, whom he has named José, the narrator visits Manila and sees there a statue of Rizal, who looks just like his brother. So he imagines that his big brother changed his name from José Rosal to José Rizal to fool their father and then had become the national hero. Here Villa displays in ironic sense of humor, as he does in the pathos of "The Fence" and in his truncated version of the origin myth.

The final important set of stories are the three related to lost youth: "Footnote to Youth," "Death into Manhood," and "Young Writer in a New Country." The first, which brought Villa to the attention of American readers when O'Brien published it in *The Best Short Stories of 1932*, is constructed as four scenes. In the first scene Dodong's father, afraid to visit a dentist, is at home sucking on a painful, broken tooth. It will presage the situation years later between Dodong and his own son. When Dodong tells his father he wants to marry Teang, his father stops sucking on the tooth and there ensues a long silence in which there is a "strange helplessness in his father's eyes" (Villa 14). The second scene is the birth of Blas, Dodong's first child, when the terror of fatherhood begins to sink in. In the third scene Dodong has realized that with manhood and marriage and family, his youth has been lost as he asks, "why Life did not fulfill all of Youth's dreams. Why it must be so. Why one was forsaken . . . after Love" (Villa 19). In the fourth scene the tables have turned. Blas has come home to announce that he will marry

Tona, and Dodong can only ask, as his father once asked him, "Must you marry?" As the story closes, "Dodong looked wistfully at his young son in the moonlight. He felt extremely sad and sorry for him" (22).

"Death into Manhood" is perhaps the most tightly structured of the stories in *Footnote to Youth.* As the story opens, "Tona did not realize that when she gave herself up to Doro she was seeing him for the last time" (Villa 289). Though abandoned, she devotes her life to Berto, the child of this union. The reader senses that as Berto grows, Tona feels a vague sense of doom. When he's fifteen, he demands long pants. Then she sees him bathing and discovers he is maturing. She sees him shaving. Then, when he's eighteen he puts on a white drill suit, slicks his hair, and advises his mother not to wait up for him as he's taking Maria to the cinema. "She suddenly grew afraid of Berto, suddenly apart from him. A cruel tumult was unleashed in her. Berto was no longer Berto. Berto was a *Man* . . . DORO" (296). Tona's womanhood triumphs over her motherhood as she rushes out into the night and races to Aling Pipa, Maria's mother: "'Poor Maria, Poor Maria,' Tona said wearily, futiley. 'Tell her never to go out alone again with Berto" (296).

The narrator of "Young Writer in a New Country" muses that in his homeland he wanted to marry, but his father said, "You are very young," when he meant, "I will come in between" (Villa 299-300). His father sends him to America to study, and there he meets new friends, but he tries to puzzle out his relationship to his father and, like the alien and ever alienated Villa, his relationship to his homeland. The story ends on this note of regret: "Will the native land forgive? Between your peace and the peace of a strange faraway desert—Between your two peaces—O, tell softly, softly. Forgive softly" (303-304).

Finally, there are five experimental pieces. In 1933, just as Villa was publishing this collection of short stories, he was giving up fiction altogether, believing that one had to choose between fiction and poetry. His poetry, even more alienated from his Philippine roots than his fiction, is written in the styles of E. E. Cummings, Marianne Moore, Edith Sitwell, Elinor Wylie, and, ultimately, the style of Villa where experiments with rhythm, internal rhyme schemes, and novel uses of punctuation dominate over content, theme, and imagery.[2] The three pieces that comprise the "Wings and Blue Flame" trilogy and a fourth piece, "Song I Did Not Hear," are composed of numbered paragraphs of musings on coming to America and friends at the University of New Mexico. "Little Tales" consists of eight fragments, each about fifty words. These pieces, more concerned with the pyrotechnics of language, confirm an observation made about his poetry: that "the Villa universe is . . . completely evacuated of values which we can easily recognize as human" (Tinio 724).

Villa did not lose his sensibility for fiction as he exerted a major influence on Philippine writing in his yearly lists of the best Philippine short stories, issued from 1926 through 1940, after the manner of his American sponsor, Edward J. O'Brien. Had Villa continued to write short stories after the manner of Sherwood Anderson, he might have become a considerable force in American fiction. As it is, *Footnote to Youth* is largely a showpiece, containing nonetheless some very powerful stories. Because he did not pursue the craft of fiction any longer, the collection has become, in one critic's biting assessment, a "footnote to Villa" (Casper 105).

Notes

[1] Among available short story collections are the following: Gregorio C. Brillantes, *The Apollo Centennial* (Manila: National Book Store, 1980) and *The Distance to Andromeda* (National Book Store, 1979); Jose Y. Dalisay, Jr., *Oldtimer* (Manila: Asphodel, 1984); Leoncio P. Deriada, *Night Mares* (New Day, 1988); Lina Espina-Moore, *Cuentos* (New Day, 1985); N. V. M. Gonzalez, *Mindoro and Beyond* (Quezon City: U of the Philippines P, 1979); Nick Joaquin, *Tropical Gothic* (Sta. Lucia: U of Queensland P, 1972); F. Sionil Jose, *Waywaya* (Hong Kong: Heinemann, 1980); Renato Madrid, *Southern Harvest* (New Day, 1987); Cecilia Manguerra-Brainard, *Woman with Horns* (New Day, 1988); Denis Murphy, *The Pope's Confessor* (New Day, 1985); Ninotchka Rosca, *Bitter Country* (Quezon City: Malaya, 1970) and *The Monsoon Collection* (U of Queensland P, 1988); Arturo B. Rotor, *The Men Who Play God* (Quezon City: Ateneo de Manila UP, 1983); Bienvenido N. Santos, *Scent of Apples* (Seattle: U of Washington P, 1979); Edilberto K. Tiempo, *Finalities* (New Day, 1982) and *Rainbow for Rima* (New Day, 1988); Linda Ty-Casper, *The Transparent Sun* (Manila: Florentino, 1963) and *The Secret Runner* (Florentino, 1974).

Several of these writers have turned to novels and novellas. Among recent titles are the following: F. Sionil Jose, *Ermita* (Manila: Solidaridad, 1988); Ninotchka Rosca, *State of War* (New York: Norton, 1988); Bienvenido N. Santos, *The Man Who (Thought He) Looked Like Robert Taylor* (New Day, 1983) and *What The Hell For You Left Your Heart in San Francisco* (New Day, 1987); and Linda Ty-Casper, *A Small Party in a Garden* (New Day, 1988).

Imprints of the University of the Philippines Press are distributed in the United States by the University of Hawaii Press. New Day imprints are distributed in North America by the Cellar Book Shop (18090 Wyoming, Detroit, Mich. 48221). Cellar is also the best single source for out-of-print books published in the Philippines.

[2] José (lately spelled "Xoce") Garcia Villa, *Have Come, Am Here* (New York: Viking, 1941); *Volume Two* (New York: New Directions, 1949); *Selected Poems and New* (New York: McDowell, Obolensky, 1958); *Appassionata: Poems in Praise of Love* (New York: King and Cowen, 1979).

Works Cited

Anderson, David D. "Sherwood Anderson," in *American Short-Story Writers, 1910-1945, First Series,* ed. Bobby Ellen Kimball, *Dictionary of Literary Biography* 86. Detroit: Gale Research, 1989.

Arcellana, Francisco. "Period of Emergence: The Short Story," in *Brown Heritage: Essays on Philippine Cultural Tradition and Literature,* ed. Antonio G. Manuud. Quezon City: Ateneo de Manila UP, 1967, 603-617.

Casper, Leonard, ed. *New Writing from the Philippines: A Critique and Anthology.* Syracuse: Syracuse UP, 1966.

Lopez, Salvador P. "Literature and Society: A Literary Past Revisited," in *Literature and Society: Cross-Cultural Perspectives,* ed. Roger J. Bresnahan. Manila: Philippine-American Educational Foundation, 1976, 6-17.

Tinio, Rolando S. "Villa's Values; Or, the Poet You Cannot Always Make Out, or Succeed in Liking Once You Are Able To," in *Brown Heritage,* ed. Manuud, 722-738.

Villa, José Garcia. *Footnote to Youth: Tales of the Philippines and Others.* New York: Charles Scribner's Sons, 1933.

Yabes, Leopoldo Y. "Pioneering in the Filipino Short Story in English (1925-1940)," *Philippine Short Stories, 1925-1940,* ed. Yabes. Quezon City: U of the Philippines P, 1974.

Midwestern Literary Identities

Theodore Dreiser: Changing Trains in Chicago

Philip L. Gerber

In 1944 Walter Damrosch, then serving as president of the American Academy of Arts and Letters, invited Theodore Dreiser to come to New York to accept the Award of Merit Medal in honor of his contribution to American fiction. In addition to his gold medal and cash prize of $1,000, Dreiser was allowed $400 for his planefare from Los Angeles, where he was then living. But at the last moment the novelist chose to travel instead by rail, this despite the vast distances to be covered, the notorious wartime crush on railroad transportation, and the fact that he would be obliged to change trains in Chicago both going and returning. Why? Dreiser, on the verge of seventy-three, was not really a well man and in fact had just a year and a half to live. He was not above frugality, to be sure, but there must have been a more compelling reason for undertaking a grueling schedule, and I like to think that it had something to do with the magical spell which Chicago had cast upon him during his boyhood, this and the inescapable likelihood that the trip might be his final opportunity for re-experiencing the thrill he had always felt upon approaching the midwestern metropolis.

The 1944 trip almost exactly marked the sixtieth anniversary of Dreiser's first solo entry into Chicago, a wondrous moment for him, preceded by intense anticipation. He always mined the facts of his own life for his fiction, and it is in *The "Genius"* (1915) that he portrays a young adventurer such as himself (in the persona of small-town boy Eugene Witla) dreamily thumbing the weekend edition of a Chicago newspaper and thrilling to the "subtle wonder of the city." Every column of print speaks of marvels not to be experienced within the confining limits of tiny Alexandria: a great hotel a-building, a famous pianist coming to perform, a new comedy-drama opening at a grand theater, a street so long that its designated addresses could reach to the number 6200—"What a tremendous city Chicago must be!" (34)

For the small towns and middle-range cities of the midwestern plains Dreiser had little but contempt, scorning them for their narrowness of viewpoint, their bleakness regarding anything that might be called culture. His own native Terre Haute—what did it conjure up for him except reminders of his boyhood poverty and a harsh winter climate against whose threat he had little protection? In later years when he was established as a writer of both prominence and importance, Terre Haute had offered him no recognition, had attempted, in fact, to bury its connection with him. But Chicago? Chicago was another matter entirely. Here existed not only golden possibilities, but there was greatness in the making. Over and over again, in fiction and nonfiction, Dreiser attempted to communicate the sweet essence of his boyhood vision of The City. Such obsessive attempts always had the power of bringing out the lyricist in him, as exemplified when he apostrophizes the city in his autobiography *Dawn*: "Hail, Chicago! First of the daughters of the new world! Strange illusion of hope and happiness that resounded as a paean by your lake of blue! . . . Of what dreams and songs were your walls and ways compounded!" (156)

Even as he rhapsodized, Dreiser understood that his praise for Chicago was compounded largely of his own overbrimming subjectivity. In *Dawn* he confessed it openly:

> The city of which I am now about to write never was on land or sea; or if it appears to have the outlines of reality, they are but shadow to the glory that was in my own mind. Compassed by a shell or skull, there was a mirror inside me which colored all it reflected. There was some mulch of chemistry that transmuted walls of yellow brick and streets of cedar block and horses and men into amethyst and gold and silver and pegasi and archangels of flaming light. . . . The city of which I sing was not of land or sea or any time or place. Look for it in vain! (156)

How, asked Dreiser, could any mortal writer hope to "hymn"—or even *suggest*—a city so tremendous in spirit as Chicago? He acknowledged the impossibility of ever being capable of duplicating for a reader those unimaginable sensations which had been his at age sixteen when he, a country bumpkin if ever there was one, had stepped off a northbound train at the old Pennsylvania depot along Canal Street into "a hurly-burly of trunks and porters and bags, lines of cabs and buses outside." And then wandering the Chicago streets, Madison in particular, in a daze of delight: "Beautiful! Like a scene in a play; an Alladin view of the Arabian nights" (296, 298).

Although convinced that it was impossible to communicate the ineffable impact of the city, Dreiser not only made the attempt but repeated it over and over again. It is in *The "Genius"* that he most specifically replicates his own youthful entry into the City Beautiful. Eugene Witla comes north from the same hinterlands as Dreiser, a route providing a panoramic overview: first the unimaginable miles of empty streets already paved and set with gas lamps; then the thousands of modest cottages occupying raw suburbs; a wilderness of railroad tracks, as many as thirty iron roads laid side by side; clusters of immigrant Lithuanians, Poles, and Czechs, representative of populations pouring in at the rate of fifty thousand per annum; then a conglomeration of factories, foundries, warehouses, grain elevators, boats plying a river, and churches.

On Dreiser's pages the history of this small but crucial portion of the Midwest, in actuality a flux of daily and drastic change, is flash-frozen into imperishable scenes, one of many in *The "Genius"* being Eugene Witla's arrival at the Pennsylvania depot, that point at which he ceases being spectator and becomes a participant:

> The train threaded its way through long lines of cars coming finally into an immense train shed where arc lights were sputtering—a score under a great curved steel and glass roof, where people were hurrying to and fro. Engines were hissing; bells clanging raucously. . . . This picture of life, this newness, fascinated [Eugene]. He stepped down and started leisurely to the gate, wondering which way he should go. He came to a corner where a lamp post already lit blazoned the name Madison. He looked out on this street and saw, as far as the eye could reach, two lines of stores, jingling horse cars, people walking. What a sight, he thought, and turned west. (38)

It is the "newness" which so captivates Eugene, this "world of hope and opportunity" which the city appears to offer scot-free for the newcomer's taking; this is what receives Dreiser's full emphasis.

The adjectives "new" and "raw" come into play; everything is in the making; on every side stand hints of things to come: solid four-story buildings of brick, as yet isolated among an ocean of more humble frame structures; impressive banks, office blocks, retail stores, grand hotels in what would become the Loop; that entire business heart "running with a tide of people which represented the youth, the illusions, the untrained aspirations, of millions of souls." Here were concentrated the eagerness, the hope, and the desire of youth. Chicago was a city that made one's adrenalin spurt, injecting "vitality into almost every wavering heart; it made the beginner dream dreams" (39).

Dreiser felt himself foremost among those dreamers. A sudden conversion was underway here, on his part. Intuitively, he had found his metier and embraced it, even if recognizing the fact only mistily in an intellectual sense during those active 1880s and not possessing any sure foreknowledge of the uses to which all this newness might be put. But once he began to take pen in hand—and that within a half-dozen years of his arrival in Chicago—Dreiser instinctively turned his back upon his previous life, that of the small town. His discarded life represented the past, the rural/agricultural culture that had been America. In its place, as the dominant and near-universal setting for all his literary works, Dreiser chose instead the metropolis, the human adaptation to and reflection of the industrial giganticism of the new America. One might say, without much fear of exaggeration, that the moment of his arrival at Pennsylvania depot was Dreiser's first step toward his preeminence as a city novelist. Thoreau and his cohorts may have sought truth in the unoccupied woods surrounding Walden Pond, and found it, leaving the village of men to do so, but Dreiser's heroes follow a reverse pattern, abandoning rural roots to become dwellers in the rabbit-warren city. This is invariable.

Eugene Witla is selected to be the Dreiser persona who will represent that overpowering first impact of the city upon the *parvenu*. I say "selected" because there is no inherent need as concerns plot for Eugene to make a stopover in Chicago, *The "Genius"* being the story of an urban artist who works chiefly in New York. His residence in Chicago and early training at the Art Institute there are purely gratuitous, autobiographical, and serve the purpose of illuminating that moment of Dreiser's discovery. The hero, as it were, merely changes trains in Chicago and then continues his quest, speeding on toward the East, where his true destiny waits.

But there were other, darker aspects of Dreiser's midwestern city experience to be dealt with in fiction, and it lies with other novels and other personae to serve this function. Nearly a dozen years prior to *The "Genius"* Dreiser had begun the process of exorcism with *Sister Carrie* (1900), and it is eighteen-year-old Caroline Meeber who is employed in dramatizing the ragtag world of toil and struggle that awaited the newcomer once the first glad blush of contact with the city had faded. It is Carrie who walks the pavement, as young Dreiser had done, footsore and weary of soul, with scarcely enough pennies for carfare, in search of employment. It is she who is compelled by necessity, as Dreiser had been, to accept work where she can find it, grinding, menial labor at subminimal wages. It is she who, timorously and with rising apprehension, approaches close to the imposing new business blocks only to be intimidated, as Dreiser had been, by impenetrable walls of brass and brick, and thick plate-glass which allow a tantalizing glimpse of wonders within while effectively barring entry to any intermediate rung of the economic ladder which all must climb in order to survive in the new "money" society taking shape beside Lake Michigan.

Like Eugene Witla, Carrie Meeber "changes trains" in Chicago, ultimately going on from there to Montreal, New York, and London. But her stopover is considerably more extended than Eugene's, occupying fully half of the novel, so that Dreiser might give full rein to his portrait of the city of the big shoulders, the story, husky, brawling hog butcher, tool maker, stacker of wheat, player with railroads and freight handler of the nation—a portrait executed in much the same spirit as Carl Sandburg's defining verses of "Chicago" but set in print considerably prior to Sandburg's time. In *Sister Carrie* Dreiser's midwestern experience is mined in order to release the memory of his traumatic immersion in the world of toil, a strangling grip from his past.

The canvas is large, the spectrum broad. Dreiser moves his reader from the dawn-to-dusk drudgery inherent in Sven Hanson's swamping out of dirtied refrigerator cars at the Union stockyards to Carrie's near enslavement as a mere cog in a primitive assembly line of machine operators busily sewing footware.

Hanson is impressed into feeding the millions, Carrie into shoeing them. In Charles Drouet we experience the world of the traveling salesman, that essential agent for the immense manufacturing houses, feeding the products of industrialism into every midwestern hamlet and village as the modern consumer society is created. He and Carrie connect also with the newest of mercantile creations, the department store, where those wares are dispensed for coin to the urban thousands—establishments such as Marshall Field's and Carson, Pirie, Scott & Co.—made accessible by another great urban triumph of technology, the streetcar. Carrie's first visit to The Fair on Dearborn Street stands out here, with its smorgasbord of lingerie, earrings, bracelets, pins, skirts, jackets, and warm winter coats. George Hurstwood takes us a rung or two upwards on the socio-economic ladder, into the realm of managers, "the first grade below the luxuriously rich," as Dreiser puts it (44). As the official greeter at Hannah and Hogg's "truly swell" saloon on Adams Street across from the imposing new Federal Building, Hurstwood is the first public relations man in our literature, selling his personality to the upper crust as openly as Drouet peddles his pots and pans to small-town merchants. Through her friend Mrs. Hale, Carrie catches—from a respectful distance—a fast glimpse of those favored few who coast atop the crest of the new society, as she views the grand suburban mansions of the wealthy North Shore women whom she has envied whenever she has seen them dashing along Chicago boulevards in private carriages. And through Carrie's first cautious experience on the stage in "Under the Gaslight" a door is opened—later to be flung ajar for a closer look—onto the emergent world of celebrity, where dollars in abundance and luxury untold are showered upon those whose personalities in some manner touch the public pulse. These are modern times indeed, if only in the formative stages. Dreiser grasps this point and makes the most of it.

In 1911, after the decade of hiatus in fiction writing caused by the publishing debacle accompanying his debut with *Sister Carrie,* Dreiser managed to complete *Jennie Gerhardt* and have it published by Harper & Brothers. The story is midwestern through and through, centering upon Columbus and Cleveland, Ohio, but it makes its obligatory bow to Chicago nonetheless. Lester Kane, attempting to have his cake and eat it, too, by continuing his unconventional liaison with Jennie even while preserving his very necessary public image as conservative bachelor businessman, hits upon Chicago as a solution to his dilemma. His family's decision to expand its business by establishing a warehouse in Chicago is fortuitous:

> Lester decided to move to Chicago immediately. He sent word for Jennie to meet him, and together they selected an apartment on the North Side, a very comfortable suite of rooms on a side street [Schiller Place] near the lake, and he had it fitted up to suit his taste. He figured that living in Chicago he could pose as a bachelor. He would never need to invite his friends to his rooms. There were his offices, where he could always be found, his clubs and his hotels. To his way of thinking the arrangement was practically ideal. (195)

Rather clearly, the selection of Chicago here is as arbitrary as in *The "Genius."* Any sizable American metropolis would have served to furnish the anonymity which, in this case, is not to be feared but actually to be desired. Given the motivation, New York would have been an even more plausible choice. By 1910 Dreiser had lived in New York for fifteen years and knew it as well, or better perhaps, than he knew the Midwest. In any event, the eastern experience was more immediate. But just as clearly, for deeply-rooted reasons Dreiser wished—needed—to bring Jennie to Chicago; his loyalties ran deep. And so Jennie Gerhardt boards the westbound train for Chicago and is installed at 19 Schiller Place, where her lover also lives while not obligated to be in his suite at the Grand Pacific Hotel or to meet a business colleague at an evening appointment in the Union League Club.

The pattern of place established in *Sister Carrie* (where the first half of the story concerns Chicago) is now reversed, the second half of *Jennie Gerhardt* focusing upon the Chicago environment. His mistress's apartment being accidentally disclosed by a careless employee, Lester moves Jennie to then suburban South Hyde Park, to "an old-time home of eleven large rooms, set in a lawn fully two hundred feet square and shaded by trees which had been planted when the city was young" (256), a site which allows Dreiser to delineate the comfortable and expansive, and, for a time, serenely private life made possible at that time and in that place.

The great final scene of *Jennie Gerhardt*, following Lester Kane's funeral at St. Michael's, a southside Catholic church, takes place, as perhaps is fitting, amid the clanging bells and pulsing steam of locomotives. Herself an outcast now, her lover's corpse in the possession of his family, Jennie at the depot observes from the shadows of a concourse linking the depot waiting rooms with the tracks while Lester's coffin is loaded for its final trip:

> Throughout the great railroad station there was a hum of anticipation. . . . People were going away for the holiday. Carriages were at the station entries. Announcers were calling in stentorian voices the destination of each new train as the time of its departure drew near . . . and then finally [came the call] for "Indianapolis, Louisville, Columbus, Cincinnati, and points South." The hour had struck . . . a long red train, brilliantly lighted, composed of baggage cars, day coaches, a dining car, set with white linen and silver, and a half dozen comfortable Pullmans, rolled in and stopped. A great black engine, puffing and glowing, had it all safely in tow. (430)

And then, after the various Kanes have dashed for their Pullmans, comes the porter pushing his rumbling, iron-wheeled truck toward the baggage car, atop it the wood, cloth, and silver coffin nailed into a rough wooden case, and the call of a blue-clad freight handler in the baggage car: "'Hey, Jack! Give us a hand here. There's a stiff outside!'" Jennie remains while trunks and valises are packed aboard, the warning bell sounded. The call of "All aboard" being heard, "then slowly the great locomotive began to move. Its bell was ringing, its steam hissing, its smokestack throwing aloft a great black plume of smoke that fell back over the cars like a pall . . . She looked, and looked until the last glimmer of the red lamp on the receding sleeper disappeared into the maze of smoke and haze overhanging the tracks of the far-reaching yard" (430-31).

Without a doubt, Dreiser's most illustrious arrival in Chicago by train came in 1912, bringing him back from New York this time, not as any penniless boy from the provinces but as the local-boy-made-good, a real "success"—to many, as W. A. Swanberg points out in his *Dreiser*, "a literary Samson, a slayer of philistines" (164). Riding high on the success of the previous year's *Jennie Gerhardt* and enjoying the considerable local acclaim for his newly released novel *The Financier*, Dreiser caught Chicago in the midst of its own literary renaissance. Harriet Monroe had just launched *Poetry*, opening a door for *vers libre* and pumping courage into a horde of Chicago writers just then at the inception of important careers, among them Edgar Lee Masters, Carl Sandburg, Floyd Dell, Arthur Davison Ficke, and Sherwood Anderson. Dreiser was lionized, much written up in the press, invited to Maurice Browne's groundbreaking Little Theater, and introduced to Margaret Anderson, soon to found *The Little Review* and attempt the serial publication of James Joyce's *Ulysses*. As an established star in the New York literary firmament, Dreiser was looked to for assistance by many, and he did give significant boosts to Sherwood Anderson and Carl Sandburg (*Letters* I 279), even though his taking the train to Chicago was aimed at another purpose entirely.

Dreiser, in *The Financier*, had hit upon the subject of a lifetime, one which would combine his fascination with railroads and his obsession with Chicago and the Midwest: the life story of Charles Tyson Yerkes, owner of those "jingling horse cars" which had so entranced him upon his first visits to the city. Yerkes, a multi-millionaire, had died in 1905, and Dreiser, researching the man's life, had found it an ideal "fit" with his plans for fiction. *The Financier* was the first part of what eventually would become a trilogy. The novel dealt with Yerke's boyhood in Philadelphia and his early career there as a financial shark and streetcar owner, culminating in his arrest, trial, and imprisonment for shady deals involving municipal funds. Following his release from Eastern Penitentiary, Yerkes had moved to Chicago and there resumed his career in finance. In the penultimate pages of *The Financier* Yerkes, to whom Dreiser had given the fictional name of Frank Algernon Cowperwood, sits aboard "a train, speeding through the mountains of Pennsylvania and over the plains of Ohio and Indiana . . . to Chicago" (775).

This scene took Dreiser back into familiar territory and invited—or tempted—him once again to reprise his own first encounter with Chicago, by 1912 already treated in *Sister Carrie* and in his as-yet-unpublished *The "Genius."* At this time Frank Cowperwood is nearly forty years old, wealthy, highly experienced, supremely sophisticated, born and raised in a great city, and yet his reaction to encountering the western metropolis for the first time is purely that of young Dreiser (and occurs historically at the same time). Arriving by Pullman, Cowperwood notes the flat tablelands of Indiana, then, far out, the telegraph poles strung with wires and sparsely planted cottages. He is impressed by the multitude of railroad tracks, side by side, evidence of the thirty lines then coming into Chicago. Cowperwood spies next the one- and two-story homes of the burgeoning suburbs, the clogged grade crossings where wait wagons and muddy-wheeled buggies; then a branch of "the filthy, arrogant, self-sufficient little Chicago River . . . with its mass of sputtering tugs, its black, oily water, its tall, red-brown, and green grain-elevators, its immense black coal-pockets and yellowish-brown lumber-yards" (*Titan*, 3-4).

At journey's end Cowperwood, like Dreiser, like Carrie Meeber, like Eugene Witla, arrives at the depot, under the roofed shed, "and amidst a clatter of trucks hauling trunks, and engines belching steam, and passengers hurrying to and fro he [makes] his way out into Canal Street and [hails] a waiting cab" (*Titan* 4). Excitement has seized him; the adrenalin pours into his blood-stream. "What a city!" he thinks. "Here was life; he saw it at a flash. Here was a seething city in the making. There was something dynamic in the very air which appealed to his fancy. How different, for some reason, from Philadelphia! . . . [Chicago] was more youthful, more hopeful. . . . This raw, dirty town seemed naturally to compose itself into stirring artistic pictures. Why, it fairly sang! The world was young here. Life was doing something new" (*Titan* 3-4).

Once again the insistent rhapsodist in Dreiser pushes to the fore asking (as with an invocation to the gods) to be the laureate of this Florence of the Western World:

> This singing flame of a city, this all America, this poet in chaps and buckskin, this rude, raw Titan, this Burns of a city! By its shimmering lake it lay, a king of shreds and patches, a maundering yokel with an epic in its mouth, a tramp, a hobo among cities, with the grip of Caesar in its mind, the dramatic force of Euripides in its soul. A very bard of a city this, singing of high deeds and high hopes, its heavy brogans buried deep in the mire of circumstance. Take Athens, oh, Greece! Italy, do you keep Rome! This was the Babylon, the Troy, the Nineveh of a younger day. (*Titan* 6)

With a lack of restraint that is near-crippling in its effect, Dreiser continues to apostrophize the city by the lake. But this was—would prove to be—his final opportunity to wax lyrical over "this new-found wonder" as well as the last time that he would indulge himself by yielding to the temptation. New York he could handle, and London and Rome and Florence and even

Monte Carlo, but the thought of Chicago, *his* Chicago, invariably broke him up.

The novel which Dreiser came to Chicago to research in 1912 was called *The Titan* (1914) and was devoted wholly to depicting Yerkes during his ascendancy in the Midwest during the 1880s and 1890s (it would be Dreiser's only novel having Chicago as its sole locale). Yerkes had settled in Chicago sometime around 1882, gotten a start in public utility franchises, and then gravitated back into rail transportation, the field he recognized as being his natural metier. In the novel, Dreiser depicts the moment at which Frank Cowperwood recognizes his key to future wealth and power:

> The little yellow, blue, green, white, and brown street-cars which he saw trundling here and there, the tired, bony horses, jingling bells at their throats, touched him. They were flimsy affairs, these cars, merely highly varnished kindling-wood with bits of polished brass and glass stuck about them, but he realized what fortunes they portended if the city grew. Street-cars, he knew, were his natural vocation. Even more than stock-brokerage, even more than banking, even more than stock-organization he loved the thought of street-cars and the vast manipulative life it suggested. (4-5)

Cowperwood begins where Yerkes had begun, by obtaining control of the North Chicago City Railway. Realizing that rail expansion is blocked by the Chicago River, he obtains control of an unused tunnel beneath the water on LaSalle Street and runs his streetcar tracks south into the business district, eventually constructing a turnaround circle for his cars' return trip. In this fashion is born the Chicago Loop and Cowperwood's great dream of weaving all of the city's diverse streetcar companies into a single, unified transportation monopoly with which he can bleed the populace dry.

Writing *The Titan* gave Dreiser opportunity and reason to deal in quite specific terms with the history of Chicago during a pair of crucial decades. He followed Yerkes's career painstakingly. The local newspapers had risen in bitter opposition to Yerkes's hoped-for streetcar monopoly and had made headlines out of a number of appalling facts, including the news that the LaSalle Street tunnel, built at taxpayers' expense, had been turned over to Yerkes for approximately 1% of its true worth. All of the important editors of the day were united in their opposition to Yerkes, including Joseph C. Medill of the *Tribune,* Victor F. Lawson of the *Morning News,* and H. H. Kohlsaat of the *Times-Herald,* who warned his readers with the headline PLAIN GRAB OF TUNNEL PROPOSED, called Yerkes a "hustler," and laid bare his plan to loot Chicago and return triumphantly to Philadelphia "with the blood of the lamb safely bottled" (Harpel 251-259). The Chicago *Daily News* uttered a mocking prayer of thanks that Yerkes had not been given the Chicago River along with the tunnel under it, and Medill's *Tribune* disclosed that while Yerkes was obliged to maintain the tunnel, the city had agreed to allow him a stipend of $20,000 a year for tunnel upkeep, a sum which would provide amply for the maintenance. Clearly, the tunnel deal was a giveaway (*Tribune* 8 July 1886 1-4).

The Yerkes-Cowperwood story involved any number of well-known Chicago personages, and many of them were brought into *The Titan,* their stories told under assumed names. These included Chicago's great merchant Marshall Field, the meatpacking king Philip D. Armour, Governor John P. Altgeld, and Mayor Carter Harrison, Jr., as well as those notorious and apparently indestructible aldermen from the First Ward, "Bathhouse John" Coughlin and "Hinky Dink" Kenna. The aldermen are thinly disguised in *The Titan,* Coughlin as "Smiling Mike" Tiernan of the Silver Moon Saloon and Kenna as "Emerald Pat" Kerrigan, so-named for his "trademark," a $14,000 jeweled stickpin. Altgeld was famous for turning down a million dollars offered by Yerkes as he requested that legislation favorable to him be allowed to slide through the state legislature and become law. Altgeld's refusal of the bribe was praised by newspaper columnist Forrest Crissey and by cartoonist John McCutcheon, and Dreiser followed their lead as he incorporated the tale into his novel. Yerkes was exposed by crusading writers such as William T. Stead, who, in his sensational muckraking book *If Christ Came to Chicago*!, called the streetcar monopolist an "immigrant from a Philadelphia penitentiary" and declared his franchises no better than stolen property. To place Yerkes in control of Chicago transportation, said Stead, was tantamount to leaving a wily fox in charge of a henhouse (94-6; 202-03). Peter Finley Dunne, Chicago's most widely read columnist, caused his Irish saloonkeeper creation "Mr. Dooley" to declare in dialect that the anniversary of Yerkes's arrival in Chicago should be celebrated the way that other great disasters were remembered:

> "Why don't we have a band out an' illuminated sthreet cars f'r to commimerate th' day that Yerkuss came to Chicago? An' there's cholera. What's th' matter with cholera?" (Ginger 109)

The Titan provided its author with an unmatched opportunity to exploit the Chicago locale. The action culminates, as the career of Yerkes had, in a showdown at City Hall on 12 December 1898. It was Yerkes and the legion of aldermen whose votes he had purchased reputedly at $20,000 apiece on one side against the organizations formed by an outraged citizenry (The Independent Anti-Boodle League and The Municipal Voters League), on the other. Two hundred thousand badges had been printed for distribution, showing a gibbet from which dangled an empty noose; everyone knew whose neck it fit. Alerted by their own newspapers, citizens of cities across the country awaited the outcome of the vote which would determine whether Yerkes would be given the "eternal franchises" for streetcar transportation which he was demanding. The Council chambers were packed that night. A brass band played. Photographic flashpowder exploded. From the galleries, indignant citizens dangled rope nooses and hooted at aldermen on the floor: "How much *you* paid?" The public pressure was too great. One by one, the "gray wolves" caved in, even "Bathhouse John" and "Hinky Dink" being forced, ultimately, to abandon Yerkes and "join the forces of decency." Chicago was saved. (DMN 13 December 1898)

Yerkes had traveled to Chicago by train from Philadelphia. Now, giving up on the Midwest, he retreated to his new home in New York, where he had built himself a splendid mansion on Millionaires Row. To carry him there, along with his antiques and his sensational collection of paintings and sculpture, required an entire special train of Pullman cars. Dreiser eventually carried his fictional story of Yerkes to its end, the Chicago phase being a central panel in the completed mural. In dealing directly with a millionaire, Dreiser was able to indulge his compulsion for using the Chicago locale in what was, to him, a very legitimate manner, fiction following fact. At the same time, he pursued the anti-capitalistic theme which always exists in his novels, sometimes concealed just below the surface of a story, often rising into view, and on occasion—but not very often—receiving an overt stress. His novels are among the most subversive in our literature, his disagreement with the built-in lack of equity that exists at the center of a profit-driven society never being wholly extraneous to the story he tells. More often it inheres like the pattern in a carpet. It satisfied Dreiser immediately to drive Cowperwood to his conclusion, to depict the fall of this financial plunderer, to chronicle the dispersal of his ill-gotten spoils at auction, and to declare the failure of the elaborate plans he had laid for immortalizing himself as an American philanthropist.

Dreiser's argument with capitalistic society dominates his masterpiece, *An American Tragedy* (1925), wherein a poor boy, the son of street missionaries, is seduced by materialistic values, eventually murdering in order to climb the ladder of Success toward the status and the wealth which his environment had caused him to covet. The story of Clyde Griffiths begins, not in Chicago, but in another midwestern rail center, Kansas City, and moves from there to upstate communities in New York and pine-shrouded Adirondack lakes, Dreiser's obligatory bow to the "truth" of his sources. But Chicago is not ignored, interestingly enough. Clyde Griffiths creeps out of Kansas City (riding a box-car rather than a Pullman), retreating from a motor accident in which he is culpable. Dreiser arranges that he shall find his way to Chicago and retrace some of his author's own youthful steps, driving a delivery wagon and inhabiting a rented bedroom on Chicago's West Side. Here, after a decent interval, Clyde will "change trains" for New York State. He has become a bellhop at the Union League Club on Jackson Boulevard, that same capitalistic fraternity house which Lester Kane had employed as a "cover" for his alliance with Jennie Gerhardt and which (in its exclusive concentration upon business matters) gives the appearance of being separated entirely from the sexual concerns of life and society:

> No women were admitted to this club. These various distinguished individuals came and went, singly as a rule, and with the noiseless vigor and reserve that characterizes the ultra successful. They often ate alone, conferred in pairs and groups, noiselessly—read their papers or books, or went here and there in swiftly driven automobiles—but for the most part seemed to be unaware of, or at least unaffected by, that element of passion, which, to [Clyde's] immature mind up to this time, had seemed to propel and disarrange so many things in those lesser worlds with which up to now he had been identified. (173)

It is at the Union League Club that Clyde, by chance (and Dreiser), is brought together with his wealthy uncle, Samuel Griffiths, manufacturer of men's shirts. Before he knows it Clyde is aboard an eastbound train out of Chicago heading for Lycurgus, New York, a job in Uncle Samuel's factory, and peril unimaginable.

Until the day he died Dreiser never published another novel after *An American Tragedy*. But during his last years he hauled out of his Hollywood storehouse the idea and partial manuscript of a book which he called *The Bulwark*, concerning the dilemma of a staunch Quaker family attempting somehow to retain their traditional spiritual values amidst the powerful Vanity Fair of conspicuous consumption promoted by the capitalistic world in which they are immersed. It might be asking a good deal too much to expect that after all this time Dreiser should continue his interest in those smoking locomotives that chug in and out of Chicago depots, particularly in a story whose focus is Philadelphia. But when *The Bulwark* appeared, posthumously, in 1946, it could be seen that the old lure of the Midwest still held. Dreiser had arranged his plot so that Etta Barnes, a daughter of his Quaker hero, should leave her family environment and accompany a radical friend cross-country to the University of Wisconsin. Concerned lest she be lost to her Quaker faith, Etta's aging father, Solon Barnes, endures the long trip by rail nearly halfway across the continent solely in order to argue for Etta's return—in the course of which travel, naturally, he must change trains in Chicago: "He had a lower berth between Philadelphia and Chicago, but had decided that a coach seat would suffice for the shorter trip to Wisconsin" (209). Solon takes pleasure in observing the environs, a backdrop of land- and cityscapes along Lake Michigan; however, he is no youngster aflame with life's ambition but, much like Dreiser in 1944, older and even approaching his terminus, and "in the background of his mind ran more somber thoughts" (209).

Works Cited

Chicago *Tribune*, 8 July 1886, 1, 4.

Dreiser, Theodore. *An American Tragedy*. New York: Boni & Liveright, 1925.

—. *The Bulwark*. New York: Doubleday, 1946.

—. *Dawn*. New York: Boni & Liveright, 1931.

—. *The Financier*. New York: Harper & Brothers, 1912.
—. *The "Genius."* New York: John Lane, 1915.
—. *Jennie Gerhardt*. New York: Harper & Brothers, 1911.
—. *Sister Carrie*. Philadelphia: University of Pennsylvania Pres, 1981.
—. *The Titan*. New York: John Lane, 1914.
Dreiser's manuscript notes [for *The Financier*]. University of Pennsylvania.
Elias, Robert H., ed. *Letters of Theodore Dreiser* 1. Philadelphia: U of Pennsylvania P, 1959.
Ginger, Ray. *Altgeld's America*. New York: Funk and Wagnalls, 1958.
Harpel Scrapbook [of Chicago newspaper clippings]. Chicago Historical Society.
Stead, William T. *If Christ Came to Chicago*! London: The Review of Reviews, 1894.

Texts, Subtexts and More Texts: Reconstructing the Narrator's Role in Sherwood Anderson's "Death in the Woods"

William V. Miller

The nature of Sherwood Anderson's short fiction has elicited much critical attention not only to the "texts" of Anderson's life but also to the "texts" created as his readers encounter the stories. For, on the one hand, Anderson was a very lyrical writer: the range of his character types is narrow, and the most common character type in the stories is largely a projection of his own artistic identity.[1] On the other hand, his oral narrators encourage readers to participate in the creation of the stories. The omniscient author of *Winesburg, Ohio* pleads for poetic assistance in telling the stories, and in a number of the best stories the first-person narrator engages the reader in the epistemological search for meaning with such cries of the heart as "I want to know why."

It is no wonder, then, that critics of Anderson's stories seem unencumbered by warnings about critical "fallacies"—intentional, affective, psychological, etc.—in their interpretive strategies. I, too, find that a greater fallacy may be the perception that the written artifact is hermetically sealed, interpretatively impervious to biographical, psychological, and sociological insights that bear on written texts. Nevertheless, these artifacts resist total, nihilistic deconstruction. One of the virtues of Wolfgang Iser's reader-response criticism is his countering the subjective problem by insisting on the integrity of the basic text.[2]

One of Anderson's texts that has attracted much critical attention is "Death in the Woods." It has the most richly documented genealogy of all of his stories, and no other story more incisively reveals both Anderson's characteristic techniques and his characteristic artistic vision. Yet the studies of this story, even in aggregate, are not totally satisfactory. And recent studies which properly identify the story's chief interpretive crux as the reader's understanding of the narrator's role seem so fixated on Anderson's very real, troubled sexuality that the surface text itself is too often neglected. The intent of this study is to confirm some of these earlier insights about the narrator from a broader textual perspective and to restore the validity of the ostensible text against the claims of certain subtexts.

The version of the "Death in the Woods" appearing in the 1933 collection *Death in the Woods* has been used by most anthologists and scholars. But the story's textual history provides valuable information about perspectives, emphases, and insights, both implicit and explicit, which the "informed reader" [Stanley Fish's term for one "who does everything within his power to make himself informed" (145)] can employ in making literary judgments. A brief survey of the genealogy of "Death in the Woods," then, is a starting point for this reexamination of the narrator issue.

Four complete versions of the essential story have been published, the earliest of which may be "Death in the Forest," which first appeared in 1969. This updated version stresses the boy narrator's youthful impressions and aspirations and lacks the resonance provided by the fuller biographies of Ma Grimes and the reflective adult narrator in the final version. Of the two versions published in 1926, the *American Mercury* narrative is closest to the final version, lacking only a paragraph explaining Ma Grimes's "bound girl" status before she was married and differing stylistically in relatively minor instances. The second 1926 version appears as chapter twelve in Anderson's fictionalized autobiography *Tar: A Midwest Childhood;* but while this version includes most of the final version, it is written in third person without the vital memory structure provided by the adult narrator and deflected from the Ma Grimes focus by details of Tar's life. Manuscript evidence suggests how Anderson revised the *American Mercury* version for the 1933 volume.

A number of other documents are important to a study of the genealogy of "Death in the Woods," including manuscripts, published fragments and other, more oblique material. The three most useful manuscripts are the typescript and two carbons prepared for the 1933 edition: the more valuable, heavily-revised

Tar manuscript; and the fragment recently discovered by Ray Lewis White. The latter, typed on the back of the *Winesburg* manuscript, presumably about 1916, includes among other materials, the familiar elements of the finished story: the frozen body of the woman found in the woods, the circling dogs which tear chunks of meat from the woman's pack, and musings by the protagonist which are particularly germane to the present study. One immediate observation is that this manuscript corroborates Anderson's assertion that he "tried to write" the story "at least a dozen times over many years" (*Memoirs* [1942] 286).

Two published fragments, *Paris Notebook, 1921* (1976) and "Father Abraham," which he was writing in 1924, concentrate on the episode on the farm where Ma Grimes had been a bound girl (Fanning 62-65 and *Reader* 530-602).[3] The earlier fragment is interesting particularly for the dreams of the young farm girl in which the "feeding" motif of the later versions is stressed. In the uncompleted, highly imaginative biography of Lincoln, Abraham the lawyer identifies with both the young German father *and* the young girl whom he has raped and injured, after the farmer is given a ten-year sentence (580).

Two other episodes or sketches appeared first in Anderson's *Memoirs*. Anderson wrote that an experience in Palos Park, Illinois, in the winter of 1920-21 provided the "impulse" for writing "Death in the Woods" (425).[4] He went walking one moonlit winter evening with a troop of dogs. In a clearing he stretched out on an inclined tree trunk and perhaps dozed. Anderson was suddenly awakened by one of the dogs, standing with his forelegs on Anderson's chest and peering into his eyes. Then the dog rejoined the pack of dogs silently running in a circle, a scene which Anderson felt was "transplanted suddenly to a primitive world." Other dogs stopped to peer at Anderson and then returned to the strange moving circle. The scene is built on the contrast between the primitive impulses of the dogs and their need "to be reassured," to retain a man's confirmation of their domesticity.

The second important episode in *Memoirs* concerns a voyeuristic experience when Anderson was twelve or thirteen (90). One night he and another boy saw through a window a naked young girl warming herself by slowly turning in front of a stove. Anderson was first absorbed in the scene but then grew angry and hit the boy. This same ambivalence of attraction and guilt is suggested when in the same passage Anderson specifically states that he collocates in his mind this image of the girl with two experiences: one, the revulsion that he felt when a surgeon was about to cut the naked body of a girl—the other, the epiphanic scene in which the frozen body of an old woman is the focal point.

Knowledge of all of these texts, as well as other statements and biographical information, fortifies the "informed" reader as he engages the chief elements of the final version of "Death in the Woods." Three nexus of real and imagined materials deserve special attention: Anderson's experiences growing up in Camden, then Clyde, Ohio in the last quarter of the nineteenth century; the genealogy of Ma Grimes; and the complex role of the dogs in the story.

Just as he stressed his adolescent experiences in the three main autobiographical works and in most of his best stories, Anderson draws on these experiences in "Death in the Woods," but in a somewhat different way. The texture of sensuous, concrete details of his youth in other tales is a chief source of their power; but in revising "Death in the Woods"—for example, in changes from "Death in the Forest" and the *Tar* version—the focus shifts away from the youth's diurnal pursuits and even the experience of discovering Ma Grimes's body toward those additional recollections which are notes toward the composition of Ma Grimes's identity. While the narrator does have childhood memories of eating liver, Grimes's surliness, and the old woman passing their house one "Summer and Fall," much of what the narrator learned about Ma Grimes was discovered in that long, indeterminate period after the death epiphany. This shift in emphasis does move from the boy to the woman; but it should also be noted that while the death scene may be a foundation episode, it does not dominate the narrator's imaginative construct. To insist on the dominance of either the narrator's paralyzing sexual immaturity (Sheick) or his rapist mentality (Colquitt), for example, obscures the legitimacy of dramatizing the artistic process.

More significant to our understanding of the story are the images of Anderson's own father and mother. During the 1920s Anderson's autobiographical and fictive representations of Irwin Anderson appeared to mellow. Earlier portraits such as that of Windy McPherson and Tom Willard in *Winesburg* stress the irresponsibility and exploitation of women which are epitomized in the characterization of Pa Grimes. More to the point, as the biographers have noted, Anderson often distorted the facts about his parents, idealizing his mother and projecting into the father his own uneasiness about relationships with women. Pa Grimes, the quintessential "feeder," is not so much a veiled portrait of his father as the hyperbolic expression of Anderson's own ambivalence about the male role. We recall the ambivalence of Anderson as a youthful voyeur, Lincoln's twin-minded empathy both for the victimized bound girl and for the basically kind farmer who cannot control his lust, and beyond versions of this text, other stories such as "The Untold Lie."

However, the story features Ma Grimes, not her husband, and energizing her characterization is Anderson's powerful, idealized, guilt-ridden remembrance of Emma Anderson, who died in 1895 when Anderson was eighteen. His descriptions of Emma in *A Story Teller's Story* and in the dedication to *Winesburg, Ohio* romanticize her beyond the factual evidence. Contrary to Anderson's claims that his mother had been a "bound girl" like Ma Grimes and a mysterious beauty of Italian descent, her heritage was German, and these other claims run counter to the specific biographical evidence. Among the documents we are considering, the early "Fred" fragment most specifically links the dead woman with Anderson's perception of his own mother, as Fred, the typical Anderson protagonist, compares the two women and ponders how animality erodes the dreams of mothers. Clare Colquitt, who thoughtfully discusses Anderson's view of the sexual roles and Anderson's guilt [See also Howe (212) and "Earth Mother" (196-206)], charges both Anderson and the narrator of "Death in the Woods" with selfishly ("for Anderson, self came first" [180]) ignoring "the grim particulars" of the lives of his mother and Ma Grimes. The cogency of this subtextual argument receives further potential support in texts considered here but not in her study, and I find parallels between her argument and the conflicting texts in such Faulkner stories as "Was," in which the reader responds both to the humor and to the countering racism. However, it is troubling that Colquitt grants nothing to intentionality and begs the questions that the story must be about either the "real" woman or the selfish "I" and that the digressions of the narrator—which are a staple technique in Anderson's art—discredit the narrator and constitute an elaborate stratagem to mask his victimizing male role.

Although Anderson did work on a farm during the summer of 1899, there are, thus far, no confirmed, factual experiences which may have served as analogues for any segment of the fictive biography of Ma Grimes. However, a comparison of the finished story with earlier fragmentary versions yields important perspectives on the Ma Grimes's characterization. The "Father Abraham" episode teems with sexuality as Abraham identifies with the farm girl's sensibility shaped by a milieu of constant desire for sex and food. Ma Grimes (named Mother Winters) is also identified with animal life in the *Paris Notebook* fragment to the degree that in a significant dream, in which she is young again and wearing a torn dress, she seeks to free herself and farm animals from a great building in which they are trapped as the air supply diminishes. But she cannot reach the iron bar which blocks the exit. "There was life, joy, happiness, for herself and all the imprisoned animals to be got by lifting the iron bar" (63). The boy is identified by Anderson as death, and the implication is that the failure to lift the bar thwarts one from escaping the mortal bonds of animal life. The "Fred" fragment shows most explicitly that this same ensnaring animality wars constantly against the dreaming, imaginative side of people.

To be sure, these contextual clues to the nature of the characterization of Ma Grimes underscore the animality of her life and therefore may denigrate her humanity. But it is reductive to ignore the dimensions of feeding beyond the strictly sexual in all of these versions, the fact that the steaming sexuality of "Father Abraham" is much diminished in the final version by specific intent and achievement, and the categorical stressing in "Fred" of how the imagination and art help one to transcend the chronic circularity of animal existence that anticipates the artistic motif in the definitive story.

Yet another document, the so-called amnesia letter written by Anderson in 1912, in the immediate context of his abrupt departure from his Elyria business, includes a cryptic section about other "gaunt" dogs (Sutton 37).

> Why do the children cry. They / are everywhere underfoot. Among / them run yellow dogs with brown / dirt stuck on their backs. The / dogs howl and the children / cry. At night the dogs / howl and the children cry / and your head hurts. There / are so many children and / so many dogs and so many long streets filled / with dirty houses.

William Sutton reported that in discussing this letter along with

"Death in the Woods" with a psychologist, the latter suggested that the dogs "represented dominant or male sexual factors" (28-9), more corroborating evidence of the sexual emphasis in the story. To be sure, in many of the "dog" passages as well as in the final version of the story the dogs are brutal feeders, with heavy male sexual overtones; but more often the dogs—and especially in the Palos Park narrative and in the "Fred" fragment—symbolize warring forces within human beings: the atavistic, primordial life force struggling against the domesticating, civilizing control of the human community. In the story, as well as in the other version and fragments, the dogs are not wolves; the dogs do not touch Ma Grimes's body; they "identify" themselves as "servants of man."

Anderson's avowed purposes and specific techniques in "Death in the Woods" are revealed in bolder relief against the background of the foregoing genealogy. Anderson typically relied on "negative capability," on inspiration rather than craftsmanship in, for example, the conscious, intellectual sense hyperbolically reflected in Poe's *Philosophy of Composition;* however, he did state the theme and his intent in "Death in the Woods" in very rare comments on a specific story, and he did revise *and* rewrite the story many times, as we have seen. Significantly, the final version incorporates two of his most successful and characteristic techniques: the epiphanic ordering of materials and the oral narrator.

Even casual readers of *Winesburg, Ohio* and a few of his best stories have noticed what has been called here "epiphanic" ordering, that is, constructing stories not by means of a strict, linear, conflict-to-climax-to-resolution plot line, but around luminous scenes which gather up and epitomize all of the data of the particular story, for example, the youth viewing Jerry Tillford and the prostitute in "I Want to Know Why." "Death in the Woods" is, of course, built around the scene in the wintry, moonlit clearing. But while this scene is the dominant image of the story, its full significance depends on the complementary images which serve to illuminate the chief image.

Directing the reader's search for the expanded meaning of the forest scene as he himself gropes toward it is the story's first-person narrator. "Death in the Forest" and "I'm a Fool" also have first-person narrators, but the narrator in "Death in the Woods" is an adult recalling a full range of experiences leading up to his present "dissatisfied" state. This device of the oral narrator controls the tone of the story and, as noted earlier, encourages the reader to join in the mental and emotional investigation into the nature of a particular experience or character. In the very best of Anderson's stories the narrator himself is an adult character to be understood and evaluated. The possibility of dramatic irony of a different order than in "I'm a Fool" claims attention in these stories, and certainly in the case of "Death in the Woods" the question of evaluating this adult narrator is perhaps the chief crux in interpreting the story—the deepest concern of Sheick, Colquitt, Lawry, and this study.

Although difficult, it is useful to discriminate between two aspects of the narrator's role: the speaker as a reflection of Anderson's powerful, lyric vision and the speaker as the artist, the most ubiquitous of all character roles in his stories. To stress the former may lead one to insights about the sexual anxieties of the narrator as well as the author for whom he is, to a degree, a surrogate. But the reader who denies and denigrates the artistic role in analyzing the narrator excludes dimensions of the story resident in the characterization of the old woman. Anderson himself outlines both the structure of the story and an important level of meaning in "Death in the Woods" in a passage deleted from the *Tar* manuscript, which is also a self-conscious statement of his artistic role: "It was to one later just a story picked up in childhood. . . . There was an impression made on the mind. Something got fixed. The seeds of a story had lodged in my mind and had to lie there until they were fertilized by the experience of my own life. Then some of them got told. Others never did. It all depends upon what happens after a man has got through with his childhood" (*Tar* MS 131, the Newberry Library). To a degree, at least, the story is, as Pearson wrote, "the narrative of his artistic fulfillment" (55).

But the narrator himself insists on more profound meanings emanating from the central image. Understanding the story requires, first of all, paying attention to the narrator before we identify him as sexually fixated, for example, or cleverly manipulative. He stresses the unity of the old woman's life of feeding animal life and then says that "a thing so complete has its own beauty." Perhaps in a very elementary sense the boy responded to the beauty of the scene, but only the adult narrator "knows" and admires aesthetically the deeper, unified pattern of the woman's cradle-to-death mission. Anderson typically looked beyond superficial beauty to gestures and patterns of actions like those of Kate Swift and of Elizabeth Willard in *Winesburg* as bases of the truly beautiful.

In addition to the narrator's statements, Anderson explicitly gave his notions of the story's theme in two rare direct statements. Neither is conclusive and the first certainly reflects male guilt, but both reveal at least Anderson's intent to heighten and establish the significance of the old woman's life in the "community." The first long statement [abbreviated here] appears in a heavily revised manuscript in a "Death in the Woods" Newberry folder:

> It seems to me that the theme of this story is the persistent animal hunger of man. There are these women who spend their whole lives, rather dumbly feeding this hunger. . . . As for technique, it was quite definitely thought out. Over the period of years I have made several attempts that had to be thrown aside. For example I thought it necessary to lift definitely the animal hunger I wanted to get out of the realm of sex. Therefore my tired-out, sexless old woman, the dogs feeding from the food attached to her body after her own death. And there is always the desire to get your story embedded [sic] in the whole life of the community.
>
> The story has its particular form, attempts at flashes out of a community life [here Anderson lists a number of episodes] . . . all of this to get a certain effect. It is a little hard to define. What is wanted is something beyond the horizon, to retain the sense of mystery in life while showing, at the same time, at what cost our ordinary animal hungers are fed.

This statement is quoted at length for what it reveals about Anderson's intentions regarding the important thematic problems of "feeding," sexual consciousness, and mystery as well as for his sense of community. The second quotation expresses Anderson's familiar theme of the sordid sameness of our lives (the circularity theme in "Fred") and the value of those like Ma Grimes who are vital to the human community. "Many lives have little or no variation. Men and women are born [sic] live and die and remain nameless, forgotten. They, in their conscious selves have little or nothing to contribute to the life around them but the lives seen whole do contribute" (*Tar* MS 130-1).

All of these statements are in essential consonance with the story. Necessary qualifications for subtexts of vision and sensibility must and have been entered. Each reader who engages the story with his or her own texts must decide whether and to what degree the geographically-supported sexual views of Anderson undercut the apparent structure and rhetorical intent in the story, but the oral narrator does function primarily to achieve Anderson's "effect," to meld the disparate experiences, his own and that of Ma Grimes, into the symbolic figure of woman-feeding. The tone of compassion validates the uniqueness of one Ma Grimes, while the disparate experiences universalize her life as archetypal for his, the narrator's and for the larger community. Her frozen body has a sensuous loveliness of formed white marble, but her "beauty" is less that of a nude object than that of Dr. Reefy or Kate Swift, an inner beauty perceived by the initiated in gestures. Her truth of "feeding" may make her grotesque; but "seen whole" through art, the unity and value of her isolated life are beautiful.

To carry this line of thought a step further we might briefly consider the style of the story. Unlike a story like "Hands," where Anderson sought the essence of a particular person, in the memorable opening paragraph of "Death in the Woods," Anderson wants both the essence and that quality which connects her more with the whole human community. Therefore, instead of the repetitive proper nouns of "Hands" (and other *Winesburg* stories), Anderson employs the less personal pronoun *she* seven times in his brief paragraph. The short, repetitive, subject-verb sentence patterns become an incantation which is appropriate for the stark matter and the narrator's sustaining tone. These stylistic qualities and others in the story, especially the refrain-like use of the verb *feed*, are not evidence of the author's fixed immaturity, but rather a combination of the typical verbal mannerisms of his oral narrators and, more importantly, of the specific technique organic to expressing "something beyond the horizon."

Something beyond the horizon. Benjamin T. Spencer directed attention to this "mythopoeist" dimension of Anderson's best fiction when he asserted that "his imagination achieved its finest expression in narratives such as 'Death in the Woods' . . . where the preternatural or archetypal not only gave it unity and direction but also evoked a connotative style approaching the idioms of poetry" (3). Clare Colquitt argues formidably that such universalizing is a tactic which demeans the historical Ma Grimes and masks the narrator/author's complicity in victimizing women, including his own mother, with his fictions. The impetus for this view is fed by Anderson's sexist statements and his profound guilt; but as I have attempted to demonstrate, a fuller consideration of the textual history of the story rebuts some generalizations which ramify from this conspiratorial reading and tends to corroborate Spencer's emphasis. To recapitulate: through her repetitive acts, the ritualistic language which figures forth those acts, and the emphasis provided by the narrator, we perceive that Ma Grimes incarnates the earth-mother role of feeding animal life. The revisions of the earlier versions show how her characterization has been universalized in the final version, and the "bound girl" analogues reveal even deeper dimensions of the feeding role. As the Palos Park and "Fred" analogues more specifically attest, the dogs in the story are primordial feeders, epitomizing in their primitive, regressive circling the feeding without end which is the complement of the feeder role. Finally, Anderson explicitly stated his intent to prove these deeper mysteries of life.

The narrator of "Death in the Woods" is a problematic creation. Certainly he does not piece together all of the fragments "with utter clarity" as one critic seems to require (Scheick 145); and Anderson's private vision of womankind, for whom he feels both guilt and compassion, influences the reader's response to the myth making. But whatever the reader may require as evidence of sexual and social maturity, the textual evidence supports the view that the adult narrator has gained in sympathy and understanding and has returned compulsively to the central image and the other images, not out of anxiety but with the artist's desire to find inner form and to express that form. Like Fred in the early fragment, who feels unequal to the task of expressing his vision of the circling dogs as a symbol of the circular, driven lives of human beings, this narrator/artist may also find compensation in experiencing the beauty of his insight about the old woman. The oral narrator's very limitations can be counted as a dimension of Anderson's aesthetic triumph in the achieved story. As members of the larger community, we have shared this ritualistic celebration of one of the myriad forgotten ones whose life "seen whole" has "contributed."

Notes

1 See Miller "Portraits."

[2] Iser's influential literary theory finds the locus of a text in the area between the written text and the reader. The text is most important ontologically in the reader's act of reading. The reader's experiences impinge on the written text, but the written text resists those interpretations that are not inherent in the written text. My paper emphasizes this resistance by first examining the written text and its genealogy and then setting forth my own interpretive reading—a response that also incorporates the more cogent responses of others.

[3] See also *Letters* 121, 125, 126 and 130.

[4] The White edition supersedes the 1941 edition. Since it appears that the account of dogs running in a circle in the "Fred" MS was written about 1916, the "impulse" may have resulted from a confluence of two experiences, either of which or even any facet of either might have been the catalyst for this episode in the final story.

[5] Thaddeus B. Hurdson, one of Anderson's boyhood friends, reports that his father spoke of the death of an old woman in Clyde, Ohio, vicinity in circumstances perhaps similar to those described in "Death in the Woods." Indianapolis, Indiana, November 8, 1979.

Works Cited

Anderson, Sherwood. "Death in the Forest." Ed. William V. Miller in *Tar: A Midwest Childhood* Ed. Ray Lewis White. Cleveland: Case Western UP, 232-236.

—. "Death in the Woods." *Sherwood Anderson's Short Stories.* Ed. Maxwell Geismar. New York: Hill and Wang, 1962. 121-132.

—. *Letters of Sherwood Anderson.* Ed. Howard Mumford Jones and Walter B. Rideout. Boston: Little, Brown, 1953.

—. *Sherwood Anderson's Memoirs.* New York: Harcourt, Brace, 1942. Superseded by the White edition.

—. *Sherwood Anderson's Memoirs: A Critical Edition.* Ed. Ray Lewis White. Chapel Hill: U of North Carolina P, 1969.

—. *The Sherwood Anderson Reader.* Ed. Paul Rosenfeld. Boston: Houghton Mifflin, 1947.

Fanning, Michael. *France and Sherwood Anderson: Paris Notebook, 1921.* Baton Rouge: Louisiana State UP, 1976.

Fish, Stanley. "Literature in the Reader: Affective Stylistics." *New Literary History* 2 (1970): 123-162.

Howe, Irving. *Sherwood Anderson.* New York: William Sloan, 1951.

Iser, Wolfgang. *The Act of Reading.* Baltimore and London: Johns Hopkins UP, 1978.

Lawry, Jon S. "'Death in the Woods' and the Artist's Self in Sherwood Anderson." *PMLA* 74 (June 1959): 306-311.

Miller, William V. "Earth Mothers, Succubi, and Other Ectoplasmic Spirits: the Women in Sherwood Anderson's Short Stores." *MidAmerica* 1 (Fall 1973): 64-81. Rpt. *Critical Essays on Sherwood Anderson.* Ed. David D. Anderson. Boston: G. K. Hall, 1981, 196-206.

—. "Portraits of the Artist: Anderson's Fictional Storytellers." *Sherwood Anderson: Dimensions of His Literary Art*. Ed. David Anderson. East Lansing: Michigan State UP, 1976.

Pearson, Norman Holmes. "Anderson and the New Puritanism." *The Newberry Library Bulletin* 2 (December 1948): 52-63.

Scheick, William J. "Compulsion Toward Repetition: Sherwood Anderson's 'Death in the Woods.'" *Studies in Short Fiction* 11 (1974): 141-146.

Spencer, Benjamin T. "Sherwood Anderson: American Mythopoeist." *American Literature* 41 (March 1969): 1-18.

Sutton, William A. *Exit to Elsinore*. Muncie, IN: Ball State UP, 1967.

White, Ray Lewis. "'Death in the Woods': Anderson's Earliest Version." *The Winesburg Eagle* 7:2 (April 1982) 1-3.

Donald Ogden Stewart—
Le Humoriste Malgré Lui

Scott Donaldson

I

Donald Ogden Stewart died of a heart attack at his home in London on August 2, 1980. Three days later his wife Ella Winter, herself a writer and radical and the widow, to stretch back another generation, of Lincoln Steffens, suffered a fatal stroke. He was 85, she 82. At the time of their passing the Stewarts had lived nearly 30 years as expatriates, driven across the Atlantic by the force of the HUAC-McCarthy storm. Stewart's reputation did not survive this long exile intact. During the 1920s he was probably the nation's most widely read humorist. Later he became a successful playwright and actor on Broadway, and then a Hollywood screenwriter of such skill that he continued to get the best assignments even after embracing communism in the mid-1930s. Yet when his name comes up in college classrooms today, it is usually as the model for the character Bill Gorton in *The Sun Also Rises*. Or he is remembered not for himself but for his famous friends, among them Ernest Hemingway, Scott Fitzgerald, John Dos Passos, Gerald and Sara Murphy, Dorothy Parker, Robert Benchley and James Thurber (one obituary categorized Stewart, inappropriately, as "a member of the fabled Algonquin 'round table'"), not to mention Katharine Hepburn (who wrote a foreword to his 1975 autobiography, *By a Stroke of Luck*) and other Hollywood luminaries, Jock Whitney and others among the 400, W. E. B. DuBois and others of the radical left. One of the most fascinating things about Don Stewart was his capacity to move in wildly contradictory worlds. As *The*

New Yorker observed, he must have been "the only member—or even ex-member—of the Racquet Club who was a pal of [labor leader] Harry Bridges."

Characteristically, Stewart does not seem to have felt any resentment about his fading reputation. The emphasis in his autobiography is on his good fortune: how he progressed from middle-class, middle western obscurity to become a Big Man at Exeter and at Yale, a commercial success during the 1920s and 1930s, and finally, as he saw it, a triumphant convert to Marxism. Along the way he was elected to Skull and Bones and welcomed to the swellest houses on Long Island and made his million in Hollywood. In short, he'd had the American dream dumped in his lap, and yet wasn't it "marvelous," he kept insisting, that he'd seen that the dream really wasn't any good, or at least not good enough? Lucky Don. He could no more change that Panglossian outlook than he could stop wanting people to like him. But both traits, he realized, had done him harm as a writer. As a humorist he was entirely too good-humored.

II

A third and last child—he was ten years younger than sister Anne, 14 years the junior of brother Bert—Donald Ogden Stewart was born Nov. 30, 1894, in Columbus, Ohio, where his father, Gilbert Holland Stewart, practiced law with modest success. The family was "in Society" but only barely, for the Stewarts lacked means. Young Donald grew up aware of this distinction, knowing what everyone else's father did for a living. At 14, he was overjoyed to be sent off to Exeter where he could get "the best education possible" and meet all the right people, or at least their sons.

Gilbert Stewart, who had once served as a circuit court judge, was more ambitious for his children than his finances warranted. First he could no longer afford the Exeter tuition, a crisis which passed when scholarships were forthcoming. Then "Judge" Stewart, as he was known at the Columbus Club, was indicted for dipping into law library funds to finance his daughter's wedding in style. He died in shame during the fall of Don's freshman year at Yale, leaving no money and a potentially alcoholic wife.

These troubles only intensified Don's determination to get ahead. He believed in all the right things: God and country, honesty and hard work, purity and the Republican party. He would be a lawyer himself, or a businessman, or "second vice president of the First National Bank" of Columbus.

He was just beginning to pursue that conventional career, as a trainee with A. T. & T., when he came to the Twin Cities in 1919 and met Scott Fitzgerald, another young man of talent who despite attending the best schools and colleges remained a relatively impoverished outsider. Fitzgerald's father, like Stewart's, had failed in business. Both young men were having girl trouble as well. Scott had been jilted by Chicago's Ginevra King and was being strung along by Zelda Sayre, 1,500 miles away in Montgomery, Alabama. Don had been spurned by another Chicago belle who was a friend of Ginevra's. And both were destined for early success which they were quite unprepared to cope with.

Fitzgerald was rewriting *This Side of Paradise* in the summer of 1919 and used to read portions of it to Stewart for his comments. Most of the time, though, they partied together. In a story for the *St. Paul Daily News*, Fitzgerald tried to capture the flavor of Stewart's charm. He pretended to be a ventriloquist at a party, though anyone could see that the doll in his lap "was not a doll. It was a real fellow." He enrolled as a freshman at a brandnew college in southern Minnesota, made the football team, joined a fraternity, and then his vacation was over and he returned to "putting up telephone wires or tearing them down or something." He "made all the women feel beautiful and all the men feel witty." St. Paul was sorry to see him go. As a female contemporary put it, "Don was just a circus." Three years later Stewart, now an author instead of a telephone man, inscribed Fitzgerald's copy of *Perfect Behavior*

> In memory of the happy never-to-be forgotten summer in the Mammoth Cave, Ky—with much love from The Author

In the meantime Don Stewart had come to New York in search of Bohemia and a writing job. He found the first in Greenwich Village and the second at *Vanity Fair*. He presented himself at the magazine on the recommendation of Fitzgerald, who was now, with Zelda, frantically being famous around Manhattan. Asked for a sample of his wares, Stewart wrote a parody of

Theodore Dreiser, which he shakily committed into the hands of Edmund Wilson, Fitzgerald's old Princeton friend and now a *Vanity Fair* editor. Wilson frowned at first, then broke into laughter. Stewart never had to worry about money after that evening at Bunny Wilson's apartment in the winter of 1921.

He wrote a funny book nearly every year during the decade ahead. His first, *A Parody Outline of History* (1921), combined his gift as literary mimic with the vogue for popular history stimulated by H. G. Wells. The method was to imagine how some memorable event—the Miles Standish-Priscilla Mullins-John Alden triangle, for example—might be told by a modern-day author, in this case Fitzgerald. Other pieces parodied the famous—Eugene O'Neill, Sinclair Lewis, and Ring Lardner—and the forgotten—Thornton W. Burgess, Harold Bell Wright, and Mary Raymond Shipman Andrews. In *Perfect Behavior* (1922), Stewart mocked the Emily Post boom, advising his readers, for example, to plan their conversation in advance: to be prepared, in case the talk took a medical turn, with "two or three amusing anecdotes about adenoids." There followed *Aunt Polly's Story of Mankind* (1923), *Mr. and Mrs. Haddock Abroad* (1924), *The Crazy Fool* (1925), *Mr. and Mrs. Haddock in Paris, France* (1926), and *Father William* (1929). Of these, only *Aunt Polly* attempted to convey a serious message; Stewart wove an anti-war theme into its Van Loon framework. But *Aunt Polly* didn't sell, while the *Haddock* books and *The Crazy Fool* made it to the best-seller lists.

Stewart next conquered Broadway, first as an actor in Philip Barry's *Holiday* (1928-1929), and then as a playwright in *Rebound*, like Barry's a high society comedy, and the musical *Fine and Dandy*, both 1930. In that same year he made a couple of Benchleyesque short subjects and wrote the script of the motion picture *Laughter*, all for Paramount. But it was MGM that called him, early in 1932, to the land of mink and Honey.

Don prospered in Hollywood. He had wit and a good ear for dialogue, while the camera could make up for his weaknesses, evident both in his fiction and the autobiography, in description and scene-setting. During the next 15 years he wrote dozens of films, from *Smilin' Through* to *Cass Timberlaine*. He won an Oscar for his adaptation of Barry's *Philadelphia Story* to the screen, with Hepburn and James Stewart in the starring roles. For a short time, he was Irving Thalberg's "white-haired boy." For a long time, he minted money—until the Blacklist caught up with him in 1950.

Unlike most writers, Don and his first wife Beatrice, whose social credentials were impeccable, were soon accepted by Hollywood's elite, including the David O. Selznicks, just as during the Broadway years they had been more or less permanent house guests of Joan and Charlie Payson at the Payne Whitney estate on Long Island. Together, the Stewarts made a bright, attractive couple who enjoyed life and could fit in anywhere. Don, especially, radiated geniality and good nature.

III

Though he was somewhat put off by Stewart's apparent "obsession with social status," Dos Passos recalled in *The Best Times,* still the two of them "laughed like fools" in the Paris and Pamplona of the 1920s, since Don "managed to be funny about almost everything." This exuberant good humor served as a *carte d'entree* to the inner circles which the son of the failed lawyer in Columbus early set out to penetrate. "I worked eight years to make Bones," he claimed. Yet the work was not onerous, for it always came naturally to Stewart to play the clown. "The Queen of Sweden is here," he cabled Marc Connelly from Capri in the winter of 1923. "What shall I do?" Connelly cabled back a one-word reply, "Compromise." Nearly half a century later, when an interviewer observed that Stewart's dog Fidget was getting the worst of it in tooth-and-claw flurries with Pussy the cat, since Pussy was in full possession of his claws while Fidget was toothless, Don immediately hushed him. "Please," he intoned. "We don't talk about such things in Fidget's presence."

A born comedian, Stewart was sometimes impatient with those who tried to be funny. Fitzgerald's idea of a joke, he maintained, was to crawl under the table and bite the legs of dinner companions. While still an aspiring writer, Hemingway showed Don some pieces for *Vanity Fair,* but he didn't even pass them along. "They weren't very funny, really." Later Hem's humor turned nasty, and the two broke off their friendship after Ernest insisted on reciting his scurrilous poem about Dorothy Parker during a 1926 gathering at Archibald and Ada MacLeish's.

Dorothy Parker *was* funny, and Don liked her a lot.

Robert Benchley was still funnier, and Don "loved and admired him" more than any other man. Yet when Parker and Benchley took Stewart to lunch at the Algonquin Round Table, he didn't feel comfortable there. The atmosphere at the Algonquin, Don thought, was over-competitive and basically unfriendly, and he didn't enjoy exchanging barbs.

In his best-selling books, Stewart rarely aimed any barbs. His characters have foibles, but the author is obviously inclined in their favor, even in favor of so bratty a child as the Haddock's Mildred. In any case, Stewart's humor depends far less upon characterization than upon language and situation. In *Mr. and Mrs. Haddock Abroad,* reissued in the Lost American Fiction Series, the fun lies largely in the commentary. Sometimes the author belabors the obvious. The Haddocks hail from a middle-western town "called Legion, being named after an old Indian Squaw called Legion, who was said to have been buried there originally." A lady wonders if the family is going to Paris. "'Yes,' replied Mr. Haddock, in the affirmative." Sometimes he insists on *non sequiturs* or curious causal relationships. "Mildred was Mr. and Mrs. Haddock's ten-year-old daughter who had come to them late in life but was having her teeth straightened by Dr. Hawley." The train conductor called "New York!" and "it *was* New York, because the conductor had been with the road forty-two years." Sometimes he treats the remarkable as commonplace. At the captain's dinner, "there was a great deal of popping of corks and informal crouching." As the ship drew nearer "to what the captain hoped would be France, the excitement of the passengers gradually increased, until on the last day there was no holding them back, and in spite of strict orders to the contrary many of them during the day foolishly jumped over the bow and began swimming ahead in their eagerness to set foot once more on land."

Social incongruity provides another source of humor in the book. The Haddocks meet a New York street cleaner who discourses patronizingly on the Parisian *haut monde* and looks forward to the day when he will be assigned to sweep outside the Racquet Club or the Ritz. A tough-talking sailor recites "To be or not to be" perfectly. A second-class passenger confesses to a slumming first-class passenger that it was booze that ruined him. The captain runs a tight ship.

> "Tomorrow will be Sunday," said the captain late Saturday night.

> "Ay, ay, sir!" said a sailor, saluting and backing out of the cabin.

Toward the end of the voyage the second-class passengers revolt, a circumstance that enables Stewart to make fun of social inequity generally and collective bargaining in particular.

These comic devices add up to what Stewart calls "crazy humor," which may have achieved its apotheosis in a skit entitled *I Gaspiri—or the Undertakers,* written by Ring Lardner and presented to the 1923 Author's League dinner by Stewart, Connelly, and Benchley. One typical gag went like this:

> Stewart: I know a girl who was born out of wedlock.
> Benchley: That's mighty pretty country around there.

Benchley himself was the living embodiment of this pre-absurdist mode. Once while visiting the Stewarts, Bob crept across the tiles of the bathroom floor to shout "Boo" at a bird perched outside the window. The creature flew away in panic, later to die—so Benchley, who was terrified of birds, devoutly hoped—of a heart attack.

Stewart's humor of the 1920s took little seriously. His parodies poked fun at O'Neill's dramatic posturings about hunger and poverty and pilloried the solemnity of Lewis and Dreiser, authors who kept writing—annoyingly to Stewart's taste—about people who were defeated by life. His own brand of brittle comedy, though it struck the public fancy, was ill suited to the ambition Don had originally set for himself: "to be the new Mark Twain, fearless, uncorrupted." Eventually, when he turned to communism in the late 1930s, he repudiated his past as crazy humorist, but he could not dispense with the temperament that made the humor possible.

IV

There was a hint of what was to come in the two sketches Stewart wrote for the *transatlantic review* in 1924. One recounts the bittersweet tale of former football star Luke Dean, who annually returns to campus to see the big game and to bore his undergraduate brothers in Alpha Psi with yarns about his gridiron accomplishments. They were living the happiest days of their lives, the aging Dean insists on telling the unresponsive collegians. "And he spoke what was to him the truth." The other depicts the "Morning of Mrs. Gordon Smythe," an English widow with no one to care for her, "an old woman with a bit of money and a dog travelling around from one place to another."

Neither of these tales necessarily predicted Stewart's subsequent conversion to the Left, but they did announce a compassion and awareness of the plight of the lonely and bereft that one would scarcely have expected from the creator of the Haddocks. Don wrote them at the behest of Hemingway, who was serving as Ford Madox Ford's sub-editor on the *review*, and he may have figured that he could afford not to be funny in a journal of such limited means and circulation. In fact, these brief and moving sketches stand up as well as anything he ever wrote. Hemingway may have had them in mind when he observed, in the mid-1920s, that "Don Stewart had the most [talent] next to Cummings. Sometimes in the Haddocks." Sometimes in the *transatlantic review*.

Both Luke Dean and Mrs. Gordon Smythe were unhappy though rich. In the following decade of boom and bust, it came to Stewart that the poor were still more unhappy, and with less justice. The world was a good place, he thought, and everyone deserved a share of the good things in it. So in 1937 he rose before the second Congress of the League of American Writers to declare himself a "horrible example" of what could happen to a young man who had started with every intention of writing the Great American Novel and then become sidetracked into ten years of successful commercial writing. Don blamed his overcompensated plight less on Hollywood than on humor itself.

The trouble with humor, he said, was that it functioned to deaden out pain and make us forget our dreams. Like religion, humor was an opium of the people, designed to let them laugh at their own defeat. A man "first learns to be humorous about the problems of life," he commented, "when he begins to admit that he is licked." He looked back on his own days of writing crazy humor as a kind of nightmare. "When a humorist feels deep down inside him that there is no outlet to his life, that he is surrounded by blind alleys, then his humor becomes mad, fantastic; then in his utter despair he creates illogical dream worlds and the sounds of his crazy laughter echo in the empty house." Crazy humor, he speculated, might go down as the distinctive contribution of "American Capitalism" to the world of letters.

He was through with such defeatist humor, Stewart insisted—but made his declaration with such engaging wit that the members of the audience were unable to suppress an occasional smile.

At the end of his talk, Stewart issued a militant call to action. Writers should "step out of the museum" into the open air and participate actively in the struggle against fascism. In fact, they should "enlist" in that fight, as he put it two years later in his introduction to *Fighting Words,* a collection of pieces from the League of American Writers' third Congress. Words were weapons, and good anti-fascists must learn how to use them. Stewart clung to his pro-communist position even after the Hitler-Stalin pact. At the fourth—and final—Congress of the League, held in June 1941, he spoke out against defectors he'd observed dashing madly toward "Nearest Exits."

Don's politics introduced him to Ella Winter. When they met in the fall of 1936, he expected her, as Steffens' widow, to be somewhat superannuated, and was stunned by her black-eyed beauty: "There she was, my sex object." They were married two and half years later, after Beatrice Stewart got a divorce to marry the Count Ilya Tolstoy and Ella's son decided he approved of Don. Meanwhile, Stewart kept getting lucrative screen assignments and espousing communist causes (he served, for example, as president of the Hollywood Anti-Nazi league).

Don's public conversion to communism did not sit well with many of his friends. Bob Benchley was alienated, and John O'Hara, and Scott Fitzgerald, who was to collaborate with Stewart on the screenplay for *The Women* during 1938. Two years earlier, before Fitzgerald settled in Hollywood, O'Hara wrote him that

> Don Stewart, who is full of shit, has converted himself to radical thought, and goes to all the parties for the Scottsboro boys. . . . Don talked to me for an hour one afternoon about how he makes a much better radical than—well, than I. Because, he pointed out, he'd *had* Skull & Bones, he'd *had* the Whitney plantation, he'd *had* big Hollywood money. He is certainly scared about something, and it isn't only the Revolution. But he is such a horse's ass that it doesn't matter very much.

Fitzgerald responded in similar vein. "If this [letter] seems toilet paper you can use it to wipe Dr. Daniel Ogden Stewart's mouth when he finally gets the kick in the ass that he has been asking for so long." In his notebooks, Fitzgerald elaborated his distaste for the course his old friend had followed. Stewart, he wrote, was a "wily old Kiss-puss," an "intellectual simpleton" making "a spiritual exercise" out of communism. The bitterest passage of all speaks of Don's "efforts to pull down the pillars on all our heads and hide in the ruins. We were through, he said,—then, satisfied he returned to suck. The Whitneys bought him up cheap and turned him out to grass on the private golf links." Unlike O'Hara, Fitzgerald had some left-leaning sympathies of his own, but both were offended by the jarring contrast between Stewart's political convictions on the one hand and his obvious financial and social success on the other. Don traveled in circles that O'Hara, who didn't make it to Yale, much less to Skull and Bones, could not penetrate and that Fitzgerald, with his drunken gaffes and excessive inquisitiveness, could never penetrate for long.

In fact Fitzgerald considered himself rather better off than Stewart in social background. "Why and where I caught a petit bourgeois attitude I don't know. But it's not like Dot's [Dorothy Parker's] and Don's who revolted from being eternal poor relations." Still, he and Stewart were both middle-class middle western youngsters who understood that charm could open doors. Don "pleases you not by direct design," Fitzgerald commented, "but because his desire to please is so intense that it is disarming. He pleases you most perhaps when his very words are irritants."

In his late screenwriting assignments and the plays that he later wrote, Stewart tried to put aside his eternally pleasant manner in an attempt to hammer home one political statement or another. *Keeper of the Flame* (1942), starring Hepburn and Spencer Tracy, warned that a Mussolini-style dictatorship could indeed happen here, if we let the Few wrest power from the Many. That motion picture, the one Stewart was proudest to have been associated with, launched the final phase of his writing career. In his play, *Emily Brady*, he tried to show that "the struggle for power in competitive Big Business inevitably incorporates anti-human practices, including gangsterism and murder. It involves defiance of democracy, especially of the Bill of Rights. It demands that human beings be regarded as commodities, to be manipulated for profit, without regard to their worth as individuals or their natural need for self-fulfillment." No one wanted to hear all that in wartime, and the play went unproduced. But another drama, *How I Wonder*, actually reached

Broadway for 63 performances in the fall of 1947. The play, which has a strong autobiographical flavor, sketches the growing political awareness of a professor of astronomy. Though inclined to retreat to his ivory observatory, the professor eventually realizes the wisdom of getting involved in political activity. His inspiration comes from the Talmud: "If not I, who? If not now, when?" George Jean Nathan panned the play in his *Theatre Book of the Year for 1947-1948*. The author "had pretentiously reached for the stars" in his quest for profundity, Nathan wrote, but "had brought down only a bunch of klieg lights, all burnt out from Hollywood overuse."

Considerably more successful with critics and audiences alike was *The Kidders*, produced in London during the 1957-1958 season. Taking a middle western suburb for its locale, the play dramatized the expatriate author's exasperation with American life. Most of the characters seem odious:

> the horribly clear-sighted young drunk with his nostalgia for the fine, heroic moments of the Pacific war, his ambitious wife given to sleeping her way round his friends, . . . the hyper-efficient secretary/mistress with her costume jewellery and her yearning for simplicity, the slick young man with a relentless eye on the main chance and a smile like a salesman's. . . .

But the real villain of the piece is the Corporation which controls the characters' lives and has, presumably, produced all their nastiness.

In *The Kidders*, which Stewart considered his best play, he tried for the first time to put his gift for humor to thematic advantage. The characters are constantly wisecracking and "kidding" each other, but with an edge to the comedy. *The Spectator* deplored the tendency of the author, "an obsessional kidder" himself, to "dress up every statement in a comic hat." *The New Statesman*, on the other hand, applauded the technique. Some of the wisecracks are very funny, the review noted,

> but just as you are opening your lips to laugh at them, the smile is wiped off your face by a sourness that seeps out from them . . . this 'kidding' is a smoke-screen thrown up to conceal the sharp edges of anxiety and hostility with which any moment you may collide; and then someone is likely to get hurt.

Even this review rebelled at the play's hopeful ending, however, on the grounds that a sunny conclusion did not seem to follow from the previous revelations. Perhaps not, but Stewart consistently contrived sky-blue endings for his characters. Unlike Moliere's or Twain's, his satire did not cut deep into human nature. His quarrel was with capitalism, almost never with individual persons. He could not help liking most people and having faith in them. Besides, some of his best friends were stockbrokers.

V

It took him nearly 50 years, Stewart wrote in his autobiography, to discover that his childhood gods had played him false, that his quest for social and financial success had led him down the garden path. Among the teachers who guided him to this realization was a character in a novel of E. M. Forster, whose pithy advice, "Only connect," Stewart would have placed on the crest of every university. Ella inspired him by her example, too, and so did men like Kyle Chrichton, who under the *nom de plume* of Robert Forsythe managed to be angry rather than merely amusing about what was wrong with America. In films like *Keeper of the Flame* and plays like *The Kidders,* Stewart attempted to transform his late-blooming convictions into art, but the attempts were not entirely successful, for he could never quite muster the requisite indignation. Nor would he give up his bourgeois existence and renounce his upper-class friends. Though a communist, he wanted still to be "old Don," well liked by everyone.

The story of his political awakening was both the least interesting part of his autobiography and the least persuasive. What a joy it was, he admitted, when Hitler invaded Russia and he was no longer ostracized by his friends. Just so: Stewart always cared tremendously about people and gave more of himself to them than to his writing or his politics. His great gift was a charm made up partly of an inner sweetness, partly of that overwhelming bias in favor of his companion that characterized Jay Gatsby, partly of *joie de vivre,* and partly of a virtually unquenchable humor. Hemingway captured some of that charm (in what, to Don, seemed a mere transcription of the way it was) in the talk between Jake Barnes and Bill Gorton, and particularly in the scene following Bill's return from Vienna, when he and Jake venture out in search of strong drink and stuffed animals. Read aloud, the Gorton-Barnes passages are funnier than anything Hemingway ever wrote—and Gorton/Stewart has the best lines.

He still had them in the fall of 1972, when I went to talk to him while on leave from William and Mary. "How *are* William and Mary?" he wanted to know as he opened the door to the London drizzle. Inside his elegant house on Frognal, in Hampstead, once the domicile of Ramsay MacDonald, we spent a long afternoon talking about his career and about Hemingway, Fitzgerald and others. Then 78, Stewart ordinarily permitted himself nothing at all to drink, he said. But he did drink wine on birthdays, and had memorized any number of them, including those of wives of defeated vice-presidential candidates. We toasted one such lady, often. In time I stopped furiously scribbling notes and gaping at the collection of African art that competed for wall space with Klees and Mondrians, Chagalls and Groszes, and simply enjoyed myself. Don told me something of his daily routine, which included a walk with Fidget to pick up the *Evening Standard*. ("Actually, he explained, "the dog does not read the *Standard*.") He knew old men were supposed to get cranky, and yet the girls he saw seemed prettier, the people nicer than ever. Could he help it if they seemed that way?

A few days later we went to luncheon at the Savoy. As the five of us—Stewart, Ella, my wife, a friend of hers, and myself—were inspecting menus, Don discovered to his joy that the hotel offered Soup Garbure. Nothing would do but that he try the soup to see if it lived up to the promise of its name. After lunch, we bundled my wife and her friend into a cab to take them to the train to New Haven and then the boat to Dieppe, where they were to learn what a week could teach them about French cooking. "I don't know if you'll understand what I mean," Don told the travellers, "but *au revoir*." Then he and Ella were off in their own taxi, back to Hampstead and the art treasures and his continuing exile as the most engaging of all traitors to his class.

Midwestern Writer: A Memoir

John E. Hallwas

"It's the place that matters, the place at the heart of things." —Loren Eiseley

Most literary scholars illuminate the familiar: they discuss writers and works of undisputed significance. But I seldom do that. I am attracted to the forgotten writers of the Midwest, the obscure figures whose works are seldom read now and perhaps never were read by very many, so I recover the lost and explore the unfamiliar. I am interested in how writers relate to place, and that can be fascinating whether or not a person wrote well enough to be widely known and subsequently remembered. And I am a writer, too, as well as a resident of Illinois, so I understand how it must have been for so many others—writing to locate themselves, to be at home here in the Midwest.

Most of the writers I have taken an interest in were dead long before I discovered them, but not all. One who wasn't lived in a neighboring county. He was Warren Van Dine, a man who shared much with me during the closing years of his life—as much as he ever shared with anyone. Not that we were close friends, but I knew him and liked him; and he enjoyed spending time with me. Although he was more than twice my age, we had much in common.

I saw Warren for the first time only ten years ago, in the summer of 1979. I was in nearby Carthage, seeking historical information about early Hancock County, where the Mormons had settled in the 1840s to pursue their dream of a millennial theocracy, an American Zion, and to assert their identity as God's chosen people. Like their Puritan forebears, they were pioneers with a special sense of destiny, and their main community, Nauvoo, was a frontier version of John Winthrop's "city upon a hill." At least, they thought so. The non-Mormons around them, like those throughout the nation, were possessed by a different dream—more secular, pluralistic, and democratic—and eventually drove the Mormons out after a miniature civil war in which both sides felt they were struggling for the future of America. And perhaps they were.

Ever since then, the people of Hancock County have had a remarkable sense of history, as if they were in touch with something basic about the American experience. The great political-religious conflict of the 1840s is their deepest cultural memory—for the county was still being settled when the Mormons arrived—and it is, perhaps, symbolic of the struggle for meaningful community in a nation devoted to freedom and diversity. In any case, the Mormon Conflict is a psychological wound in Hancock County, and it has been irritated in recent years by the restoration of Nauvoo as a shrine to the vision and purpose of the Mormon pioneers. Nowhere in the Midwest does local history bear a more profound burden.

Carthage itself is bound forever to the great struggle, for on a quiet street is the old county jail where Joseph Smith was murdered in 1844—now a shrine to the memory of the prophet-martyr. And in the center of the tree-shaded square is a lovely, turn-of-the-century courthouse, topped by a magnificent white cupola with a red-shingled dome. There the local historical society keeps masses of records relating to the country's past.

That was where I went on that summer day in 1979 and where I first heard of Warren Van Dine. Even among such well-informed, history-minded people, he was considered unusual. When I asked a difficult question, one of the Carthage natives said, "Warren Van Dine would know. He's a regular encyclopedia of the local past. And he's a writer, you know. Written lots of things about the county."

I met Warren later that afternoon. He was a tall, thin, bald-headed man, 75 years old and somewhat stooped. His medium-brown suit, with its wide lapels, seemed too large for his bony frame, and it surely hadn't been cleaned in years. His dingy, multi-colored necktie hung loosely under his collar, and the small, tight knot suggested that he never re-tied it, just slipped it off and on over his head. He looked like a hobo, but he spoke with the intelligence and insight of a college professor.

He knew all about the so-called Mormon War. His ancestors had been involved. On his mother's side of the family he was related to Joseph Smith, whose theocratic political ambitions had precipitated the violence. Warren's roots went deep into the county—which is to say, deep into the heart of things that mattered, as far as his sense of identity was concerned.

But I am getting ahead of my story. On that day in 1979 I was interested in cemetery records. I am an archivist, too, so my professional duties include the preservation of records about the ordinary people who have embodied and transmitted our culture. In western Illinois I am a man known largely for my commitment to the past, to what can be discovered about the dead, and nothing is more basic to that effort than cemeteries and graves.

Warren was the right man to see. In the previous twenty years he had compiled burial records from one graveyard after another in Hancock County, and he had correlated that information with obituaries and other sources until his files were crammed with data about the dead in well over 100 cemeteries. He knew much about the residents of now-forgotten places like Sutter and Elderville, and he was familiar with the past inhabitants of now-dying villages like Basco, Ferris, St. Marys, and Fountain Green.

Cemetery work was never just a casual pursuit with Warren. It was a kind of mission, a special duty he had assumed in the rural Illinois county where his family had lived for generations. Beyond that, it was a means of engaging himself with countless men and women of the past who had contributed to his cultural context—and who were no less fascinating to him because they were gone.

Warren combined excursions to little-known cemeteries with continuous reading in old newspapers and other local records—what he called his "research." By the time I met him, he could talk with fluency about vast numbers of people who had once lived in Hancock County. He was therefore useful to an archivist like myself, who struggles to preserve the past in one corner of the Midwest and, within limits, to comprehend it.

It was Warren who told me about Frances Gilchrist Wood, for example, whose love for nineteenth-century Carthage prompted her to write a now-forgotten novel of community life called *Gospel Four Corners;* and Colonel Levi Williams, the hotheaded vigilante who burned the Mormon settlement at Yelrome in the 1840s, and Amzi Doolittle, the frontier businessman who, it was said, could swear longer without repeating himself than any other man in the county.

In Warren's mind the dead were still part of the fabric of local culture, and he asserted their continuing presence with his detailed and rambling comments about them. Graveyards fascinated him. He started doing serious cemetery work long before it became a national movement, and when the modern history of Hancock County appeared in 1968, his main contribution was a chapter entitled "Hancock's Silent Cities of the Dead."

The thinly populated, richly historic county was his native ground—his spiritual home. He felt connected to it by a thousand strands of experience there—a web, perhaps, that was the ultimate influence on his life.

As one might expect, Warren took Memorial Day seriously. He understood it in the old sense as a kind of ritual, a yearly affirmation of community between the living and the dead, marked by the visiting of graves and the placing of flowers. I recall driving him around the county one May 31st, so he could show me a few of his favorite cemeteries. Along the way, he resurrected one person after another in a continuous stream of talk. He reminded me of the famous Memorial Day speech that Justice Oliver Wendell Holmes delivered a century ago: "As surely as this day comes round, we are in the presence of the dead. . . . I see them now, more than I can number." It was like that with Warren, too.

The last stop we made was at the McKay Cemetery in Burnside, the village seven miles north of Carthage where he had spent most of his life. Warren's parents were buried there, beneath a white marble headstone that he had erected to memorialize them. I noticed that this mother had died way back in 1920, more than twenty years before his father, and when I mentioned that, he said a curious thing: "Yes, sometimes people have to continue on alone, even in Burnside."

However, I later found out that his father had married again several months after his mother's death. I had misunderstood what he meant. Herbert Van Dine's second wife was a sturdy, uneducated, farm-type woman who had in turn outlived him by many years. She was buried there, too, but her grave was not marked. That was when I began to realize there was a mystery about Warren, some inner darkness that had deeply affected his life. He had been referring to himself.

As we drove back to his home on that Memorial Day, Warren mentioned that his own burial plans had already been made—that he had acquired a lot and purchased a headstone. He would have been the last person to leave such a matter to chance.

The more time I spent with Warren, the more I realized that he was a brilliant man, in his own way. He was very widely read and could discuss great historical events and famous literary works with equal facility. He often spoke to local groups on topics like "The Purpose of Education" and "The American Revolution," and he took those matters seriously.

His powers of recall were astounding. I once asked him to tell me about the history of Burnside, and he talked for more than an hour without stopping, pouring forth a barrage of names, dates, and other details without looking at a note. He described the founding of the town as if he had witnessed it back in the 1840s, and he spoke warmly and personally of the people who had lived there over the years, as if they were family members. He carried the whole history of the community in his head, so it seemed to me, and his rambling commentary ended only because I had to leave.

Perhaps that was the ultimate difference between us: I could get away from the past, but Warren could not.

On another occasion, when I knew him better, he told me the story of how his parents had moved to Burnside from a neighboring township in 1912, when he was a small boy. He recalled the village as a thriving farm center, with its own drug store, pool hall, blacksmith shop, state bank, lumberyard, and other businesses that made a complete town in those days. All of them were lined up along the dirt road that was Main Street, where the children played together after school and their parents gossiped into the evening on Saturday nights.

The Van Dines lived across from the two-story frame schoolhouse, in an elegant Queen Anne-style home that Warren's father had built. Herbert Van Dine was a carpenter, and the beautiful twelve-room house was a testament to his skill as a builder—and to his success in a community that recognized his skill. Indeed, his work was well known in nearby villages like Adrian, Ferris, and Fountain Green, where he built churches and schools as well as homes and businesses.

His wife Flora had been a schoolteacher before Warren's impending birth had ended her career. "She was a woman with high ideals," Warren said, "and when she could no longer teach school, she taught me." He was the product of her intellectual commitment—a profound kind of maternal self-expression—and there had been a strong bond between them.

My relationship to Warren took on a deeper dimension as I began to be more interested in him than in the information he had accumulated. There was something about his preoccupation with the local past that intrigued me. I have known dozens of local historians in western Illinois, all of them fascinated with the past and glad to recall it for an archivist with a tape recorder, but for Warren, remembering was an obsession.

So was writing—or at least, it had been for most of his life. One day he casually commented that decades ago his poems were appearing in periodicals like *The Midland* and *The Literary Digest*. I was surprised. He had never before mentioned his work as a poet. A diffident man, he was slowly starting to relate to me. He produced a slim volume entitled *Unchanging Gold*, a collection of mostly sentimental poems that he had written many years ago.

He said it was the first book ever published by the Decker Press, located in nearby Prairie City, and he told me the story of his association with James Decker, an ambitious young publisher who thought that Warren would one day be a noted American poet. Decker was wrong, of course, but he was not wrong about William Everson (Brother Antoninus), David Ignatow, Kenneth Rexroth, Louis Zukofsky, and others whose books he published when few other presses, in the Midwest or elsewhere, would produce volumes by unknown poets. Started with Warren's book in 1938, the Decker Press soon became the most active poetry publisher in America. It ended some years later with a murder-suicide case. Warren knew all about that, too, even though it had happened in the next county, for he viewed himself as a co-founder of the ill-fated press, which had failed even as his poetic career had failed, for deeply personal reasons.

On another occasion he talked about his work as a fiction writer. He mentioned that one of his stories had appeared in *The Best Short Stories of 1924*. When I got back to my office at Western Illinois University Library, I looked up that volume. Sure enough, there it was: "The Poet" by Warren L. Van Dine, reprinted from the pages of *The Midland*. Some of Warren's other stories were included in the list of notable works published every year in the Best Short Stories volumes.

As I later found out, Warren had attended the University of Iowa during the early twenties, when young midwestern writers were excited and inspired by the poetry of Edgar Lee Masters and Carl Sandburg, the fiction of Sherwood Anderson and Willa Cather. By and large, the literati at the university—faculty and students—were concerned with family and community life in the Midwest, as well as the pioneer experience, so Warren fit in—as well as a shy, insecure youth from Burnside could fit in anywhere.

He studied under such talented men as John T. Frederick, editor of *The Midland*; Edwin Ford Piper, a noted Iowa poet, and Frank Luther Mott, who later won a Pulitzer Prize. His classmates included Paul Corey, Marquis Childs, Ruth Lechlitner, Charlton Laird, and other subsequently successful writers.

None was considered more talented than Warren Van Dine, whose works began appearing in print while he was still a student. Along with his short stories he was writing poetry then, too. In 1925 he was included in *The Poets of the Future*, a collection devoted to promising poets at American colleges.

None of Warren's poems and stories seems impressive now, but I find them interesting simply because he became increasingly interesting to me. He had literary talent, but there was something that kept him from fulfilling his early promise. It had to do with his family life, I was sure, so that was the direction of my inquiry as I looked into the mystery of Warren Van Dine.

His mother was not only an ardent reader and a lover of poetry, she "possessed an unfathomable nature," according to her obituary—for I looked it up in the yellowed pages of *The Carthage Republican*. She was apparently a very bright, capable, committed woman, and she had sparkled in the limited social world of Burnside. Before her marriage she had studied at Graceland College, associated with the Reorganized Church of Jesus Christ of Latter Day Saints. She was devoted to the church that her great uncle had founded—and for which, she believed, he had died. She regarded Joseph Smith as the greatest figure since Christ, and she felt deeply connected to the Mormon heritage of Hancock County. To her, the murder of the Prophet and the expulsion of his followers from Nauvoo were unspeakable tragedies that somehow verified the sacred importance of the Latter Day Saints, even as they confirmed the world's wickedness.

Warren was Flora Van Dine's only child for a dozen years, until his sister was born, and there was a deep communion between mother and son. They spent long golden days together while Warren's father was away, working out of town with his building crew. "She was very fond of music," her obituary says, "and it was through her singing of inspirational songs that she was sustained as she did her household duties." Warren must have been deeply impressed with the sound of his mother's voice, to which he was so often the only listener, for he could still remember parts of the songs she sang after sixty years. Included among them were hymns that reflected Mormon righteousness and millennialism—in lines like these:

> All that was promised the Saints shall be given,
> For they shall be crowned when the Savior does come;
> And earth will appear as the Garden of Eden,
> Where Christ and His people will ever be one.

Warren's mother wanted him to be a writer, especially to chronicle and celebrate the Mormon experience. That was her dream, her deepest desire. She urged him to write poetry while he was in his early teens, and she sent him to the high school at Carthage—where he did, in fact, distinguish himself as a student. She must have been pleased when the editor of *The Carthage Republican* wrote an article about Warren in 1919, referring to him as "a gifted youth" whose poetry "had real merit." By that time, surely, her dream had become his as well.

A few months before Warren graduated, his mother died. She had been ill with cancer for some time and was eventually confined to her upstairs bedroom. In her last days she continued to make plans with Warren—college plans, for she wanted him to attend Graceland College, just as she had, and to continue to grow in the faith that had been so important in her own life while he prepared for the career she had chosen for him. Of course, as her condition deteriorated, he suffered with her, and when she finally died, he was bereft.

After the agony of the funeral was over, Warren and his small sister remained with his father in a house that must have seemed incredibly quiet and empty. Herbert Van Dine was a tall, muscular man who had not finished high school, and he was apparently never close to his bookish son. He had no interest in poetry or literature of any kind, and he had, of course, wanted a son who could work with his hands. He made sporadic efforts to involve Warren in his carpentry, but it was evident that his son was committed to other things.

Beyond that, I don't know much about Warren's family life. A couple of the old-timers in Carthage mumbled about "what Warren had been through," but they did not, and would not, explain what they meant. And Warren never discussed it.

I didn't need to know. An archivist learns to live with the unexplained. Besides, I too, had come from a shattered, troubled family in a small Illinois town. My father had also been a carpenter, a distant man, and my mother had died while I was in high school—a death that had changed everything. I knew the unutterable sense of loss, the collapse of psychological support, the inescapable antagonism, the temptation to withdraw. I didn't tell Warren any of that; I never talk about it either. But I was in a position to understand. And I knew that with his mother's death, something of Warren had gone to lie in the cemetery at the edge of town, and something of her had remained with him.

As the weeks and months passed, he apparently feared that he was slowly forgetting her—a common response to the death of someone deeply loved—but the dream they had shared still united them. In one of his poems from this period Warren refers to "A face that slowly faded in the darkness / And a voice that drifted into gray memories," while "out of the depths of death came a marvelous dream!" Writing became a way of renewing the bond between them.

In the following fall Warren left Burnside for the University of Iowa to study English and become a writer. Why he did not attend Graceland College I don't know, but I am sure that enrolling instead at the university was the most fortunate decision of his life. Shortly after he left town, his father remarried.

Of course, while he lived in Iowa City Warren longed for Hancock County. Perhaps the best poem of his college days is "At the Grave of Joseph Smith," a meditation on the famous religious leader, who is buried at Nauvoo. He depicts Smith as the Christ figure, walking alone in "his Gethsemane" while the city slept and "this Judas of a world sought him." Like his mother, Warren was a devoted Mormon, at least in his early years, and he viewed the lights and shadows of his own experience in relationship to the life of the Prophet. Significantly, he portrays Smith as an isolated individual, undergoing spiritual agony.

It was also in college that Warren wrote "The Poet,"

which had appeared in *The Best Short Stories of 1924*. It is a revealing story, told by a small-town carpenter whose son had recently died—a son that he didn't understand. At the outset he tells of marrying an educated woman, a schoolteacher who read books and "dreamed of doing great things." She wanted him "to climb up in the world and get to be somebody," but he liked the "rough work" of a builder. She urged him to be an elder in the church, but he disliked church and wanted to spend his Sundays "getting ready for the next week." She encouraged him to run for local office, but he was happy "with a home and plenty to eat."

When her urgings met resistance, she turned her attention to their son. She dreamed that he would one day make his mark as a writer. She died too soon, but her influence on the boy made it impossible for him to enter the world of his father—the only world that was open to him. The carpenter felt that his son "was queer that way—more of an onlooker in life than someone mixed up in it." There was always a gap between them. But after studying at a state university, the youth returned home and joined his father's work crew. Soon he received word that his collection of poetry had been accepted by a New York publisher. Then he died in an accident there in the village, leaving the carpenter to ponder his mysterious son, whose need "to pour himself out in writing" had isolated him from others in the village: "He had been lonely, I saw; yes sir, just plain lonely."

"The Poet" is obviously a wish-fulfillment story in which Warren re-shaped his life so as to satisfy both of his feuding parents: he became a carpenter who worked alongside his father, in a world where poets had no value, and he became the literary success that his mother had wanted him to be. Then he suddenly died, for he couldn't imagine himself as fulfilling both of those contradictory roles.

While at the university, Warren discovered *Spoon River Anthology*, and the controversial book had a big impact on him. What impressed him most was not the poet's "revolt from the village," but his sympathy for the ordinary people who composed it and who carried their hopes and frustrations into the grave.

One day we discussed the book, for it was a favorite of mine, too, and he said something that I failed to note exactly but was approximately this: "In Spoon River the dead are doomed to remember. They linger in the village graveyard and bear witness to their lives in the community. That shows us something important: the human heart is local; it has roots. And nothing lends meaning to our lives like the persistence of memory."

Masters's famous book probably helped Warren to clarify his own purpose as a writer. It certainly enlarged his sympathy for the lives that had touched his own back in Hancock County—both the living and the dead.

After studying for most of four years—in religion and history as well as English—Warren left Iowa City and returned to the county that he had never spiritually been away from. While his classmates were planning to launch their careers, he simply wanted to return home. He was terribly afraid of rootlessness, and no other place appealed to him. So he went back to Burnside, population 300, a village that was starting the long process of cultural decay and dissolution that had been initiated by the coming of cars and hard roads. It was becoming a place where the old remained in a secure but diminishing social environment and the young grew up and left. But Warren stayed. He worked briefly for the Santa Fe Railroad in nearby Fort Madison and for a rubber factory in Keokuk, also just a short distance away. Then he was a house painter in Burnside for many years. He apparently did not work with his father.

Not many houses needed painting in Burnside or other nearby villages from one year to the next, but Warren liked it that way. He worked to support himself so he could write. That was his real vocation. He strove to wrest meaning from his relationship to the place and people that had contributed so much to his identity. He wanted to be at home in the world.

But he found it very difficult to write well in Burnside. He was apparently too close to the source of his insecurity and loneliness. Much of what he wrote he later threw out, and he seldom sent poems and stories anywhere. In a suggestive poem called "The Poet," written sometime in the late 1920s, the speaker cries out, "I dip my pen in blood; / I trace my words in dust," but "My writings are destroyed / And destroyed."

Warren was apparently unable to assert himself. He needed to articulate a personal vision, a critical perspective on the social context that was his unique subject matter, but he was afraid to break the bond that united him to everything that really mattered. His failure was surely bound up with the memory of his mother and his overwhelming insecurity after her death.

Warren Van Dine was a George Willard who couldn't bear to leave Winesburg.

In the mid-1930s he decided to write a massive biography of Joseph Smith, his famous relative, and he worked on it for more than ten years. But he never finished it. Warren was a man to whom family and community were everything, and all his work on the book began to threaten his sense of relationship to both. As he told me one afternoon, "I couldn't fuse the two halves of the Prophet's life—his importance as a religious leader, which my mother believed implicitly and I always accepted, and his actions as a frontier politician and community leader in the closing years of his life. I was afraid of what would happen if I went any further."

A talented and sensitive man, Warren knew that his vision as a writer was a powerful force, an expression of his individuality and therefore inherently threatening to his sense of connection, his feeling of social context, especially where family and community and religion were so deeply intertwined. His enlightened, individualized perspective could isolate him from others who embodied but did not transcend their culture. Fear of alienation was, in fact, the reason he had returned to Burnside after launching his career at the university and had begun studying local history. Unable to comprehend his loneliness, he had struggled to regain a sense of belonging.

He had thought that a biography of Joseph Smith would be an ideal means of affirming what mattered most—his complex relationship to Hancock County and his Mormon heritage. But he found that biography, too, is a kind of literary art that makes high demands on the author. Withholding his judgement while he examined and evaluated, he eventually realized that he would have to challenge his family's faith, in some respects, to fulfill his lifelong dream. Warren abandoned serious writing after that, for he lacked the courage to pursue it.

Instead, he plunged deeper and deeper into genealogy and local history until the county's past somehow merged with his own. From time to time he wrote historical pieces for the Carthage newspaper, but those demanded little of him. Among them are some biographical sketches of Hancock County pioneers—men and women of little distinction, really, but heroes, of a sort, to him, for they had established the cultural framework of the county. He often referred to such early residents as "our ancestors," for to Warren local history became an intensely personal thing, a quest for communion. More importantly, perhaps, his continually expanding cemetery research, aimed at rescuing earlier residents from oblivion, became a means of embracing Mormons and non-Mormons alike—and thus, of transcending the antagonism of the 1840s, which had been latent in his mother's literary hopes for him.

But as he worked, Warren became preoccupied with death—not physical dissolution but the inevitable fading of the self from human memory. Many of his poems suggest this. In one of them, entitled "Pioneers," the speaker, who symbolizes the early settlers of the Midwest, is mysteriously "Drawn through the darkness" to a vague eternity where he mingles with "the gray drifting shadows of the dead." Despite his culture-making effort, his identity is lost.

As time went by, Warren amassed the encyclopedic knowledge of the county's past residents which later brought him to my attention. He became a leader in the war of memory against forgetfulness, and he thereby achieved a sense of purpose and a measure of gratitude from the people of Hancock County. But he paid a heavy price, for it is dangerous to linger among the dead: one becomes so easily bound to them. For Warren the past became a world that was increasingly hard to get away from. He became a recluse.

When his father died in 1941, Warren acquired the old two-story Van Dine home in Burnside and lived there alone. He never married—or had much to do with women throughout his life—and he seldom had any visitors. The once-elegant home that had symbolized his father's place in the community gradually fell into disrepair. The front steps began to sag. The attic window became broken. Moss covered the wood shingles, and a tree grew into the roof of the front porch. By the time I saw it, the house looked like a crumbling relic of the past.

Of course, in Warren's later years there was little of the old sense of community in Burnside. The town had steadily diminished until there were perhaps 150 people remaining and virtually no businesses. But as the old residents died or prepared to move away, auctions were commonly held, and Warren attended most of them, often buying up items that had been made or owned by people that he remembered from years ago. The old Van Dine home became the attic of the community, where fragments of the local past were gathered and cherished.

As the years passed, Warren became engulfed by the many

things he could not bear to throw away or otherwise part with: old appliances, sets of china, outdated furniture, faded paintings, broken clocks—the clutter of a lifetime. When I first saw the inside of his house, I wondered how anyone could walk through it. I remember thinking that it was emblematic of Warren's mind—incredibly full but unfocused, and overly committed to the past.

After I had known him for about two years, he decided to show me his inner sanctum—the place where his writing had been done, and not done, over the years. I followed him up the dusty stairs. The treads were stacked with old dishes, silverware, tools, lamps, and toys. His study was apparently the master bedroom. It was cluttered with hundreds of books. A photograph of his mother stood on the dresser. She was a full-figured, distinguished-looking woman of about 40, with great waves of prematurely white hair pinned up on her head. "My mother," he said, handing me the photograph. "She was a remarkable woman." She must have been, I thought, to have exerted such an influence for so long.

But Warren had led me up to his room, the one room he really lived in, because he wanted to show me something else. He opened a closet door. Stacked on the floor was an extensive run of *The Midland*—from 1920, when he enrolled at the University of Iowa, until 1933, when John T. Frederick gave up trying to keep the periodical alive and it folded. Warren showed me his stories in it, and he discussed his experience at Iowa during those magical years in the twenties. He thought I would be interested, and I was. Alongside the magazine was a huge set of University of Iowa yearbooks, from the time he was a student there until the 1970s—decades of yearbooks through which he had watched the university slowly change. Obviously he had never gotten over the experience of being among the writers there, at a time when modern midwestern literature was being born and everything seemed possible—even for a shy and lonely youth from Burnside.

After that I never again visited Warren at his home, but I saw him from time to time at nearby Carthage, where he carried on his research at the courthouse. That is where I spoke with him now and again or picked him up to go visit some place in the county that I wanted to see or Warren wanted to show me.

I have never met a more reliable guide to the history of

any community or county, and I have known many. He was an archivist's dream—and a writer's nightmare.

Warren died in the fall of 1983. We had no mutual friends, so by the time I found out about it, he was already buried. But as soon as I had the chance I drove over to the Nauvoo City Cemetery to visit his grave. The headstone he had ordered for himself confirmed much that I had suspected:

Warren L. Van Dine
November 25, 1902
September 25, 1983
American Poet and Short Story Writer

At first I was surprised that he was buried there instead of in the McKay Cemetery at Burnside, near his mother, but the more I reflected on it, the more I felt that perhaps this was his way of asserting the independence that had eluded him during his life, except for his years at the University of Iowa. Or maybe his marker in the much-visited cemetery at Nauvoo was a means of gaining recognition. After all, he was a man who had received so little for so long. Or he may have simply decided that since Nauvoo was at the heart of things, as far as his Mormon heritage was concerned, that was where his grave needed to be. I don't know. We can only interpret other lives; we cannot really know them. And the dead we feel connected with are always partly an expression of ourselves.

As I walked away, looking at the vast expanse of graves that Warren would have been familiar with, I couldn't help reflecting that the dead in Hancock County were more remote from us now that he was gone. Surely many people of the past that he knew something about are no longer a presence in anyone's mind.

In the years since Warren's death I have often thought about him. To me as a literary scholar, he has come to symbolize all the frustrated and forgotten writers who struggled to express themselves and relate to their cultural environment in the Midwest—and never achieved anything significant. But to me as an archivist, a man who rescues what he can in a hopeless race with oblivion, Warren has taken on a kind of tragic stature. In the face of massive and inevitable forgetting, his life was an act of stubborn resistance. He strove to remember—and in the process, to dispel his loneliness and be at home on his native ground.

It would be unbearably ironic if Warren Van Dine, of all people, should be completely forgotten, so I wrote this about him, and now he won't be. In the process, of course, I have pushed my own roots more firmly into the same ground. I have affirmed my place here—and salvaged something of myself as well.

As I have said before, Warren and I had much in common.

Midwestern Discontinuities

A Cutting Art: Sharpness of Image in the Fiction of Jonis Agee

Jill B. Gidmark

One can be riveted by any number of things when cracking a Jonis Agee story—the setting of unpretentious cities and rural towns of Minnesota and Iowa in some stories that contrasts with nameless no-man's lands in other stories, the variety in her narrative voices, the compression of energy in her plots, and, most of all, the images that, in Marge Piercy's words, are "sharp enough to cut your fingers on." The emotions Agee conjures up are certainly not simple or one-dimensional; many of them are not even pretty. None of them is ordinary. And the stories telling of obsessions and cruelties may not end in epiphany or forgiveness or even cessation. But there is a kinky truth in them, a slice of behavior we can believe even when we cannot identify or sympathize with it, a texture and feel of reality and courage, and a total effect of neon flashing at night and the color staying with you a long time.

Aside from a few early (and slight, by comparison) chapbooks and scattered periodical publication of fiction, Agee appears in her true and vivid colors in three important works—*Stiller's Pond*, a 1988 collection of upper midwestern fiction that Agee co-edited and for which she wrote the title story; *Pretend We've Never Met* (1989), a collection of two dozen stories, half of which were previously published; and *Bend This Heart* (1989), twenty-three new stories.

It is possible that readers not used to new fiction may be more drawn to an earlier Agee story such as "Stiller's Pond" than to pieces in her most recent collections because that story is so accessible, so satisfying, and so obviously human and mythical in its strivings, its glimmers of a kind of tarnished glory, and its more frequent failings. It is rooted in values of the human heart—ancestry, place, family, passion, privacy, and love. The opening (and first sentences are uniformly wonderful in Agee) is conversationally agreeable and inviting: "Look, I just want to tell you what it's like out there, what the wind and water do." It's a cold January; little waves are starched into peaks by the wind, the rough surface of no consequence because for a long time children have been forbidden to skate on the pond. The eerie and evocative plot is slowly revealed—a dead woman (great aunt of the narrator) found drowned many years ago with hair tangled in cattails near the body of a man "bobbing like a cork in the hold that stayed warm over the spring." The woman's burial was rude ("in a homemade box with the dull nickel nails winking out of the mismatched corners"), the parents hard and tight as those nails in refusing to identify the male body as that of either the hired man or the oldest son, both of whom disappeared the same night. The mystery of exactly what happened remains unsolved as the story closes, but what is revealed is the work of the turtles and the fishes on the drowned bodies (Grandmother tells the children that the woman is coming back for her eyes, which the turtles plucked) and a whispered secret that both disappoints and conceals: "They weren't wearing skates. 'And that's why . . . you can't go there—ever.'" The prohibition, though, "seal[s] forever in our hearts the desire for the place, a desire that can never be satisfied, a desire we give our children for Stiller's Pond."

The mystery in later Agee stories is not so literal, so defined, or even so benign. It is more like hallucination. One of my favorites is "Side Road," where the narrator parks a semi-truck sideways, races across it ("I may have a gun, and I may not"), then gives up to pursuers who bring her to "a place that is nearly not one," where genderless, alien people in an assembly line are passing in clear heavy plastic bags butchered human livers—"something intimate red, something closer, something deeper, and there is a mounting feeling that this might be a place you could get hurt in." When blood suddenly begins to spurt and fly and everything becomes "a frenzy of feeding" in the silvery grey room, the narrator, thoughts empty, knows there is no way out, knows that she has seen "something I was not supposed to see," that she has come "too far this time." Yet, despite the bizarre trappings and machinery, the spirit of the impression here can strike home in a concrete way; more readers than not have probably gone perilously "too far" with something dangerous at one time or another.

The more you read of the book, the more you are surprised by the richness there is to the spectrum of Agee's narrative voices. If we overlook "Stiller's Pond," we are a third of the way into *Pretend We've Never Met* before encountering a first-person narrator, and yet it is the immediacy and directness of first person that Agee uses to best advantage and employs in most of the rest of the book.

The earlier stories, in the third person, share the common denominator of obsessive behavior, which is played out in different ways and which must be cast at the distance of the third person to get the full story—we would distrust a subjective narrator's rendering of any of these scenarios. "Mercury" gives us a man in love with his car which he parks outside of his too-small garage and which, over the course of several months, simply disappears piece by carefully excised piece, from the outside in, until "there was nothing to insure its memory—not a bolt, not a shred of glass or metal, not even grooves where the weight of its bulk had settled into the ground. . . . He was certain it had been there once, but it was clearly not there now. It seemed better that way."

In "CybeLee's Life Story," the title character decides that it would be nice to think she's crazy: "Then you wouldn't know that confusion of the erroneous appearance of sun on a cloudy day. . . . CybeLee had always failed. Now she was stuck with her senses pinching at her like new shoes and her memories sucking her down the pipe like bathwater. Curiosity dragged her along like a willful dog on a leash." In a piece that is scarcely more than a page, "This is a Love Story," the obsession is for a pet dog who replaces a wife: "A man and his dog, on an invisible track that moved the dirt aside, pulled the birds down, swam them into the water and out again. As the man smoked in the living room late at night, he watched the dark turn gray, through the swirls, turn shapes, turn dog and lie down at his feet." The protagonist in "Historical Accuracy" has a fetish for his large toe nails which he clips on important occasions, numbers, and stores in a small metal box. Here is sharpness used as a metaphor for memory; collecting the nails, in fact, is more important to the man than the occasions he thus commemorates. In "A Pleasant Story" Lucille imagines becoming a tomato vine to spite her husband and, to spite her neighbor, nurtures a strange tree in her garden which bears paring knives, an image of Lucille's spite, for fruit. Lucille harvests them wearing a pith helmet, a fur coat, a flak jacket, and goalie pads. "The Man of Sorrows" is obsessed to obscenity with his telephone and structures his daily tasks and his sexual urges around using it. Physical contact with it is the one thing that gives his life meaning. He prefers the rotary dial to the touch-tone model because "A man could slip off one of those little squares marked G4HI onto T8UV or # or into space itself. Forever. No contact."

Three of the stories in *Pretend We've Never Met*—"Young," "At Last," and "A Farm Story"—read like grim fables which hold the narrator at some distance. There is only *incidentally* a first-person narrator here, and that perspective takes a back seat to the developed image. The brief "Young" is only two sentences long, yet packed with potential and expectancy—"car lights bend the night into its coming" and the young gather, waiting "for time to go faster." The same poise and suspension appear in "At Last," a frightening extended image of fatal dryness and stillness—hollyhocks "frozen in the heat," turtles decaying in their shells, moths dead on porches and windowsills. The suspension smartly springs to death and menace. In "A Farm Story" a rural wife gathering chicken eggs fends off a bull snake with a pitchfork—"Look, I see myself buried in the snake, its blackness my blood coating straw, staining the egg red and yellow, now broken coils, broken shells, brittle straw."

Agee uses the narrator as a fully developed character recounting a personal experience in six of the stories in this collection. Four of these have female narrators: "Today," "After the Movies," "Cousin Taber's," and "The Dead of July." Two stories, less successful, use the male persona—"My Story" and "Working Iron." Underlying the episode in both types is that sharp image, hot and clear, that Agee so impressively concocts. "Today" begins with homespun philosophy:

> Around me the house, the people, the animals make decisions. The toaster produces the amount of brownness it considers right. I can't get it browner, burned almost as I like it. No matter how many times I punch it back it returns just as quickly. It makes these decisions. I am not certain that they are made in my interest. I suspect that I have little to do with it.

The narrator, a writer, searches for her typewriter stool to begin her day. Remembering that it sometimes does double duty as a television stand in her daughter's room, she happens upon her daughter in bed with her boyfriend.

"After the Movies" and the piece which follows, "The Story of the Belt," are stories of child abuse. "The Story of the Belt" is told in the third person with a Brothers Grimm lilt. Two boys are beaten by their father, egged on by a mother who has a "red coal of hate in her mouth." The belt rises "like a scarf in the wind, then settl[es] down on him, its silky touch . . . ended in a sting." One beaten boy grows up to live in a house whose very foundations erupt:

> Somewhere so deep, the giant back of the snake humps and writhes, the house on its back jiggles and cracks with the strain. Someday, the concrete will burst, the crack will become a chasm, the skin of stucco will shed, the rooms sloughed in a tangle, a pale outline of dark and light.

The narrator in "After the Movies" remembers being ten years old, walking home with her brother on a winter afternoon when "thin, runny sunshine . . . made everything look like it just woke up or something." The shortcut they take brings them through an abandoned amusement park and near a group of older boys playing hockey, one of whom steps in front of the girl, using words and gestures she doesn't understand. She "knew the sun was starting to drop because it got real sharp and orange over the houses. . . . And when [the boy] whispered again, bent down so close to me, his red hair [was] like a sun burning the top of his head off." Although in the older boy's touch she felt a "warmth that made the winter go away for a while," she knows such a feeling is wrong and, in fear and shame, she runs away.

In "Cousin Taber's," a farmer and his wife assaulted by drought and economic failure are visited by the narrator and her husband unexpectedly. The narrator sees "the daisies glow like coins in the yard light and the susans are as dark as animal eyes: come closer come closer, they whisper with a dark rustle." Her husband, a successful gambler, slips the older couple $50,000, and the narrator envisions the farm productive once again, "the scent of round, hot, red tomatoes as the knife punctures the skin with a squirt." The scene ends more bleak than hopeful, though, as they all stare out of the window—the breeze has died and help is too late.

But better and sharper than these is "The Dead of July," which begins, "I go all day wearing Mama's face. I feel it sliding over mine in that tight rubber-glove way as I drive to work. . . . It's that way so the mouth can't do anything drastic, like smile. It can only get thin as paper. . . . And the eyes, well, they're blank, neutral as flour." Agee defines the scene well; almost every sentence gives a new and sure image that physically manifests the suffocation of heat seen through the narrator's oppressed and inherited blank eyes. Birds are squabbling, "rising like cinders and burnt scraps of paper from a fire." In a laundromat, "the clothes thumping hot against the hot dryer walls, when you pull them out, they grab hold of you like they're going to keep thumping."

Three stories in *Pretend We've Never Met* use the first-person narrator as more or less objective observer—"What the Fall Brings," "Aronson's Orchard," and "Emma May Sievert." The three narrators themselves are relatively insignificant, but the study they produce of their subject—in each case, a crazed or obsessed person—is searingly clear and complete. Within this structure, Agee's chosen narrative voice shines, for it allows both observation and evaluation, at the same time resulting in the best plots she's written. As either an acquaintance or a close friend, the narrators have firsthand knowledge of their subject, but they have distance, too—the subjects are neither family nor intimates. The narrators have no reason to fabricate or falsify. "Emma May Sievert" seems the slighter story beside the other two; the tale is backed into with deliciously tantalizing and leading hints such as "Emma May Sievert probably just went down for preserves like always" and "So yes, I did know about the root cellar that was dark enough." The narrator prevaricates and hypothesizes and tries to put the most civilized construction possible on Emma's death, but the innuendoes prove that she has killed herself, distracted by her husband's slaughter of three newborn calves. The truth is also a truth of strongly personified images—"The mama cows calling so it sounded like human sobbing . . . the babies squealing and tugging, panting, finally broken out in a sweat because they're so afraid and the rope is burning through their new hair." At night, Emma hears their cries and feels as if "the moon had blown into pieces." By day, she cooks plums that "seemed to separate into strands of red, raw meat that she almost mistook for chickens she must gut and prepare for dinner . . . plums swimming like small bloody fish in the stew pan . . . , as if she would have to kill each one of them first before they could be of use." The fact that her husband decided her death was due to "her heart" is a meaningful double entendre.

"What the Fall Brings" uses animal death for an equally shocking and brutal effect. The narrator begins by saying that in the fall in Divinity, Iowa, "such memories [as she will relate] . . . come ghosting up high over the buildings, or leaking out of doorways like someone's washer running crazy and crazy." She is thirty years old, recalling events of her first year in high school. Her subject is Billy Bond, the second boy she ever kissed, who becomes more attracted to his prize-winning hog Bluebell than the other 4Hers do to their pets. Top honors at the Iowa State Fair mean that Bluebell will be displayed at Reese's A & P and then butchered and roasted for the football homecoming celebration. Billy, however, was "driven crazy by the sight and smell of his beloved Bluebell turning slowly over the coals in the late afternoon sun" and embarks on a shooting spree from the roof of the downtown bank.

Likewise told through memory, "Aronson's Orchard" blends brutal human death with distraction and obsession. The provocative first sentence sets the tone: "And in the fall, it is being haunted by the dried vines that have left their darker mark along the wooden fence behind the house on the farm I remember as my first home." As in "What the Fall Brings," the setting here is the same small Iowa town, and the narrator is "haunted by the sight of those dark red, almost mahogany apples at Aronson's Orchard." This is a story of nurture and ancestry. Aronson's emigrating great-great-grandfather had brought across the ocean tree seedlings cupped "in his hand like a kitten" to start an orchard. Aronson himself nurtures the family, having spoiled his son Reinhardt and now coddling the town with a new feature added to his orchard every year—dumplings, cider, doughnuts, etc. The narrator believes this is his way of making a public "apology," for this is also a story of betrayal of nurture in a violent, criminal way; Reinhardt has grown into a rapist and a murderer.

If death and heat predominate the sharp images in *Pretend We've Never Met, Bend This Heart* is filled with heat that is even more suffocating, animal imagery more vigorous, and an urgency that pulses and throbs like blood. Significantly, most of the pieces are set in summer, when heat is insistent and oppressive, and "the insects' raw hum seems to turn the heat up." Pulsating is a prevailing motion. The last sentence of the first story, "I Can't Stop Loving You," sets the vibration that resonates throughout the book: "And when I met someone finally, I trapped his heart like a small animal and held it, held it, held it." In the penultimate story ("Private Lives"), also trapped, but in an ambiguous and threatening embrace, mouth to pulsing throat, are two men in their late fifties, partners in a tumultuous, long-term relationship. "Just Your Friend" tells of a series of newspaper clippings left under an office door that rustled and "throbbed like a small animal's heart." When the magician's hand touched his assistant ("The Magician's Assistant"), her skin "shook for minutes afterward, as if he had half the heart of an elephant." In "What in the World," a missionary out jogging is threatened by an Indian holding a brick, and "felt his heart take a huge surge and knock, as if the assembly line [of a brewery] had faltered and the bottles were swaying, threatening to topple."

The images in *Bend This Heart* are more startling than those in *Pretend We've Never Met*; the characters are more bizarre, filled with religious guilt or fervor, or lewd compulsions they themselves encourage. The tone is wry and sardonic; Agee's vision is dark and seems unredemptive. The point of view is more distanced; the ratio of the number of stories here that use the third-person narrator to those using first person is greater than two to one. Her preference reveals experimentation and near perfection of the technique. The stories tell of social and psychological ills—deteriorating relationships, depression, death, disinterest, dead ends. Some of the stories feel like exercises in emotional ventriloquism; odds are that we readers have not experienced such things. One lightning-fast story throws the reader into a bloody terrorist massacre; another shows a diabetic, widowed missionary returned to his St. Paul home after forty years serving in a Third World country. Yet another shows an ex-nun waiting with a stranger for the arrival of spacemen in the mountains of Washington state. A few of the stories seem to be excuses for playing around with brilliant metaphor. In "The Only Thing Different," hair being cut over the bathroom sink gathers like "pine needles, curved slivers of heart." In "See the Pyramids," another short story, more episodic, a comforter has tufts of yarn "like laziness sticking out," hair dyed red grows out in black fingers, and dreams slither as pools of snakes. In the longer "Hunting Story," geese killed on a hunting trip had "blooms of blood in the breast . . . like medals."

The title of the book *Bend This Heart*, as well as the titles of most of the stories, taken from songs, is deceptively innocuous and inviting—"I Can't Stop Loving You," "Lady of Spain," "Cupid," "I Wonder Who's Kissing Him Now," "Each Time We Meet," "You Belong to Me." These signify love and its problems, which Agee specifies as the concern of the book. The love here, though, is not young and pure but jaded and prurient, sometimes drug-sodden, the relationships kitschy and Kafkaesque. The love is not sweet—it's deluded or controlling or lustful. It's love by default, almost in spite of disinterest. A car that has been wrecked is perceived by the owner as "an act of love, a promise of more to come." A middle-aged adulterer fingers the nipple of his young lover "like an ignition button on a powerful boat." (In *Pretend We've Never Met*, another illicit liaison described "hands rolling my nipples like they were balls of beer-soaked napkin on the table back at Sleepy's where we'd been drinking.") A poet and his groupie pickup girl friend snort cocaine, attend his performance, and then have loveless sex in a hotel room bathed in the soundless glare of the television. The most "conventional" love story in the book, "Private Lives," traces a long-term homosexual relationship between two middle-aged men, and represents one of the best developed plot lines in the book.

However nasty or grotesque or revolting they may be, many of the stories recount incidents of the real human tendency to retreat when life gets too strong or when feelings of inadequacy set in. Most of the characters are not aggressive or pugnacious. As victims of circumstance or their own neglect, they strive not to lose what shaky ground they have gotten hold of. Reba's Buddhist ex-husband in "And Blue" clenches his hands watching soap operas and prefers leftovers to other food; he himself is left over, and love is clenched shut against him. The narrator in "Stop Loving Me" is sloppy, lazy, and hopeless, but complacent in her solitary life. The woman in "In the Blood" feels trapped and repelled by her cancer-wracked husband in much the way that she had trapped her pet dog in the garage once—fear and frenzy make "her body ache . . . as if it had been filled with stones."

Many of the characters in this collection are not admirable. They almost revel in their lapses and misses. The hunter of geese in "Hunting Story" steals from his uncle, shoots over his limit, and causes the death of a prize black labrador. Jeremiah in "Someone Else to Love" takes his plain wife for granted until she leaves him. Jo in "You Belong to Me" cinches an argument by throwing all of her lover's belongings onto the backyard in winter.

Most relationships are dysfunctional. In "Time Only Adds to the Blame," there is bitterness between a daughter and her domineering mother when family members gather in Chicago for the funeral of the daughter's older sister. Though arthritic, the mother is still powerful and cruel. On the airplane, "Her fingers test the metal buckle of the seatbelt for sharpness like a knife blade." Her "big hands . . . can hurt us again." When the daughter, by way of leave-taking, presses her cheek against her mother's, she feels a shock "like the numbing buzz on the electric fence on the day the plastic grip split and the current leaked into my closed hand." We infer that her relationship with her now-dead sister, whom she consistently refers to as "the body," was marked as well by hatred and jealously.

A sequel to that story is "Each Time We Meet," an elaboration on the character of the mother. The setting this time is the mother's home in South Carolina, and getting there is "like driving into the hot damp mouth of a dog." The mother's welcome is forbidding, her body is "lethal," her uncombed hair "a half of orange clumps thick as snakes." During the visit, a family decision is made to institutionalize the schizophrenic mother, and she is driven to the mental hospital and left sitting "in the chrome and orange vinyl chairs of the modern patient lounge, marooned in her angry colors."

"I Wonder Who's Kissing Him Now," placed between "Time Only Adds to the Blame" and "Each Time We Meet," ties up motifs of funeral, loveless families, and infidelity into the mystery game Clue—who did it? in what room? with what weapon?

At times in *Bend This Heart* an object—a cremation urn, a magazine clipping, a dead and refrigerated pigeon—takes on the vigor of a human character. It literally "glows" with significance, as the telephone in *Pretend We've Never Met* had glowed with "power." In this collection, scissors "glitter with possibility" during a haircut. A firebombed motorcycle leaves a stain that won't go away. A ruby ring winks "like a lewd gesture."

The most compelling and the most sinister of such objects is the television set. Beginning with the first story, "I Can't Stop Loving You," it becomes a symbol for retreat from life and chance and contact, a false panacea and a consolation: "I was busy eating, being alone with the television's sympathetic light bathing me blue and more as I slept on the sofa." The television gives a reason not to bother communicating; it anesthetizes all feeling. Many characters—even whole families—are willing or indifferently pulled under its addictive spell. Jeremiah in "Someone Else to Love" is too numb to admit it, but he prefers "the tube"—"it fed him, he fed it"—to legitimate communication with his wife. The schizophrenic mother in "Each Time We Meet" keeps the television turned up to discourage her husband and adult daughters from conspiring against her. The family in "Lady of Spain" is so addicted that the line between real life and televised game show has been erased completely. Physical love made in the glow of the television screen is devoid of meaning or emotional contact.

If the television symbolizes a dead end to communication and, hence, to loving, Agee's animal imagery symbolizes the possibility, at least, of hope or the justification of entrapment. Agee's pets—a horse, two parrots, and goldfish—and a statement she once made during an interview attest to the importance of animals in her life and writing. She offers, as the "underlying vision" of her fiction, that "we have torn at the connection to every living thing." Harm done to animals is sometimes worse than what we do to humans, she says, because animals are helpless. In her stories a horse is beaten, cats are abused, one dog is locked away and another needlessly drowned. A fence around one unfortunate house can't keep the snakes out, and, of course, more than literal snakes are implied. Metaphorically, men are described as "dogs" or "snakes" lusting after a woman, coffins "hunch like dogs," and steam "like a snake goes writhing through the house, rubbing all the windows shut with moisture." Animals add a vigor, a primal urge, to Agee's quest to give readers a pulsating slice of life.

The majority of Agee's characters and most of her narrators are nameless. In fact, body parts in place of names may identify characters—"the hand" ("Lady of Spain"), "the black bag" ("Lady of Spain"), "the body" ("Time Only Adds to the Blame"), and "the legs" ("Someone Else to Love"). The point is that the experience, vividly conceived, or the image, sharply rendered, carries more weight than any personal identity. Agee's odd and passionate images, as she says of gossip in "Someone Else to Love," are "like penknives they would gladly attack him with." She forges and cuts with care, and the polished images glow—hard, memorable, and gemlike. If we readers feel the images at times "rub . . . [us] raw with . . . broken glass edges," then that is, as in "Time Only Adds to the Blame," "a solution none of us imagines. That makes it the best one."

Book-Length Works by Jonis Agee

Authored:
Bend This Heart (Coffee House Press/short stories/1989)
Houses (Truck Press/long poem/1976)
Mercury (Toothpaste Press/chapbook/1981)
Pretend We've Never Met (Peregrine-Smith/short stories/1989)
Two Poems (Pentagram Press/chapbook/1982)

Edited:
Border Crossings (New Rivers Press/Midwestern writing/1984)
Stiller's Pond (New Rivers Press/Upper Midwest fiction/1988)
These Women and Secrets (Gallimaufry Press/women's fiction/1978)

Eliot's Contrasts:
From the Regional to the Universal

Bernard F. Engel

Critics have been aware that T. S. Eliot's double regional identity, as a product of both the southern Midwest and New England, spurred his use of contrast and comparison in poems and in prose. These logical processes are inherent in thinking—my cat knows me from a mackerel, at least when he's hungry—but in Eliot's work they become structural devices as well as instruments for supporting argument. Arthur Mizener, for example, sees as basic to Eliot's thought the contrast between St. Louis, his boyhood home, and the New England that retained family loyalties. This double affiliation, Mizener says, led Eliot to build his poems around "contrasts among different ways of life" (12-20).

Interest in strongly differing positions began early. Robert Crawford points to a story Eliot wrote at the age of 10 which tells of the betrothal of Miss End and Mr. Front; in another story in the same childhood magazine, Eliot wrote of the elopement of Mr. Up and Miss Down (1). By the time Eliot composed "Portrait of a Lady" (written 1909-10), the custom of lining up opposites had led to the idea that, as the "lady" says, "our beginnings never know our ends." But by 1942, when he published the "Little Gidding" section of "Four Quartets," Eliot was aware that apparent opposites often have connections: "What we call the beginning is often the end / And to make an end is to make a beginning."

That awareness of regional differences contributed to this habit of seeing polarities seems likely. It is possible, moreover, to argue that these differences help to account for other, more subtle characteristics of Eliot's thought. These could be illustrated in any sizable selection from his poetry and prose. To avoid working over material already subjected to thousands of interpretations, I focus on some of Eliot's own remarks on regional identity and then turn to the early poems collected by John Hayward, works that are in some instances a stage beyond juvenilia but that do not illustrate the supreme talent which first becomes apparent with the composition of "The Love Song of J. Alfred Prufrock" (1910-11) and of "Portrait of a Lady."

Most important for this argument are indications that Eliot felt some uncertainty about his geographical roots. Such uncertainty no doubt contributed to his feeling that people of the modern era, including himself, are hollow men, that the characters he observes are often evanescent, that there is now an unreality about existence that makes our world a waste land, a place where the mermaids of legend somehow represent a more substantial reality than the pathetically ridiculous J. Alfred Prufrock despite his St. Louis name and his London environment. This uncertainty, moreover, probably contributed to his frequent feeling that the poet should be impersonal and that he was himself more the observer than the participant.

Like many other citizens of America's mobile society, Eliot had even in childhood to acknowledge two regional identities. His family maintained a strong connection with the region they regarded as their place of origin. Though Eliot had his elementary schooling in St. Louis, the family customarily spent part of each summer on the Massachusetts coast, and in 1905 they sent him to Milton Academy in Massachusetts to complete his preparatory education. Eliot had no further extended residence in the Midwest.

In a 1917 review of Edward Garnett's *Turgenev*, Eliot remarked on the situation of the writer who has two geographical identities. Of Turgenev's "transplantation" to Paris, Eliot wrote that it enabled him to speak with authority about both Russian and French literature, but that it also put him in isolation. He further observed that a writer's art must be racial—which means, in plain words, that it must be based on the accumulated sensations of the first twenty-one years."

Eliot made a number of statements about St. Louis, frequently comparing it with New England or Europe and sometimes commenting on the effect of his own "transplantation." Though the St. Louis where he spent most of his own first 16 years was famous for corruption in business and politics—see Lincoln Steffens' *The Shame of the Cities*—as well as for the stench of its sewers, he told a hometown audience in 1933 that "I am very well satisfied with having been born in St. Louis" (*American Literature* 6). In 1928, noting that his family "guarded jealously its connections with New England, he said that he had come to perceive that he had "always been a New Englander in the South West, and a South Westerner in New England" (Musgrove 12). His statement emphasized features of nature, primarily the visual: "In New England I missed the long dark river, the ailanthus trees, the flaming cardinal birds, the high limestone bluffs where we searched for fossil shellfish; in Missouri I missed the fir trees, the bay and goldenrod, the song-sparrows, the red granite and the blue sea of Massachusetts" (*American Literature* 8). Two years later, he wrote that "as I spent the first sixteen years of my life in St. Louis, it is evident that St. Louis affected me more deeply than any other environment has done" (28-29). He added that "Missouri and the Mississippi have made a deeper impression on me than any other part of the world." He observed also that his parents and grandfather had all worked for the betterment of his native city.

During the years in St. Louis, New England influences were strong. The dominant force in the family was William Greenleaf Eliot, even though he had died a year before the future poet was born. William was a righteous man of whom James F. Clarke wrote "one feels rebuked in his presence" (Howarth 2). He was a native of Massachusetts who had been raised in Baltimore and had also lived in New Bedford and in Washington D. C. His Unitarian emphasis on good works led him to be an activist in civic and humanitarian affairs; his genteel idealism led him to preach against the control of society by money, a development he saw in the post-Civil War years. Long after his death he remained, so the poet later wrote, a stern presence in the family (Gordon 8).

The influence of the poet's immediate family is less certainly associated with a region: one need not assume that all notions of duty, for example, come from the Northeast. The poet's father Henry was a successful businessman who had a taste for the arts. Of most apparent influence, however, was Eliot's mother Charlotte, who, in addition to civic good works, turned out poetry all her lifetime. Though she wrote in the worn genteel tradition, Eliot showed respect for her by having her long poem *Savanarola* published in 1926. Adherence to the worn did not keep her from seeing her son's talent. He later wrote that when his early "A Lyric" appeared in the *Smith Academy Record*, she told him it was better than anything she had ever written. Eliot observed: "I knew what her verse meant to her. We did not discuss the matter further." Eliot's beliefs that the poet is responsible to the art of poetry and that the poet should purify the language, as well as his lifelong exploration of the spiritual situation of his contemporaries, arise from an earnestness attributable in good part to the influence of his civic-minded family.

An important similarity was recognition by both mother and son of a sphere beyond that of mundane reality, a recognition that perhaps helps account for Eliot's interest in religion and for his perception that the people and events of the modern city are unreal. Both mother and son talked of a source of illumination comparable to that of the mystic. For Charlotte, this was adequately represented by the traditional figure of the prophet or seer who plucks sublime truths from mysterious depths. This figure was essentially an expression of confidence in things as they are, a pragmatic mysticism. For her son, enlightenment was intensely spiritual and had no practical consequences. In early work, he sometimes expressed a notion of "the Absolute," a coherent truth that he contrasted with the chaos of metropolitan existence. But he gave more importance to experiences of what he called "the silence," moments of intense awareness of a sphere beyond this world. Describing such moments of "illumination" as they came to Pascal, Eliot wrote that "you may call it communion with the Divine, or you may call it a temporary crystallization of the mind" (*Selected Essays* 358). Eliot never claimed that a poem came to him in such a moment. The contribution of a "silence" was to reinforce his faith in the existence of experiences not scientifically describable.

The alternation in regional identities may have given rise to Eliot's observation that one needs a strong sense of place. In a 1927 letter to Sir Herbert Read (Tate 15), he wrote:

> Some day I want to write an essay about the point of view of an American who wasn't an American, because he was born in the South and went to school in New England as a small boy with a nigger drawl, but who wasn't a southerner in the South because his people were southerners and Virginians, and who was never

> anything anywhere and who therefore felt himself to be more a Frenchman than an American and more an Englishman than a Frenchman and yet felt that the USA up to a hundred years ago was a family extension.

(The last sentence in this statement, indicating the sense that his own social class had been displaced, shows Eliot's continuing participation in some aspects of that genteel tradition against which his best poems rebel).

Of the 14 poems in Hayward's compilation *Poems Written in Early Youth*, several are conventional lyrics, songs, and graduation pieces. Even here, the occasional use of the *carpe diem* convention and the appearance of some of the mild melancholy of *The Rubaiyat*—a work that impressed Eliot for a time (Bergonzi 14) as it had impressed such disparate versifiers as Riley and Twain—suggest interest in the relationship between time and identity. Speculations on this topic, scarcely an unusual one for the thoughtful poet, would culminate grandly in "Four Quartets" where, as Mizener says, the interest in contrasting ways of life becomes transmuted into philosophical or theological principle; here, Mizener says, Eliot finally brings together the world of time and that of the spiritual. Some of the early pieces also show interest in the integrity of the person, in the effort to hold oneself together in a world wherein little coherence is to be found.

The poem "A Fable for Feasters" (1905) shows Eliot adopting the voice and manner of Byron's humorous verse, employing deliberately awkward placement of sentence elements ("He even soaked the uncomplaining porter / Who stood outside the door from head to feet"), interpolation of comment by the speaker on the story he tells ("my statement nobody can doubt"), and accumulation of detail and incident that gently mock the characters (here, the listing of menu items to suggest gluttony on the part of a band of monks). Though the narrative of a ghost making off with an abbot is one that would appeal to the young reader, the writing is superior in use of detail and consistency of tone, far better work than one expects of schoolboy verse. [Hindsight, that tempter, suggests seeing the "disappeared" abbot as an early example of the evanescent.]

There is perhaps a touch of familiarity with contemporary physics and philosophy in the poem Hayward entitled "A Lyric" (written January 1905). Or the notion may have come from reading in Eastern religions. At any rate, the poem shows willingness to consider the possibility that the self and the rest of existence are tentative and changeable, rather than firmly shaped products of divine creation. The poem exploits the notion that time and space themselves "are things which cannot be" (the same line appears in the alternate version of this poem, which was printed in April 1907 as "Song"). In "Before Morning" (1908), interest in time is mingled with contrasts between the pretty and the drab, the fresh and dispirited, that also are to be found in much of Eliot's later verse. The poem develops in the manner of traditional poetry the contrast between fresh flowers and withered ones, and the fact that dawn begins a new phase of existence even as it ends an old one. Eliot writes not for pity or pathos, however, and certainly not as a disappointed romantic hero, but as the disinterested observer, free of the romantic's self-concern. The last line of each of the two stanzas is "Fresh flowers, withered flowers, flowers of dawn." By omitting verbs, Eliot causes the line to present rather than to comment.

Willingness to entertain ideas of the self as a flowing, as lacking in permanence, also appears in "Circe's Palace" (1908). Here Eliot perhaps borrows from Swinburne in saying of flowers that "Their petals are fanged and red / With hideous streak and stain." But the last two lines—"And they look at us with the eyes / Of men whom we knew long ago"—show Eliot already finding continuity in experience (the "they" may refer only to the peacocks of the poem's ending lines; more likely it refers to all the animals in the stanza—panthers and a python as well as the birds).

"On a Portrait" (1909) tells of a woman who stands apart, caught up in "tenuous dreams" not accessible to the hurried, "evanescent" as the lamia one might see in imagination. Whatever her musings, she keeps them secret, "beyond the circle of our thought." Her psychological or spiritual remoteness is emphasized by the speaker's remark that a parrot, too, "regards her with a patient, curious eye," sees her as interesting but apart from the everyday. The observer and the woman are particular individuals only, not representatives of a class. One may speculate that it was finding similar characters employed as types of the bourgeoisie in the poems of Baudelaire and Laforgue that soon led Eliot to see such people as representatives of modern humankind. The piece seems a preliminary sketch of the more fully presented woman of "Portrait of a Lady," a character who does rise to representation.

Eliot spoofs the tradition that love is undying in "Nocturne" (1909). Here the speaker, perhaps a playwright, tells of sending Romeo to court Juliet, the two meeting under a "bored but courteous moon." Seeing that the lovers themselves have little to say, the speaker reports that he had a servant stab Romeo. Posing not as a cynic but as a cool-eyed manipulator, the speaker voices his satisfaction that the resulting bloodstains look "effective" and that "female readers" weep. There is no awareness that speaker and victim inhabit the same spiritual world.

A note under the title of "Humoresque" (1910) says "patterned after J. Laforgue"; Hayward says the source is the French poet's "Locutions de Pierrot, xii." Eliot here uses the possibility of shifting identities—at least as seen by those outside the self—to mock the tradition of the Romantic hero. The central figure is a marionette which, the speaker says, is dead "though not yet tired of the game." The speaker rather liked him for his common face, "pinched in a comic, dull grimace." The irrelevance of the death is indicated by giving fragments of conversations carried on by indifferent observers. The speaker concedes that the marionette, earlier described as weak in the head (or, perhaps, the meaning is one's thoughts about it were weak) comes up with idiotic logic, yet reflects that "in some star" he might be a hero. On this earth, however, the detail finally noted is his bizarre mask, his disguised identity. The poet treats his subject courteously but somewhat aloofly, as though analyzing. The ironic stance is in the vein of "Prufrock," but in that poem the speaker presents himself, a figure who is a bit ridiculous but one whose pathos is deeply felt.

The direct ancestor to Profrock appears in "Spleen" (1910). The speaker here is conscious of the saddening disparity between the "satisfied" and "definite" procession of churchgoers following a complacent routine that amounts to spiritual death or unreality and the ardor and comprehension he presumably believes religion should provide. As he watches people leaving church, he notes details of city life akin to those Eliot would more famously present in "Preludes" (written 1909-11). The details, the speaker remarks, are part of a "dull conspiracy" he finds himself too enervated to rally against. Meanwhile "life"—representing perhaps a spiritually fulfilled existence—stands, dressed in the "punctilious" way of Prufrock (and of Eliot himself, who had adopted the dandyism of Laforgue), in wait "On the doorstep of the Absolute"—waits, one takes it, for some recognition and comprehension despite his insignificance. The speaker is not a tragic hero; rather, he is bored, without importance in his own eyes or in those of the world (though of course, as in "Prufrock," there is an undercurrent of deep feeling). The emptiness and ennui of the man of "Spleen" are borrowed from Baudelaire; one might see, for example, poems LXXVIII through LXXXI in the Mathews edition of *Flowers of Evil*. But Eliot's poem is more concentrated, his writing less diffuse.

Something of the atmosphere of "The Waste Land" and of that work's insistence that life without certainties of faith is empty is anticipated in "The Death of Saint Narcissus" (written between 1911 and 1915), in which the first five lines parallel lines 25 to 29 of the greater poem. Telling of the saint's religious ecstasies and his death by arrows, the poem opens with a seven-line stanza that uses the word "shadow" five times. It thus suggests an insubstantiality in the modern reader that is heightened by implied contrast with the saint's wholeness.

Eliot in his later years disciplined uncertainty. In "The Dry Salvages" section of "Four Quartets," he uses the river—clearly the Mississippi—and the sea—the waters off the New England coast—as different voices that convey the same warning of disaster: at the culmination of his career, that is, regional influences remained distinctive yet expressed the same comprehension. "The Dry Salvages" says that the "sullen, untamed and intractable" river remains "within us," is, one might deduce, the ultimate development of the evanescent, the flowing of the stream of time.

Finally, those who doubt the importance of Missouri for Eliot may reflect on the fact that in adulthood he combined the idea of saintliness, important to him from around 1912 on, with his reflections on Missouri's most famous literary character. He did not read *Huckleberry Finn* until he was an adult (he speculated that his parents had kept the book from him because of Huck's smoking). After he finally read it, he used Huck as one version of his ideal, contrasting him with both the pioneer and the businessman. Huck, he said, shows the independence, not of the pioneer but of the vagabond, and by his existence he questions the values of America as much as the values of Europe. Huck, it appears, resists the idea of getting ahead and therefore is to Eliot "in a state of nature as detached as that of the saint" (*American Literature* 32). He contrasts, indeed, not merely with the products of other cultures, but with a cast of mind universal in the modern world. The emphasis on comparison and contrast, apparently originating in consciousness of regional differences, had by the apex of Eliot's career become a principal tool for comprehension of the cultural and spiritual worlds Eliot perceived.

Works Cited

Bergonzi, Bernard. *T. S. Eliot.* New York: Macmillan, 1972.

Crawford, Robert. *The Savage and the City in the Work of T. S. Eliot.* Oxford: Clarendon Press, 1987.

Eliot, T. S. *American Literature and the American Language.* St. Louis: Washington University, 1953.

—. Review of *Turgenev,* by Edward Garnett. *The Egoist* IV (December 1917), 167.

—. *Selected Essays.* New York: Harcourt Brace & World, 1964. New Edition.

Gordon, Lyndall. *Eliot's Early Years.* New York: Oxford UP, 1977.

Hayward, John (comp.). *Poems Written in Early Youth by T. S. Eliot.* London: Faber and Faber, 1967.

Howarth, Herbert. *Notes on Some Figures Behind T. S. Eliot.* Boston: Houghton Mifflin, 1964.

Mizener, Arthur. "To Meet Mr. Eliot." Ed. Linda Wagner. *T. S. Eliot: A Collection of Criticism.* New York: McGraw-Hill, 1974, pp. 9-20.

Musgrove, S. *T. S. Eliot and Walt Whitman.* New York: Haskell House, 1966.

Tate, Allen, ed. *T. S. Eliot: The Man and His Work.* New York: Delacorte Press, 1966.

Babel, The Crowd, and "The People" in Early Chicago Fiction

Guy Szuberla

"I am the people—the mob—the crowd—the mass."
—Carl Sandburg, *Chicago Poems* (1916)

On April 23, 1893, the Chicago *Inter Ocean* printed a color plate titled "Cosmopolitan Chicago: State Street, Looking North—The Mingling of Many Nationalities." It ran as the cover for a Sunday "illustrated supplement," placed there, no doubt, to sell papers and to boom the city's virtues. In the weeks just before the Columbian Exposition officially opened, such appeals to civic pride and such heavy-handed pitches to the city's visitors were commonplace. The *Inter Ocean* illustration, nevertheless, represents a peculiarly localized fantasy of social peace and civic order (plate 1).

At a time when Thomas Nast and other popular cartoonists drew immigrants as bombthrowers and apelike beasts, the *Inter Ocean*'s idealized but alien crowd marches down State Street with exemplary decorum and an almost earthly solemnity. The cartoonist has typified Chicago and its immigrant population in the idiom of cosmopolitan boosterism that washed over the city in 1893. "The World's Parliament of Religions," seeking to establish world "brotherhood," would meet at the Chicago World's Fair in a mood that one clergyman respectfully called "holy intoxication" and another repeatedly characterized as "Pentecostal" (Berg 326-27). For one summer in Chicago, the search for the ties that bind the family of man seemed a high, holy, and reasonable pursuit.

Cosmopolitan Chicago.
State Street, Looking North—The Mingling of Many Nationalities.
Chicago *Inter Ocean*, "Illustrated Supplement" (23 April 1893): cover page
Courtesy of Professor Harrison Hayford,
Northwestern University, Evanston

This simple cartoon, then, enacts a ritualized gathering of the nations of the earth. But the cartoon's stylized figures—tagged and typed by costume, racial color, and physiognomy—also stand as a reminder that Chicago was painfully conscious of itself as a "modern Babel." The association of Babel and Chicago in the 1890s and the early 1900s was an inescapable one. By 1890 the city's foreign-born population had come nearly to equal its native born. According to the *Eleventh Census of the United States*, in 1890, 855,523 of the city's 1,099,850 claimed parents of foreign birth. Editorial writers, whether excoriating the patriotism of city's polyglot population or praising immigrant industry and thrift, regularly invoked the typology of Babel.[1] Exploiting the traditional associations of Babel with confusion and disorder, citing the *Census* figures on immigrant population, the city's nativist journal *America* used the example of Chicago to warn that "babel-tongued communities" threatened to crowd out "the native element" and destroy "peace and harmony" (Chatfield-Taylor 2).

But the myth of Babel, as George Steiner has shown, paradoxically carries within it the seeds of a second myth: the Pentecostal "gift of tongues" or a "return to unison in some messianic moment of restored understanding" (59). Throughout the 1890s and early 1900s, Chicago writers articulated, sometimes with humor and sometimes with high seriousness, their own version of such a "moment." The cartoon of "Cosmopolitan Chicago" outlines one variation; a flood of fiction, variously welcoming the city's "newcomers," carried many more. George Ade collected stories of Chicago under the title *In Babel* (1903), and gently reworked the ancient sign of confusion into a synonym for the city's "congress of nations" (318). The novelist Henry Blake Fuller, reviewing a scholarly study of the many languages spoken in Chicago, called his city "the Modern Babel" and confidently asserted that it was a "municipal crucible" melding a "diversity of human elements" into "peace and concord." From about 1890 to 1920, Babel—as a sign of degeneration and as a prefiguring of a pentecostal communion—proved to be a pliable symbol in the city's political debate and in its literature.

To study Babel in Chicago fiction, then, is first to study a political discourse: the voice of the mob, the silence of the crowd, or the polyglot speech of the people in, for example, strike scenes and city council meetings. But these recurring type-scenes, I will argue, will offer a paradigm for studying the forms that Chicago writers used to represent polylingualism outside well-defined political settings. Ardent nativists like Charles King, no less than Theodore Dreiser, Henry Blake Fuller, Robert Herrick, Will Payne, Brand Whitlock, and I. K. Friedman, struggled to understand and represent immigrant speech. Whether they use Babel to invoke what Steiner calls a "return to unison" or to call up an equally traditional spectre of chaos, they are animated and inspired by what they hear in the city's "confusion of tongues."

I

Toward the close of Theodore Dreiser's novel *The Titan* (1914), in "The Cataclysm" chapter, a crowd of "five hundred citizens" menaces an Alderman Pinski. They shout "in chorus": "Ho, you robber! You thief! You boodler! Hang him! Ho! Ho! Ho! Get a rope!" "An Irish-American," "a bearded Pole," "a Swede," "a Jew"—each in turn sings out a death threat or an angry insult, and the whole crowd joins in, chanting "Kill him! Brain him!" Dreiser, of course, emphasizes that this is a "conglomerate outpouring"—a polyglot and multi-ethnic crowd (486-88). Their chanting and their death threats, the ritualized and angry exchanges between the alderman and the crowd, enact forms embedded deeply in Chicago's politics and fiction.

Political discourse, Chicago style, has regularly been animated by snarling anger and bravura threats. On the night the Chicago City Council selected Eugene Sawyer as Chicago's acting mayor, December 2, 1987, some nine hundred protesters jammed into the City Hall lobby and about four thousand more people demonstrated outside. The crowd in council chambers waved dollar bills, chanting "No deal! No deal!" They shouted profanities and death threats at the aldermen they opposed, and the aldermen shouted back threats of their own. Alderman Mell, one of the white aldermen backing the black Sawyer, told a heckler: "You're dead! You're dead!"[2]

Chicago's aldermen and its novelists seem, at such moments, prisoners of language in the same prison or madhouse. The will and the words of its crowds, and the echo in those politicians and writers who give it voice, can break loose with unrivalled force and passion. Such a crowd may be said to represent the inarticulate voice of the people made articulate or the cacaphonous sounds of violence and anarchy. Chicago's fiction and the city's insistent political history have made the crowd both the symbol of democracy and the voice of a destructive and mindless force.

Perhaps in this the city's literary and political traditions differ little from those of the rest of the United States. Nicolaus Mills has recently argued in *The Crowd in American Fiction* (1986) that American fiction and political thought reveal an abiding ambivalence about the meaning and identity of the crowd. Mills has shown that the crowd, in writers as different as Hawthorne and Steinbeck, has embodied a mythic power, what our politicians and novelists alike reverently term the will of "the people." The people in the streets can prod politicians to act when they might otherwise flounder in indecision and caution. The crowd thus possesses the power to give clarity to political questions and to define their urgency. At the same time, many American writers and thinkers—John Adams and James Fenimore Cooper, principal among them—see the crowd and the mob as interchangeable names for the same bloodthirsty beast. Adams and many others view those who pursue political power on the streets as the "rabble," identifying them with what they brand the lower orders of American society. The crowd, by the terms of such exclusory definitions, can never be equated with "the people" as a whole (Mills 49). Our democratic and revolutionary history, in short, has endowed us with a double legacy: we honor "the people" and fear "the mob."

The cultural construction of the crowd in Chicago fiction in many ways rests on these same divided values. Chicago writers, unlike the writers that Mills cites, typically emphasize the crowd's polyglot voice and its multi-ethnic character. Dreiser's representations of polyglot voices do blend the speech into one language. But, that Dreiser makes free use of "homogenizing conventions"—as Meir Sternberg might call them—does not necessarily erase the multi-ethnic character of crowd. Readers, accustomed to fiction's well-established representational and translational conventions, grant the author the freedom to express polylingual speech in unilingual forms (Sternberg 223-24). Thus Dreiser can homogenize into standard English the speech of the Pole, the Jew, the Swede, and the Irish-American—without any dialectical or macaronic distractions. Babel's chaos is evoked but implicitly contained: the multi-ethnic crowd has, for the moment, been transformed into a community and its polyglot speech made over into a unilingual political discourse.

While the epic and almost operatic design of Dreiser's *The Titan* permitted such a chorus, other Chicago writers deliberately circumvented homogenizing conventions that would have had them representing immigrant speech in English. Consider the embedded silence of the immigrant crowds and their polylingual voices in Henry Blake Fuller's novel, *The Cliff-Dwellers* (1893). Fuller's central protagonist, George Ogden, after observing "the town's swarming hordes," draws up a *catalogue raisonne*, classifying immigrants by their "dialects, brogues, patois, accents in all their palatal and labial variations and according to all the differentiations in pharynx, larynx, and epiglottis." This rather full and rich description of polyglot speech leads, paradoxically, into a narrative of privation and negation. At no point, that is, does Fuller represent anyone in the crowds of "Germans, Irish, and Swedes . . . negroes . . . Chinese . . . Poles" and "Bohemians" in the act of speaking (53-55). Though he has stipulated their powers of speech, he cannot seem to imagine specific lines or words that they can speak or a situation in which such speech would be plausible. In the same narrative sequence, Ogden will confront "the confused cataract of conflicting nationalities within" City Hall, a charged reference to the confusion of tongues. Despite the apparent allusions to babble and Babel, this polyglot crowd seems every bit as silent, if not as solemn, as those represented in *Inter Ocean*'s picture of "Cosmopolitan Chicago." George Ogden, a loyal if callow son of New England, cannot speak with them or understand the "dialects, brogues, patois" that he hears. Pentecost and Babel merge ambiguously.

Somewhat like Fuller, Herrick regularly manipulates his narration so as to have American and middle-class characters cancel out the words of the polyglot crowd. In his Chicago novels, they stand between the reader and the crowd, interpreting its words and political intentions. A group of Hyde Park intellectuals performs this function in Herrick's *The Gospel of Freedom* (1898). One of them, Thornton Jennings, an ordinarily tolerant political reformer and an eminently middle-class character, acts as a spokesman for Herrick's progressive views. At one point, he nevertheless commits himself to a fearful prophecy: "Someday," he warns, the "good people of Chicago . . . will wake up with forty-thousand Polacks and other impetuous citizens tearing down their houses" (129). Two chapters later, a fire in the stockyards district seems to validate his prediction. From four miles away, in a comfortable Hyde Park living room, the principal characters watch the flames and clouds of smoke. As they argue about the meaning of the fire, some fearfully envision rampaging "mobs," while others claim that such riots represent "the 'people'" in legitimate protest against repressive economic conditions (155-56).

Bracketing the word "people" in quotes suggests that Herrick may hold reservations about the immigrants' claims to political power. His treatment of the Pullman strike and the strikers in *The Web of Life* (1900), while generally granting the justice of the strikers' cause, reprises the crowd's words through the young and idealist Dr. Sommers. The crowd itself, referred to as "the rabble," "the hot sweating mob," and "the seething mass," is said to "shout," "howl," and "roar" (189-91). But what they roar and shout, we are never told in direct discourse or through their own words. They cannot speak, in any case, because Sommers and others speak for them. Immigrants, in effect, are reduced to pop literature stereotypes, silent and sullen background figures.

II

Charles King also wrote a Chicago novel that placed the Pullman strike in the foreground, though no literary critic or historian with good sense would class *A Tame Surrender* (1896) with Fuller's or Herrick's well-wrought fiction. Perhaps because King did not share their progressive and reformist tendencies, he found it easier to let a crowd speak in its own unmediated voice. That is not to say that Captain King, U. S. A., an Indian fighter during the 1870s, practices realism in his treatment of street crowds or immigrant characters.[3] He does not. He arbitrarily gives his Irish characters a rolling brogue and lets his Germans speak English without a trace of their native speech. *A Tame Surrender* teems with lurid and romanticized characters; it is thickly larded with their cliche-ridden prose and patriotic speech making. (This novel is but one of five the ever-industrious King published in 1896.) What recommends this work of pulpish fiction to us now is the clarity with which it illustrates the conventions of popular literature. These free King to figure the crowd—and the stock political roles of immigrant characters—with reckless ease.

King's attitude in characterizing street crowds vacillates from a condescending egalitarianism to a stern Carlylean fury. He declares at one point during a strike scene that "an American street crowd is gifted with a fine sense of humor" (206); shortly thereafter, he refers to the same crowd as "that misguided, drink-crazed, demagogue-excited mob" (211). Such rapid shifts can be attributed to King's defective writing skills and to his high-speed production techniques. The full explanation may not, however, be so simple. King's aim, if the repeated strike and crowd scenes are an indication, is to magnify the fluidity of the crowd's identity and to locate its evolving animus. What is it that transforms a group of "jovial" street toughs into a mob of "maddened men" and "foul-mouthed, slatternly women" (206-7, 211)?

The key to this question's answer would appear to be lowly Max Elmendorf, a feeble and altogether ineffective rabble-rouser. This German socialist and tutor is a tireless maker of speeches, an author of inflammatory articles in the German-language paper, *Arbeiter Zeitung*, and a constant conspirator. But he is all wind and words and is quickly exposed as a rather hollow threat to the city's law and order. King himself cannot seem to decide whether he wants us to regard Elmendorf as comic or dangerous. For all his complaints about a "demagogue-excited crowd," he shows us no instance of the crowd being stirred by a demagogue or by any speaker (211). The strike begins without Elmendorf, and when the crowd begins to chant its slogans—"Down with the government" and "To Hell with the United States"—and wreaks "havoc" on the railway, he is already under arrest (211).

What King defines in the strike scenes is a contrast between the "calm, grim, and silent" men of the army and a "vast mob of howling antagonists" (211, 210). The stock epithets are at least as old as Homer's descriptions of the Greeks and Trojans in the *Iliad* (Book 3). Still, it's clear that through these contrasts King aims to undercut Elmendorf's and the strikers' claim that they are "the people." In one of his many speeches, a characteristically pompous and flatulent performance, Elmendorf blesses the memory of the Haymarket anarchists:

> The blood of the martyred men you hanged eight years ago as Anarchists cries aloud for vengeance, and the day of the people has come at last. They govern the governor; *they* are the legislature of Illinois, and when they rise no power on earth can save you. (195)

The "governor," any half-awake reader of 1896 knew, was Illinois Governor Peter Altgeld, who in 1893 had pardoned the three surviving Haymarket anarchists. When he pardoned the anarchists, editorial writers pilloried the German-born Altgeld. Since he was "an alien himself," the Washington *Post* declared, he had "little or no stake in the problem of American social evolution." The Toledo *Blade* charged that he had "encouraged anarchy, rapine, and the overthrow of civilization."[4] From their perspective and King's, Altgeld—who had also opposed the use of troops to quell the Pullman strike—had twice capitulated to the mob. Elmendorf, in contrast, asserts that it is "the people" exercising their near-mythical power who speak and act through the governor.

To King, the German Elmendorf is an authentic embodiment of the German-born Altgeld, his comically inflated defense of the Haymarket anarchists a faithful reproduction of Altgeld's political thinking. Anarchists now "govern the governor," and a foreign-born mob lays claim to being "the people"; King's irony seems painfully obvious: anarchy and the American government have merged indivisibly.

III

The cultural construction of the crowd's identity in Will Payne's *The Money Captain* (1898) rests upon almost the same repertory of political attitudes and codes as King's novel. Here, too, Babel and the spectre of anarchy haunt the city. Such beliefs and fears, of course, were the common property of politicians and many other Chicago authors at the turn of the century. A half-dozen and more Chicago novels written in this period, notably J. W. McConaughy's *The Boss* (1911) and Henry Kitchell Webster's *The Duke of Cameron Avenue* (1904), explored the subterranean connection between the immigrant crowd and the city's political leaders. But Payne's novel, in its treatment of the Chicago city council and its codification of the crowd's force, seems seminal.

The city council meeting in Payne's novel takes place at night—as it does in Dreiser's "Cataclysm" chapter. Here we see, mainly through the eyes of Victor Nidstrom, a carefully choreographed type-scene, where the aldermen and the crowd perform a ritualized dance of democracy and corruption. To Nidstrom, Payne's archetypically middle-class hero, the voices of the council blend into "a strange medley of accents" and the crowd itself composes into "a strange ragged frieze." Such images and perceptions play up the foreign or mixed ethnic character of the aldermen and the crowd, though there's no suggestion of a redemptive melting pot myth in the spectacle. Payne, instead, stresses that the city council meeting sits at the center of "a sinister world."

From the gallery, Nidstrom can hear the aldermen's shouts about "too much noise," but while he detects the "rich brogue" of one speaker and the others' repeated calls for order, he can apprehend only the vehemence and riotous laughter that punctuate the debate. Even after he was positioned himself to hear the speeches, the words that reach him make no sense:

> Near the center of the chamber a burly member whose snow-white hair was clipped close to his fat head arose with ponderous unsteadiness and began talking in thick, uncertain tones. His bulky frame swayed threateningly. Now and then he made a grotesque gesture. One moment he bellowed unintelligibly and the next his voice sank to a muttering sound. (107-108)

Repeatedly the speaker tries to pronounce the word "eligible," and repeatedly he fails to say more than "egg-il" or "edge-il." As he stumbles over his words and drunkenly fails to find out what subject's under debate, the other council members shout "vote! vote!"

The chaos of the council floor, where shouts, noise, and drunkards rule, is mimicked in the gallery crowd above. Packed tightly together, they elbow each other for room to smoke and spit. Nidstrom will later remember this night as a "saturnalia of degradation" and "dirt" (112). What first strikes him, however, are the "odd shapes and sizes" of the crowd's heads. "Many of them," he observes, "were badly set off with tousled hair." His observations on physiognomy and cephalic indexes reflect, none too subtly, the nativist 1890s' prevailing typology of race and ethnicity, a tacit statement of the Anglo-Saxon myth. The gallery crowd's physical features, their dirtiness and disorder, brand them as members of a lower social class and outcast races.

O'Toole, the crowd's favored speaker, is one of them. His disordered hair, "his rasping voice, rich . . . with hints of Ireland," suggest that the face and voice of the crowd are one and the same as the government's. He is the speaker that the crowd has waited for, and, though Nidstrom could not know it, he, too, has been waiting to see O'Toole. Seeing him—Nidstrom never seems to understand his words—makes plain that he himself has been an instrument of bribery. He now realizes that he has, unwittingly, played a part in a complicated price-fixing and franchise-buying scheme. That clinching recognition, in turn, signals to us the identity of the "trampish crowd" and the aldermen.

IV

Victor Nidstrom escapes from the crowd, fleeing the dirt and darkness of the city hall for his clean, well-lighted home. For a time, he thinks about leaving Chicago and returning to the "simple freshness" of High Grove, Michigan, where he could breathe the "air of repose," where, he believes, "his whole life" might be as "clean and innocent as his home" (112). But, at the novel's end, he reconsiders and seems ready to live out a life in the city he once despairingly called "Babel" (3). His uneasy and separate peace with Chicago, however, does not turn upon an acknowledgement of the crowd's political will or a new understanding of its polyglot voices. O'Toole's corrupt oratorical gestures and the "grotesque" appeals of the other aldermen to the crowd still burn in his memory.

Nidstrom's decision points, rather formulaically, to the saving Victorian graces of home and family—to separation from Babel's people, not fusion in the crowded melting pot of the city. Payne evokes the mythic or biblical "Babel" to project the city as the type and figure of corruption and chaos. But Babel had come to have another meaning for many Chicago writers and polemicists in this period.[5] Since "Babel" symbolizes the coming together of a "nation of nations," it can also, as Werner Sollors has suggested, prefigure that transcendent and Pentecostal moment "beyond ethnicity" (53, 60-61).

Brand Whitlock intimates such possibilities in writing about Malachi Nolan, an Irish saloon-keeper and ward boss. In these two *Gold Brick* (1910) stories, Whitlock stresses the "babel of voices" heard in the city's ward politics. "Reform in the

First," the clearest illustration of his sympathies, points toward a community transcending ethnic differences and a definition of "the people" linked to a "cosmopolitan" ideal. That transcendent unity is adumbrated in a political alliance between Nolan and the blue-blooded John Underwood. Prompted by Nolan, Underwood campaigns in "the Syrian, Arabic, Chinese, and Italian quarters" of Chicago's First Ward (246). Though his bid for office in this meets defeat, the "horrible uproar" of the crowd that signals it does not, as in Payne, dramatize political corruption or ethnic divisions (245, 261). Instead, the polyglot crowd's voices reverberate with Underwood's "stunned" sense of dejection and loss. Whitlock does not, in short, use the story to counsel flight from Babel, but to urge a compact or political union among all its people.

Which is not to say that Whitlock confronts directly the difficulties of representing the crowd's contending and polylingual voices. The story's comic and ironic effects spring from a monolingual protagonist's failure to understand the polyglot language of contemporary political discourse. Underwood, intent upon fulfilling political ambitions passed down by "one of the oldest families of Chicago," does not claim the role of translator or seek to act as mediator between Americans and the alien crowd (235-6).

That is a role rather readily assumed by Blair Carrhart, the improbably named hero of I. K. Friedman's *By Bread Alone* (1901). Other progressive novelists—from Howells with Conrad Dryfoos in *A Hazard of New Fortunes* to Robert Herrick with Thornton Jennings in *The Gospel of Freedom*—had readily granted intellectuals and middle-class reformers license to speak for the immigrant masses. But that convention breaks down in Friedman's novel. He cannot, when the logic of his plot overtakes him, substitute the rational voice of his middle-class character for the emotions and cries of the crowd. Almost inadvertently, then, he discovers the conflict between the crowd and his appointed mediator.

Carrhart grandly conceives of himself as "the shepherd who wished to guide" workers "to the promised land" (445). Though he is of the finest New England stock, he has distinguished himself as a workingman and, in the bargain, has taken a "close, repulsive" room above a Croatian saloon in the farthest reaches of South Chicago (66-67). Fired with an unshakable socialist faith, he preaches the coming of a "Cooperative Commonwealth" to Polish, Czech, Hungarian, and Slavic steelworkers. Moses and Christ, he would bring word of socialism to these poor "sheep" (90-1). He intends to be a mediator between the foreign masses and the mill owners. In the end, he fails as a leader of the people almost as completely as Whitlock's Underwood and King's Elmendorf. Injured and defeated in a violent strike, he withdraws into marriage and pledges himself to a career as a reform politician.

Blair and Friedman (in intrusive authorial commentary) espouse several contradictory or shifting attitudes towards the immigrants' political role and power. Even at his most sympathetic or sentimental, Friedman inserts ominous and fearful signs of the immigrant crowd's irrational force. In chapter twenty, "The Man of the Hour," Carrhart addresses a mass meeting of foreign-born steelworkers. His speech and the crowd's cheering assent imply that their grievances and political energy might be channeled into democratic forms. He had spoken to the crowd of steelworkers as "individuals," instructing them on "the importance of the worker as a voter," on the complexities of a tariff bill, and on the finer points of a coming election (225). Yet, in summing up the effect of Blair's words, Friedman says:

> To the foreigners, who had the thing interpreted to them and exaggerated in the interpretation, Blair became a worker of miracles—a common laborer who was able by his word to influence the most potent in the land; a mysterious but good agent acting in a mysterious but good manner in their behalf. (228)

If such passages elevate Blair to a Christ-like station and define the appeal of socialism to the workers, they also build upon prevailing racial myths by stressing the simple-mindedness and superstitious nature of the immigrants. This crowd "growled and scowled" "savagely" before he began to speak and remains a broodingly "dark foreign" mass (224).

When later, during a strike, they raise their once-muted voices into hideous cries and their "worst passions" erupt into violence, Friedman's sympathies seem shattered and confused (338). Blair himself becomes "like a keeper who had liberated a chained beast and now cowed before the beast he had liberated" (330). Earlier in the novel, when "restless crowds" had formed and chaos threatened, Blair transformed through his words "a babble of voices"—"Slav, Czek, Magyar, Germanic"—into logical and compelling speeches that the crowd echoed in chants (161-4). Now the crowd resents his words and they shout their own "babel of cries" (331).

At first, Blair perceives a "polyglot muttering," a buzzing of foreign voices about his ears. In indirect discourse Friedman gives voice to the strikers' complaints and their political intentions: "Why," the crowd is said to ask, "did this man hold them back?" The crowd then mutters a series of such childlike queries (330). Friedman answers (or Blair does in narrated monologue) in words calculated to discredit the strikers' protests: "They had the consistency that comes from one thought; the inconsistency that comes from many thoughts was incomprehensible to their narrow, sodden understanding" (330). Their "sodden" slowness turns quickly into fury and cries for vengeance. Before long, this mob of "demons" and "hideous dwarfs" has destroyed the mill and its machinery (342). Blair himself, impelled by his "super-excited brain," finally joins their maddened assault (361).

The mob's actions, to borrow Harold Kaplan's words, are never presented as acts of "redemptive violence" (120). Carrhart comes to see "the people" transfigured as a result of the experience. As he redefines his ambitions at the novel's end, he recasts "the people" into an abstraction larger and far more idealized than these Polish, Hungarian, Slavic and Czech steelworkers. With this allegorized ideal in mind, he pledges himself to "realize the Cooperative Commonwealth for the people" (479-81).

The immigrant crowd, in these works of Chicago fiction, reflects some traditional American anxieties about democracy and "the people." Since the crowd itself exists outside ordinary political and social institutions, it threatens always to move beyond all laws and all controls. Radicals like the socialist Friedman and conservatives like the iron-fisted King express almost the same fear of the crowd. Political ideology does not automatically determine a writer's understanding of "the people" or stifle the fear that a crowd, in an instant, might become a beastlike mob. King's and Friedman's repertory of images and their fears of the "rabble" often sound remarkably similar. That the crowds they wrote about were immigrants magnified their quite conventional fears and anxieties about "the people." The voices of Babel spoke, to them and others, of chaos and anarchy.

But they also spoke, however faintly, of "the people" in a second sense. That is to say, of the "nation of nations," an idealized America, an America emerging from the mixing and mingling of all people (Sollors 261). The polyglot character of the street crowds, the roll calls and catalogs of nationalities in city council and at factory gates—these project and predict the coming of such a *nation of nations.* Empowering the immigrant crowd with speech—even the babble and the chants of Friedman's strikers and the howls of Herrick's and King's mobs—grudgingly reified the immigrants' political power and validated their voice in the American polity. For these writers, each ethnic and racial group, each new tongue and voice, articulated new and separate political demands. Babel and the immigrant crowd, in the political context they and many others imagined, inevitably came to represent equivocal formulations of the melting pot myth. The crowd and "the people," in this fiction, are as liable to prefigure ethnic divisions, racial conflicts, and mob violence as they are to express a Pentecostal communion and an ideal America.

Notes

[1] See, for example, two editorials in the *Inter Ocean*: "Our Foreign Born Population" (18 March 1893) and "Cosmopolitan Chicago" (19 March 1893).

[2] Quotations and information in this paragraph are taken from David Jackson's article "The Making of Mayor What's-His-Name," *Chicago* 37 (February 1988): 110-12; and three articles from the *Chicago Tribune*: "Madhouse Inside and Outside" (2 December 1987): 1, 5; "Mayor Makes Pitch for Unity" and "The Historic Council Meeting" (3 December 1987): 15.

[3] For an illuminating sketch of King's life and work, see Clell T. Peterson's "Charles King: Soldier and Novelist," *American Book Collector* 16 (1965): 8-12.

[4] Quoted in Ray Ginger, *Altgeld's America: The Lincoln Ideal versus Changing Realities* (Chicago: Quadrangle Books, 1965): 85-6.

[5] See, for example, Rabbi Emil G. Hirsch's "Preface" to Sigmund Krausz's *Street Types of Chicago* (Chicago: Max Stern & Co., 1892): iv-v.

Works Cited

Ade, George. *In Babel: Stories of Chicago.* New York: McClure, 1903.

Burg, David F. *Chicago's White City of 1893*. Lexington: UP of Kentucky, 1976.

Chatfield-Taylor, Hobart. "Babel-Tongued Communities." *America* 1 (4 October 1888): 2.

Dreiser, Theodore. *The Titan*. New York: Signet, 1965.

Friedman, I. K. *By Bread Alone*. New York: McClure, Phillips, 1901.

Fuller, Henry Blake. "Chicago's Varied Population Made Subject of Linguistic Study." *The Chicago Evening Post* (7 March 1903): 2: 1-2.

—. *The Cliff-Dwellers*. New York: Harper, 1893.

Herrick, Robert. *The Gospel of Freedom*. New York: Macmillan, 1898.

—. *The Web of Life*. New York: Macmillan, 1900.

Kaplan, Harold. *Power and Order*. Chicago: The U of Chicago P, 1981.

King, Charles T. *A Tame Surrender: A Story of the Chicago Strike*. Philadelphia: J. B. Lippincott, 1896.

Mills, Nicolaus. *The Crowd in American Fiction*. Baton Rouge: Louisiana State UP, 1986.

Payne, Will. *The Money Captain*. Chicago: Herbert S. Stone, 1898.

Sollors, Werner. *Beyond Ethnicity: Consent and Descent in American Culture*. New York: Oxford UP, 1986.

Steiner, George. *After Babel*. London: Oxford UP, 1973.

Sternberg, Meir. "Polylingualism and Translation as Mimesis." *Poetics Today* 2 (1981): 221-39.

Whitlock, Brand. *The Gold Brick*. New York: Hurst, 1910.

America, 1945: Jo Sinclair's *The Changelings*

Ellen Serlen Uffen

Jo Sinclair's novel, *The Changelings* (1955), seems to hide no depths. It is the story of what happens to the people of a predominantly Jewish, working-class neighborhood of mostly two-family homes in an Ohio city in the summer of 1945, immediately after some Jews move up and out and some blacks would like to move in. To read the book this literally and narrowly, however, is to ignore Sinclair's carefully wrought literary architecture and the novel's thematic complexity. On a truer but more abstract level, *The Changelings* takes on little less than the big themes of human experience as they existed in post-World War II America: the book is about love and fear and friendship and hypocrisy and expectations and about the nature of prejudice. It is about the significance of ritual and the consequences of its destruction. It is also, perhaps most importantly, about loss of language and of home and of homeland, loss of childhood, loss of dreams.

The novel is presented in the form of a concentrated *Bildungsroman*, but one which involves changes in nature and in places as well as in people. The transition from childhood to young womanhood of twelve-year-old Judith Vincent, one of the changelings of the title, coincides with the transformation of nature from a summer of unusual heat to the year's first cleansing snow. As Vincent's own growth has its physical parallel in nature's change, so it has a dramatic parallel in a neighborhood's transition or, better, in simply the threat of change in "the street," as the area is known. The actual settings in which the action occurs are as much characters in *The Changelings* as are the human beings who carry out the action. The book comprises a series of important locales; as the drama shifts from one to another, tensions shift. We learn to expect from the places certain significances. These, in turn, influence the human tensions which then create the dramatic action.

In a book inhabited by immigrants (mostly from eastern Europe), the locale of greatest significance is America itself, still *die Goldene Medina*—the Golden Land—but still also a foreign place where "the habits are different" (*Changelings* 186). The locale next in size and meaning is the Ohio city which contains the action, no doubt a fictionalized and unnamed Cleveland because that is Jo Sinclair's city.[1] There is also "the street," where most of the novel's actors live, and the "Gully," where the children meet. There are other places: The Heights, never seen, but the section of the city, higher up and cooler, where the Jews move who have succeeded in their adopted land; and the black neighborhood, which we see briefly. The street and the Gully are the settings for most of the drama.

The street is the home of the six families who are the novel's center: the Goldens, Levines, Zigmans, Valentis, Vincents and Millers. While the street is in some ways a microcosm of a larger environment, it is also enclosed, family centered and loving, a safe and known place. If it is a ghetto, that is a definition imposed from without. Its inhabitants do not see it as such. The neighborhood is largely Jewish, with some Italians, and all the others whom the Jews categorize as "gentiles," or *die goyim*, making a distinction between these and the Italians. The stories of the street are of children in trouble, children in love, of loneliness, of hardworking families, cheating husbands, and of the tensions created from too little money—in short, all the fodder of life and of other novels. When the book opens, there is a threat to the street. Blacks wish to move into the enclave and the street is afraid.

The other center of dramatic action, not far from the street, is the Gully, once a dump and now a no man's land between the black and white neighborhood. It is

> a children's place, honeycombed with their ways of living. In winter, they slid down the shallow hills in sleds or sitting in discarded wash buckets. In spring, they searched as if for buried treasure for the partially burnt objects which came to the surface in certain muddy spots, through layers of old ashes. In summer—when the evenings were as open as the days—the gang un-

> locked its clubhouse, nailed tight the boards loosened by winter, and took over ownership.
>
> For in the summer the Gully really belonged to Vincent and her gang. (2-3)

The Gully is described in mock archeological terms, as if the fact of its long existence lends a kind of approval of nature and of history to its function as a place where children can find peace. Yet the layers the children sift through to find their treasure are composed of ashes. The Gully is also a wasteland, a vast receptacle for the human failures—even the treasures are "partially burnt"—of the past. The children are its inheritors. But the fact that the Gully does belong to children is itself a promise that the future can be redeemed. It is in the Gully also where lovers meet and birds sing, and it is here that Vincent encounters Clara Jackson, her black counterpart and the other changeling, and begins the friendship with her that will initiate the process of redemption. Clara cements the relationship the first time they meet by giving Vincent a knife and a St. Anthony's medal, symbols of physical and spiritual protection. They come together honestly in the Gully, without the prejudices and threats that would attend such meetings outside, and with the freedom to reveal their feelings.

The honest articulation of feeling cannot happen anywhere else. The children as well as the adults are mute outside of the Gully: Dave Zigman, for instance, Vincent's friend, loves his mother, "but without words" (66). "The silence between them was of heart things and neither seemed able to touch one word of that close, beautiful language trembling around them like delicate waves of feeling" (67). We are told of Chip Levine's crudely expressed love for Ruth Miller that "somewhere inside of her Ruth felt this inarticulate way Chip had of making love to her; no language at his fingertips, no music in his mind, to soften and color a phrase . . . " (55). Alex Golden loves his brother, Jules, the young poet and the articulate exception to everyone, "inarticulately, profusely, with awe" (72); similarly, "The rough words" of Santina Valenti, "which she spoke to the street, the excited ones to Alex, were not the language she spoke in her heart. . . . The language in her heart, like the dream of love there, was musical, beautifully pure" (79).

As the action proceeds, characters gradually gain the ability to speak honestly to themselves and to each other. For those who dare to learn, connections are made and relationships secured. But first, barriers must be broken through, sometimes at the great expense of severing other, family relationships. Dramatic tension is focused primarily on the personal. In an important sense, the book is concerned with why we are inarticulate and how it is possible to learn to speak. This distance between people, extended to a larger, social, but no more insidious level, is Jo Sinclair's definition of prejudice.

Prejudice here is a problem whose origins have nothing to do with differences in color or race. It begins with a group of like members who are unhappy, insecure, discontent, unable to communicate and, thus, to exorcise the displeasure. Frustrations fester and must be released. A place at which to aim the anger or hurt is needed. Hence, the alien group most readily available becomes both catalyst and scapegoat. *The Changelings,* in this sense, is not primarily about black/Jewish tensions. That is a dramatic byproduct of the central fictional concerns. The book is not even about blacks, particularly. It is about Jews and how they live in a land that is not theirs, how they deal with their children, whose land it is, and with their own memories of oppression, most recently the Nazi threat of annihilation. (The book mentions the Holocaust only in passing and in mostly oblique references. It is set, however, in 1945, the year World War II ended. To miss the connection is to ignore our own complex response to the Jews who live in the street. History, if not Jo Sinclair, disallows the easy assignment of guilt to those who suffered at the hands of the truly guilty.)

The Jews here, dispossessed of their past, even of their language, Yiddish, are feeling threatened again when the novel opens, but now in their new land. They are once more victims of history, this time of the blacks, the latest Cossacks to steal their freedom. They do not perceive this fear as irrational. On the contrary, as Sophie Golden explains to her son, Jules, it is necessary for the Jews to be continuously vigilant, even in America. Jules has accused her and others of maintaining what he feels to be an overly proprietary attitude toward their neighborhood. In answer, she gives her son a short history of the street: the Jews have built up the neighborhood, raised their children there, and have become the leaders. The others, she says, the gentiles, do not want to be leaders because

> They are safe. They can sit and be quiet inside. Can we? When is a Jew safe? Only when he is a landlord who watches every second—day and night. Only when

> he owns the street. . . . When he can holler out like a bell if anything comes to remind him he's only a Jew. If anybody tries to slap him in the face with the fact, like—like it is garbage! (115)

The situation Mrs. Golden describes is, of course, fraught with irony never lost on Jules. The oppressed have become the oppressors. The situation of the blacks in 1945 Cleveland more than superficially resembles that of the Jews earlier, ghettoized and abused in Hungary, Russia, Poland, Germany. What the Jews were to their official government oppressors so the blacks have become to them. To extend the ironic comparison further, later in the book Herschel Levine views the street itself as "a Palestine to the Black Ones . . . a golden place" (268). He sees neither the irony nor the pathetic grandeur of his comparison.

Levine and the others who live in the street are allowed to characterize themselves, some with profound revelation, some superficially. We see each person through Jo Sinclair's third-person narrator, whose focus shifts to the narrowed vision of whatever actor is center stage. The blacks, however, are not characterized. There is barely an attempt to make even Clara more than a cipher. But this is hardly a dramatic failure, as Johnnetta B. Cole and Elizabeth H. Oakes believe in their essay on the novel.[2] If we understand that *The Changelings* is not so much a sociological study of results as it is a psychological presentation of causes, Sinclair's methods become clearer. Clara, for instance, takes on real fictional life only when Vincent confers it upon her by projection of her own feelings and desires. This is a novel which, in general, is concerned less for social situation—unlike, for instance, the novels of the 1930s—than for the complex of human emotions which created it. Consequently, Sinclair does not judge her characters, nor does she allow us to. The Jews, who are collectively the novel's focus, are alternatively innocent and guilty, sympathetic and blind. Were they able to stand outside of themselves and articulate the situation in which we see them, these people would view as a perverse trick of fate that, after having gained their own freedom, to keep it they are forced to deny others theirs.

Their inability to comprehend what is occurring is suggested in the narrative by a hazy unreality which has caused and is pervading what otherwise appears to be the very real action of the book. The "exceptionally hot summer" is itself making things happen and affecting people's perceptions and behavior.

Nature is masking clarity. Those who live in the street, senses stultified and movements lulled, witness the life of the street, made phantasmagoric by the oppressive heat. They watch the blacks enter the neighborhood, and "These black people who came so eagerly and stubbornly to ask for rooms seemed part of the heavy fantasy the heat had made of their lives" (1). The silent coming, being turned away, and leaving feels choreographed; it is a constant slow dance occurring at the back of the stage behind a gauze curtain, while the major dramatic events happen stage front. This movement, in turn, affects the tone of the book: the blacks' attempts to move into the neighborhood and their failure to do so create a palpable sadness which pervades the action. This haze which masks clarity also affects us, outside the novel. We cannot easily take sides.

Our inability to place guilt and our awareness of the ironies of history are mirrored in Ruth Miller's confused reaction to the crucial fight scene involving Ross Valenti, who mistakenly believes his sister, Santina, has been sexually involved with a black man, and an anonymous black, who has innocently come to look for an apartment. Again, the heat renders the confrontation shadowboxing to our perception, as if Ross's insubstantial opponent has been conjured up by the people who watch. Ruth, in the crowd, faint and dizzy, weakened by the heat and the violence, confuses victim and victimized, past and present, and her brother, Herb, beaten by European thugs years earlier, with the black man here:

> As she stared, horrified, the faces of her family seemed like the village faces out of her childhood, the faces of the gentiles, called the *goyim* by the village Jews. She searched for Herb's face among the gloating, excited, vengeful expressions of her family. Where was Herbie? She turned back, looking for him on the Valenti porch. Was it Herbie being beaten up there? Herbie again? With his own father, his mother and brother, fantastically changed into the *goyim* who used to catch Jews and beat them when they wandered into the wrong streets? (234)

Sinclair's method of shrouding action in fantasy may also be her comment on the unreality of what exists outside of the novel, in what we perceive to be our reality. These things happen, she suggests, but logic insists they should not. Prejudice is the product of something—the heat here—which steals reason.

The movement of blacks into the street begins, ironically, to be felt by us as an intrinsic part of the ritual life of the street, the very thing that defines its existence and their own to its inhabitants. The characters spend a great deal of time talking and watching the street from their front porches and listening to its familiar sounds: Mrs. Valenti shouting for Santina, Mrs. Levine scheming to make money, the noise of seltzer deliveries and chicken deliveries, Dave and Chip's public sparring matches, Ruth Miller walking to work in her father's pawnshop. But now there is a jarring note in the ritual: always the blacks coming, asking, being turned away. To us, silent witnesses from our vantage point off to the side and new to the established ways of these people, the constant comings and goings of the blacks searching for a place to live make them seem to belong to the life of the street and lead us to expect them to continue their quest. To the street, however, their presence is intrusive and insidious, as is evident when we hear some mention of the blacks insinuating its way into each conversation, sometimes casually and in passing, sometimes as the focus of discussion, as if they of the street were talking of a situation as natural as the all-pervasive heat. But interestingly, the life of the street continues vividly despite the perception by the older generation that the appearance of the blacks is a jarring foretaste of the death of ritual or of life as it is. This persistent vitality suggests their perception is wrong. Maybe this change is a sign of transition between the old ritual and the new one of the new land and the new generation and maybe, we outsiders are led to believe, this is not necessarily a change for the worse.

The new is, in fact, already established, not yet in the street, but in the Gully, the place of the children. That which is the basic definition of ritual, religious observance is changed here, for better or worse, in this place where the new world will begin. Although they do not make the connection consciously, Vincent's gang holds its meetings regularly at the beginning of the Jewish Sabbath, Friday night. They occasionally have had meetings at other times, "but the Friday meetings remained iron rituals because Saturday was the best day for snitching in stores" (3). The gang members, not all of whom are Jewish, gather in their small clubhouse, "big enough to hold ten people," the *minyan*, or the number, according to Jewish law, necessary for formal prayer. Vincent and Dave—the leaders, the high priests, the rabbis—sit above the others, on either side of a crate upon which are (ritually) placed "two wine bottles, to hold candles" (3). With each step of the process ritualized, the gang then bakes potatoes in a makeshift fireplace. The Sabbath dinner. In "this children's place of Gully," we are told, as in the adults' synagogue, "dream and emotion flowed like a rich language," the replacement here for the mysterious Hebrew of traditional observance. The clubhouse, to Vincent, "seemed enclosed in a magic ring" (3,4).

Much can be said, of course, about what might be viewed as the sacrilegious quality of this mock worship. It feels a bit like Fagin's boys at a witches' Sabbath. To join together in prayer of a sort as preparation for a day of thievery hardly defines serious religious observance, no matter how liberal one's proclivity in the area of faith. Perhaps we are meant to wonder—worry—about the future of traditional Judaism in such young American hands. Yet we are also meant to recognize the very real emotional comraderie of the gang. Vincent "had yearned to understand and possess her father's God" (102), we know, and her attempt to do so is honest, albeit unorthodox, in all senses of that word. In their way, the children are preserving ritual forms and clearly they are retaining magic.

This may not be true of the adults. No matter what moral reservations we may have about this new religion, at least Vincent's gang meets regularly on Friday nights. Most of their parents attend religious services once a year, on the Jewish High Holy Days (a fact that Jules Golden notes with cynicism). There is also another, even more hypocritical contrast to the children's religion provided in the novel in the persons of Sam Miller and of Vincent's grandmother, both of whom follow versions of worship so stern that they preclude human feeling, the essence of the children's ritual. Sam Miller is a founder of the neighborhood synagogue, a man of high standing in the community, regarded by all with respect bordering on awe. But in the course of the story, we find out that Miller has been a womanizer, a tyrant to his family, a snob and a religious hypocrite who sends his daughter to work in his shop on the Sabbath because Saturday is the best day for business. At the same time, he resents his younger son's refusal to do forbidden work on the Sabbath but will not himself work.

Vincent's grandmother, so impressive and elegant in her strength, is the other version of the old beliefs. She is tyrannical, too, over her family, hard and cruel, but she is also the regal matriarch of the street who holds court regularly from Vincent's front porch. She is "a tribal chief" (182) whose presence vitalizes the people and whose decision to emigrate to the "Homeland" of Palestine is interpreted by the street as an inspiration and a triumph for all of them. "An old woman," says Mrs. Golden in "dramatic Yiddish," "has the strength, the courage, to go to her true home. It is a sign that our street will be victorious. That we will keep our homes. In peace" (183). Her reclamation of the past, of religion and of ritual, that is, will, in turn, give them the strength, in America, to retain theirs. Her son, Jules, questions the logic: "My God, you're crazy," is his American response.

These are the forms of worship the novel presents. The contrasts are clear. Vincent's new religion is not a perverted version of the old. It is carried out in the Gully, the place where human connection is possible, and it establishes a bond between religion and humanity, a quality lacking, for instance, in the grandmother's piety. The fact of being tied to a continuous religious tradition is clearly still important to Vincent. Her beliefs, however, adapted to life in America, embrace an ecumenism feared by the parents' generation, who see it as a harbinger of the end of the Jews. Vincent's sister, Shirley, is their example: she has married a Catholic, had a Catholic child and is treated "as if dead" by her father and grandmother, this despite the fact that Shirley has kept an important link with her heritage by naming the child in the traditional Jewish way, after a relative who has died. Manny is also the only baby in the book, which in itself suggests that the new ecumenism will be the future. Vincent and her mother, whose love overrides law, retain the connection with Shirley. Vincent once brings her nephew to her father and grandmother, forcing them to recognize the baby. The father does. The grandmother, stolid in her own faith, which requires her to withhold love for the sake of law, does not. Manny's religion is also Clara's, whose slave ancestors chose to be Catholics when they were emancipated. Vincent sees Clara's story as a revelation of how the Church is tied "to history and to generations of people picking and choosing" (250), as if her sister did the same. To Vincent this legitimizes the lives of her sister and her nephew and links them both with Clara.

Vincent also connects Clara's history with her own family's stories of the flight from Europe to the freedom of America. The stories fill her with religious magic, which she compares to

> how sometimes when you sat in *shul* and listened to the chant of the prayers and it was like a sad, thrilling feeling of goosebumps—as if you recognized the sound even though you did not understand the words or the meaning of a prayer that made Pa strike his chest slowly with his fist as he stood there swaying, wrapped in the long tassled prayer shawl. (250)

When her family arrived in America, they tried to become American by leaving behind what they believed to be foreign habits. They learned to speak English (although Yiddish is still their language of emotion) and in Vincent's family, they no longer keep up the family Bible. This new American, denied her place in a continuing heritage, surreptitiously adds not only her own name to the Bible and her sister's and her brother Nate's, but Manny's and his father's as well, thus making them a part of the past and the future. Vincent understands America as a land which is capable of absorbing others' traditions and not a place which, as her parents fear, will cause loss of their own traditions through assimilation, a prophecy whose realization they themselves have accelerated by their decision to discontinue the listing of generations in the family Bible.

In a book so concerned with symbols and tradition and ritual, it is fitting that it is a symbolic act—a violent one in this case, the mock rape of Judith Vincent—which is responsible for allowing the future to commence. The experiences of the older generation, the movement from Europe to America, from past to present, from summer to fall, from one set of beliefs to another, parallel, even in the wrenching quality of the transition, Vincent's movement from adolescence to adulthood. The difference is that the time from summer to fall is, for Vincent's parents, how long it takes for their old life to begin to die and for Vincent, the fall is the season before the snow which will cleanse the present and make the spring happen. Her loss of childhood is her gain in humanity and in womanhood, both literally and figuratively: Judaism celebrates the transition to the moral responsibility of womanhood at the age of twelve.

The scene takes place in the Gully, the violence at once defiling its sanctity as a pure place of children but the shock of it also opening up the gully to free the children to grow. Led by Dave Zigman, Vincent's trusted second-in-command, the gang members force Vincent to the ground, pin her and strip her naked. Vincent, who always wore her brother's pants and was nicknamed *schwartze kuter*, the black alley cat, because of her ability to scurry, undetected, through forbidden places, is now revealed, even to herself, in all her "unshielded softness." What happens is disturbing, but not so much because of the actual events—this is, after all, a children's prank gone wild and not a real rape—as for its compressed revelation of all the fears come true of female adolescents. Suddenly, Vincent has become a woman. She has lost her virginity, that is, her hold on all that she once unquestioningly trusted and believed in and has forcibly traded her old confidence for a new vulnerability and, as she soon discovers, loneliness. Yet, she realizes later, her experience also "somehow had left her mind naked, ready for a different kind of awareness" (103). She has begun, in fire, the process of growing up.

Dave, on his side, has been motivated by frustration. He is an adolescent, too, on the verge of manhood. He is losing control of his life. The world outside the Gully is beginning to change and, influenced by his parents' fears, he is privately enraged and frightened at what he perceives to be the threat to his home and his life of the blacks moving into the street. He has, to Vincent, "turned into somebody sour and nervous as a man, Mr. Levine, or her father, or Mr. Miller; he acted like one of the men of the street, who were always looking over their shoulders for colored people or something" (9). Now, stimulated to anger by the gang's discussion of the changing street and looking for trouble anyway, Dave taunts Vincent and supervises the "gang rape," carefully directing the others that they are only proving she is a girl: "Nothing dirty. All we do is pull off her clothes and prove it, see?" (18). He makes her the object of his rage, as if by revealing Vincent's femaleness, his fifteen-year-old maleness will take on the strength he needs to be a man and to protect the present. The scene, from his point of view, is as emotionally charged and compressed as it has been for Vincent. During the rest of the novel—this occurs at the beginning—he will gradually learn to articulate his fears and, like Vincent, begin to grow up.

After the gang scatters and Vincent is left alone, Clara, who has witnessed everything, appears. She is the same age as Vincent, the same height, and is wearing almost the same outfit. To Vincent, "For a fantastic second, it was like staring into a mirror—except for the brown color of her face" (22), an ironic, new generation reversal of Jules's recognition that his mother's fear of blacks is her fear of herself, of the blackness in her own heart. In this first direct confrontation in the novel of a black and a white person, significantly, blackness is not an issue at all. Clara's first words to Vincent—"Hey, if you're crying, you're a jackass" (21)—have nothing to do with color differences; they refer to the girls' mutual femaleness and the need for strength to confront a mutual enemy. Clara's "outrage encompassed both of them" (23). She offers to lend Vincent her knife to "cut off that damn thing they're always talking so big about" (22), and later gives her a St. Anthony's medal, "a piece of God . . . for protection" (133).

These comments cement the relationship that inspires Jules, the sickly and dying Homer of the street and the observer, from his porch, of the life of the street, to compose his poem, "The Changelings." "Come, Changeling," reads the first stanza,

> . . . let us look into our hearts for identity!
> Let us know how they put us into the barred baby cribs,
> deep inside the walled homes of those strangers
> who call themselves our mothers, our fathers,
> Let us know that we speak a different language of
> dreams of thoughts, of love—we children who were
> never their children in the heart.
> Yes, though they feed us with bread made of their
> fears and ignorance, we cannot grow into their dark
> images: we are changelings in our hearts, we must
> be free! (304)

The poem aims to reveal to the children their role in the future. The stories in the novel that parallel the main plot are variations on the poem's theme. Many of the younger generation, in the course of the book, wake up to find freedom and to look, unintimidated by their parents' fears, at their own future. That they learn to accept the future is not necessarily to deny the past—perhaps Jules is too harsh in his own rejection—but some degree of assimilation, they learn, will occur. They learn that the transition involves pain.

The book begins in the summer, before Rosh Hashanah, the beginning of the Jewish New Year. It ends after Yom Kippur, the Day of Atonement. The first snow is falling, covering the hurts of summer. Dave Zigman and Judith Vincent, no longer estranged, are to meet Clara Jackson at the apartment of Shirley O'Brien, Judith's sister. After fall and winter will come spring. Rebirth, Jo Sinclair suggests, is possible.

Notes

[1] The city, that is, where Jo Sinclair grew up. She was born in Brooklyn, New York, in 1913, and moved to Cleveland in 1916.

[2] The Feminist Press edition of *The Changelings* (1985) includes three essays: an "Afterword" by Nellie McKay, 323-37; "On Racism and Ethnocentrism," by Johnnetta B. Cole and Elizabeth H. Oakes, 339-47; and "A Biographical Note," by Elizabeth Sandberg, 349-52. The reference here is to the Cole/Oakes essay, 346.

Catholic-Lutheran Interaction in Keillor's *Lake Wobegon Days* and Hassler's *Grand Opening*

Robert D. Narveson

Since fiction is one of the sources from which we form our ideas about life, we are interested in how well fictional representations square with the experiences of life from which they are drawn. Two recent novels by Minnesotans focus in part on Catholic and Lutheran interaction in small rural towns. Since a Nebraska anthropologist's recent study of a similar Nebraska town focuses on the same subject, and so, to a lesser extent, do observations I solicited from a group of university students from small towns, I see here an opportunity to compare descriptions drawn directly from life with fictional representations of the same phenomena.

The two novels are Jon Hassler's *Grand Opening* (1987), a neatly plotted novel with a unified story to tell, and Garrison Keillor's *Lake Wobegon Days* (1985), a novel pretending to be history, sociology, and anthropology, even to the inclusion of footnotes citing authentic-sounding but dubious authorities. The portrayals in both novels agree in their main points with the evidence presented by anthropologist Ellen Dubas and with the testimony offered by the students about the importance of religious affiliation in shaping the social, economic, and political lives of people in typical midwestern rural small towns.

Garrison Keillor became a celebrity through hosting his popular radio show "A Prairie Home Companion" that two years after its last live broadcast is still being rebroadcast weekly on many public radio stations. His novel augments and elaborates on the tales he tells as the climactic feature of each of those shows. Jon Hassler, a native of Minnesota who lives and writes in Minnesota, is better known in his native state than in the nation. Since, however, his novels *Staggerford* (1977), *Simon's Night* (1979), *The Love Hunter* (1981), and *A Green Journey* (1985), in addition to *Grand Opening*, stand in matched paperback editions on the shelves of bookstores in Washington DC and Chicago as well as in Minneapolis-St. Paul and Lincoln, Nebraska, he does seem to have a national following.[1]

While the two novels are worth attention as novels or I would not be interested in them in the first place, assessing them as artistic achievements is not the purpose of this inquiry. Novelistic elements such as technical point of view become relevant, however, in their relation to what is said about religious affiliation. Both novels have omniscient narrators, yet the points of view are quite different. Hassler's narrator writes as a novelist telling a story. He and his readers have the comfortable relation of people sharing well-known novelistic conventions. He reports the thoughts and actions of outsiders—the Foster family—attempting to establish themselves in a close-knit rural community, but interspersed are the thoughts and actions of long-established insiders in the community. Seeing Hassler's community through the sensibilities of such different kinds of characters, readers must constantly decide how much of each character's opinions to believe.

If one also must decide what to believe about Lake Wobegon, it is for a different reason. Keillor writes as one who belongs to the community though he has left it (and presumably has gained perspective on it), who is now sharing his insider's knowledge with his readers, who are outsiders. Everything about the community is interpreted for us by this not-at-all disinterested narrator in the way things are intimately known by friends, relatives, and neighbors through long acquaintance and talk.

Hassler's novel is set in the 1940s; Keillor's ranges over time from the mid-nineteenth century to the present with the emphasis on the present. The differences in time-setting are not important. Religious attitudes do change, but very slowly. Descriptions of religious attitudes in Hassler's novel are of interest for another reason. Until now, the most notable fictional small towns in midwestern literature have been the inventions of Protestant (or at least non-Catholic) writers: Winesburg, Ohio; Spoon River, Illinois; Gopher Prairie, Minnesota. Keillor, too, grew up Protestant. Hassler, on the other hand, grew up

Catholic. Both Keillor and Hassler can successfully portray characters of either faith, but in these novels each focuses most strongly on members of the denomination in which he was nurtured.

Are the fictional accounts by Hassler and Keillor of social interaction among small-town Catholics and Lutherans true to the experience of those who actually live in small midwestern communities? As a Minnesotan now living in Nebraska, I do not find the views of Minnesotans and Nebraskans substantially different on the subject of how religious affiliation affects social interaction. My impression is that what Hassler and Keillor report largely corroborates the anecdotal reports of my Nebraska students. What the students report and what the novelists report both corroborate many of the observations of Ellen Dubas, an anthropologist in Nebraska, whose dissertation studies religious affiliation and social interaction in a rural Nebraska community. The town that Dubas calls Riverview, which she studied between August 1979 and December 1981, had 3,500 residents, considerably more than either Hassler's Plum (1500 people) or Keillor's Lake Wobegon (940 people). The difference in size does not seem to me to invalidate comparisons. The answer to my question appears to be yes, the fictional accounts by Hassler and Keillor do seem largely true to life—or at least to reports of life as it is lived in the kinds of communities they depict. The fictional accounts agree with the anthropologist's account in what they say about social, economic, and political life, and the anthropologist's analysis explains features of the novels' accounts that might strike one as false notes. The more interesting question, no doubt, is "so what?" and that question is partially answered along the way and more directly answered, if too briefly, at the conclusion.

In the Nebraska town Dubas calls Riverview, which is roughly divided between Catholics and Lutherans, social and interest groups tend to have memberships primarily along sectarian lines, which are also kinship lines. Because Catholics so often marry Catholics and Lutherans Lutherans, religious affiliation in Riverview could be registered merely by hearing a person's name, "which is the way that people in Riverview first think of each other" (Dubas 7). "The term 'Catholic,' 'Lutheran,' or 'Methodist,'" she says, "implies for the speaker a significant identity, carrying a message about the person and determining to a certain extent whether they are potential marriage partners or even whether one is likely to spend any social or free time with the person" (Dubas 85). At many important celebrations—birthdays, graduations, weddings, wedding anniversaries—activities are separated by religious affiliation even though (and in fact because) the basis of the separation is the kinship group. "In nearly every local activity," Dubas reports, "either considerably less than half of the people involved are Catholic or Catholics are the clear majority. This indicates how they [i.e. members of each group] isolate themselves from the rest of the community" (Dubas 102).

Volunteer groups in the fictional towns follow the pattern Dubas describes. In Lake Wobegon a Lutheran boy scout troop meets every Tuesday night in the church basement, while the Catholics have their own troop (*LWD* 217k). Among the Lake Wobegon Lutheran women there is Ladies Circle, within which the feud of the Ingqvists and Rogneses is played out (*LWD* 108). Of corresponding importance to Catholic men in Plum is the Holy Angels Men's Club. Sectarian schools are, of course, another potent force for social division in a community. Lake Wobegon has a Catholic grade school, with nuns to teach its classes. Perhaps the minority status of the Catholics in Plum is indicated by the absence of a Catholic school as well as by plans to establish a Lutheran school. Dubas reports that "In Riverview Catholics and Lutherans maintain social isolation from each other by use of a series of subtle but real maneuvers" (Dubas 18). "Religious affiliation," Dubas writes, "is the main identity in Riverview. It controls who interacts with whom and who trades with whom" (Dubas 23). Because they recognize this to be the case in Plum, Hank Foster and his partner choose Art Nicholai, returned veteran, as their local manager: "He met their four criteria: he was husky, ambitious, polite, and Catholic" (*GO* 318).

The social and economic insularity stemming from religious affiliation tends to show up strongly in *Grand Opening* and weakly in *Lake Wobegon Days* because the focus of the two novelists is different. A dominant focus in the former is on outsiders discovering what is hardest to adjust to after they move to a small town. Hassler contrasts city Catholics with Plum Catholics to the advantage of the city Catholics because that is the way the Fosters see it. He focuses primarily though not exclusively on what divides Catholics and Lutherans in his town of Plum. The dominant focus in Keillor, by contrast, is on an insider who out of loyalty is more attuned (like my students) to the strengths than the weaknesses of a small town community. Keillor focuses on what differentiates Lake Wobegon Catholics *and* Lutherans from city Catholics and Lutherans to the advantage of Lake Wobegon. His stress is on what unites Catholic and Lutheran as Lake Wobegonians.

According to one of my Lutheran freshmen, "Catholics seem to stick together more than Protestants—not in an outward way, but in a way you can just kind of see. Often I would hear my mom or grandma complain about the Catholic women and how they were all so great and how they had their little group who did all these activities within the church and usually thought they were right about everything they wanted done." Remembering his childhood, the Lake Wobegon narrator writes: "We were suspicious of Catholics, enough to wonder if perhaps the Pope had ordered them to take in little Protestant children during blizzards and make them say the Rosary for their suppers" (*LWD* 310). One disgruntled former Lake Wobegonian remembered: "Religious intolerance was part of our faith. We believed that Catholics were illiterate peasants, foreign-born, who worshiped idols . . . " (*LWD* 317). The Protestant narrator of Lake Wobegon recalls how "On Memorial Day, two great bands of marchers assemble in the morning, the Catholics at Our Lady and everyone else at the Lutheran church. . . . " The Prairie Home Cemetery, to which both groups march, is divided, and the kids yell taunts at each other across the fence (*LWD* 148-9). Lacking adult inhibitions, these children express the biases that their parents show in private but conceal in public.

There is a historical reason for the greater conflict in Hassler's Plum than in Keillor's Lake Wobegon. Conflicts between Catholics and Protestants, especially Lutherans, are a part of German history (Dubas 17). Dubas notes that both Lutheran churches in Riverview are of German origin. A reader with a little knowledge of Lutheranism will recognize that the Lutheran church in Plum belongs to the Missouri Synod, a synod largely of German background. Judging from the names, the Catholic church in Plum, while not so German as in Lake Wobegon, nevertheless is heavily German. This source of inherited conflict does not exist in Lake Wobegon. In Lake Wobegon there is suspicion of Catholics by the Norwegian Lutherans, but it lacks the virulence of the same suspicion in Plum or in Riverview. Catholic-Lutheran rivalries in Lake Wobegon are far more benign and good-natured than in Plum, where both

Catholics and Lutherans have strong German contingents.

In Plum, one of the things Stan Kimball tells Hank Foster is that these villagers "were never so happy as when they were at odds for the love of God . . . " (*GO* 160). Certainly Hassler describes instances that lend force to Kimball's assertion. Mayor Brask and his wife, for example, come across as first-class Lutheran bigots (and social snobs as well), and on the other side, when the Fosters move to a new neighborhood, the Catholic Bea Crowley tells Catherine Foster, "I just wanted to say welcome to Bean Street and I'm so happy you're Catholic. The DeRoches were Catholic too, and when they moved away I was afraid we'd lose ground" (*GO* 175). After the Fosters are settled in a new house they give a party, to which they invite Lutherans as well as Catholics, scandalizing both. Paul Dimmitburg's Lutheran minister father is one of the few who comes and gets along fine. He brings along his wife, Paul's mother, for whom Paul finds himself making an ironic apology. "Please forgive my mother," he says. "She can't understand why God didn't create all of humanity Lutheran" (*GO* 180). The Fosters' attempt to bridge the social gap between Catholics and Lutherans is a failure.

Given a strong degree of social isolation by religious group, it is not surprising that under most circumstances, the villagers in Lake Wobegon and in Plum, like those in Dubas's Riverview, not only socialize but also spend their money with co-religionists. Division of social activities by sect feeds into the economic division, since church-sponsored events provide opportunities for finding providers of needed services among one's co-religionists. It is at a meeting of Catholic Action that one character in Lake Wobegon finds an orthodontist. Hassler's narrator describes the thoughts of Hank Foster, who has successfully revitalized a failing food store in Plum:

> The only unfortunate thing was that all of Hank's new customers, except during sales, were the same people he saw returning tonight from the communion rail. He had thought that the combination of bargains and Paul Dimmitburg [his recently hired Lutheran helper] might have won him a few Lutherans, but it hadn't happened. Stan Kimball said it would never happen no matter how superior to Legget's [the rival Lutheran-owned store] the market became. (*GO* 160)

The egregious May Brask, a bigoted Lutheran, had earlier in the novel expressed the fear that just what Hank has accomplished would happen: "This ambitious competitor was sure to drain off all the Catholic trade Legget had gained through Kermit's decline" (*GO* 71).

Plummians overlook their sectarian biases to take advantage of Hank's sales, but their bias reigns again once the economic inducement departs. Similarly: "In Lake Wobegon, car ownership is a matter of faith. Lutherans drive Fords, bought from Bunsen Motors, the Lutheran car dealer, and Catholics drive Chevies from Main Garage, owned by the Kruegers, except for Hjalmar Ingqvist (the banker), who has a Lincoln" (*L WD* 139). One other Lake Wobegonian with less social impunity than the banker comes perilously near to breaking this rule of car ownership until the Lutheran pastor points out his Christian duty to own a Ford. Dubas notes that in Riverview "Decisions on personal business transactions such as grocery shopping and automobile repairs frequently are made on the basis of kinship. She observes further: "The more significant financial exchanges of the religious institutions themselves are influenced by kin and religious affiliation" (207).

In politics, too, one would expect to find biases stemming from religious affiliation, and that is what one does find. The Lutheran Mayor Brask of Plum sees the Fosters as a threat to the political balance in the town, which favors the Lutherans. Hassler writes: "Besides being mayor, Harlan Brask was chairman, ex officio, of the five-member Plum school board, on which there were two Lutherans besides himself—a majority nearly offset by the influence of the superintendent, who was Catholic" (*GO* 71). When a vote took place on expelling someone from school, the Plum school board split on sectarian lines, with one abstention for a reason not given.

Mayor Brask's Lutheran bigotry is matched by that of certain Catholics in Plum. One fellow religionist says to Hank Foster: "A bunch of us men from Holy Angels have been trying for years to get another Catholic seat on the board and tip the balance." He asks Hank to run for election, saying, "We don't know how you do it, but you've got Lutherans buying your groceries, and you just might get Lutherans to vote you onto the board." When Hank asks: "What has religion got to to with a public school?" he is told, as an instance, that the Lutherans want to buy old desks, and that the Catholics would rather see the desks burned or trashed (*GO* 246). Hank innocently serves the cause of bigotry when he contributes money to the Holy Angels Men's Club to help buy a house. Told that the purchase is an investment designed to raise money for the parish, he is too innocent to guess that the Catholics are buying the house to thwart the Lutherans. Stan Kimball soon tells him: "You had no idea, did you, that the Lutherans intended to buy Mrs. Ottmann's house and convert it into a parochial school?" (*GO* 307). And on the other side, Catherine is defeated in her bid for school board by an orchestrated write-in campaign by the Lutherans. In Stan Kimball's view, only bigots can afford to go into politics. If you are not a bigot, you alienate both sides (*GO* 250).

The Fosters, as newcomers to Plum, attract the confidences of people in the community who, not members of either major religious group, feel somewhat excluded from both. These partial outsiders, a reader may feel invited to suppose, have an urge to exaggerate what those who are in the dominant groups have an interest in downplaying or denying. Stan Kimball, the undertaker and furniture retailer, who is neither Catholic nor Lutheran, claims to take a sympathetic and detached view of town folkways, but is actually devastatingly critical of them. Similarly, in Dubas's Riverview it was the Baptist minister who expressed the feeling that voting was based on religious affiliation and that there was anti-Catholic feeling in the community (Dubas 65). According to another of Hassler's nonreligious characters, Wallace Flint, "Holy Angels Catholic and Emmanual [*sic*] Lutheran—they compete for places on opposite sides of the cemetery" (*GO* 50). Wallace attributes all of this to "religious hate." Wallace, however, turns out to be the villain of the novel if anyone is. We soon learn that his views are not wholly to be trusted; nevertheless, there is evidence to give credence to claim.

The political issue is subtler, however, than either Stan Kimball or Wallace Flint suggests. Kimball and Flint ignore the existence, suggested in Hassler's description, of a fair body of swing voters who do not vote as members of a religious block. And while Kimball had told Hank earlier in the novel that he would never win regular Lutheran customers, according to the Catholic speaker, Hank has by now done just that and might win Lutheran votes besides.

If religious rivalry is so strong, and if Lutheran voters are in the majority, an impartial reader may be inclined to ask why there are any Catholics at all on the town council and school board. Dubas has a persuasive economic explanation for why communities rather evenly balanced between two sects often show a balanced or nearly balanced membership on elective boards: "If the people of Riverview could be said to have a common purpose, it would be the economic success of the community. Many differences of opinion are subordinated to this common goal" (Dubas 15). In Riverview, economic survival takes priority over sectarian bigotry and brings the divided sides of the town together. In Hassler's Plum, the volunteer fire department is non-partisan. In Lake Wobegon, Bud, the town engineer, notes that plumbing has a higher priority than sectarian rivalries. In Riverview, Catholics are elected to the school board to win Catholic votes necessary to pass bond issues. In economics and politics the impulse to sectarian insularity is present but is generally suppressed.

"On the public boards and councils religious affiliation never overtly generates conflict," Dubas says of Riverview. "However, consensual-style decision making often occurs in advance of a formal vote" (Dubas 22). A principle not strictly observed is that one has a loyalty to one's town. One shops there, even if the same things or better could be bought more cheaply elsewhere. In Lake Wobegon, Clifford's selection of frames is clearly based on Scripture, Keillor as narrator critically and humorously says ("take no thought for what you shall wear. . . ."), but people buy them rather than drive to a neighboring city where the selection is better. Economic loyalty to one's town has limits, but is there. The same is true of economic loyalty to one's sect. In Plum, people generally shop at the stores of their own sect, but when there is a sale, Lutherans buy at the Catholic store, and when the Catholic store had run down, Catholics bought at the Lutheran store. Sectarian loyalty was never the only consideration for either group. Communal and sectarian loyalty may be called weak principles. Dubas says that in Riverview people interact with individuals of different religious affiliations when impelled to by political or economic need. "As a result," she says, "kinship and volunteer groups demonstrate the lowest levels of religious integration in the community, and the business and political groups demonstrate the highest levels of integration" (Dubas 1), and "Despite potential conflict among the members of different religious affiliations, the city council, school boards, and other associations related to civic affairs are well integrated religiously. There is no overt evidence of religiously related conflict on the public level. . . . Those civic and volunteer groups whose membership reflects the business interests of the community are quite well integrated" (Dubas 3). The mayor of Lake Wobegon is Lutheran (*LWD* 235), along with a majority of the town council, reflecting, as in Hassler's town, the realities of political power. Nevertheless, the minority can achieve its successes by appeals to shared communal values. In Lake Wobegon, for example, Father Emil spoke to the town council against a community TV antenna on the water tower and won, though for other reasons than the persuasive force of his eloquence (*LWD* 237).

Furthermore, "membership in the community does not depend on having a good reputation; only upon having a reputation" (Bailey 1917:7 quoted by Dubas 83)—a reputation, that is, that includes membership. The villagers look after those of their own who need looking after, whatever their reputation, and to some extent whatever their religious affiliation. The closeness of all in the community is such that outsiders have difficulty ever feeling comfortable there. In Lake Wobegon, an outsider married to a town girl felt when visiting the town "as if he had walked into the wrong class, medieval history instead of civics which he had studied for, and everyone but him knew the right answers" (*LWD* 268). Dubas remarks that few outsiders last more than five years in Riverview, "even if they are Catholic or Lutheran," unless they have married into the community (Dubas 93). Hassler's Foster family lasts less than a year in Plum. Whatever prejudices members of each religious group hold concerning other groups, community identity is more real than group difference. Each group considers its behavior better than that of the other, Dubas says, then adds: "If there are real differences in behavior, however, they are difficult to define."

When I asked my UN-L freshmen whether people in their home towns were influenced by religious affiliation in deciding where to do business or with whom to socialize, they were scandalized. One would expect that encountering this influence operating in fiction would elicit their strong disapprobation. Religious suspicion and bigotry are deeply woven into the fabric of Hassler's novel, but these elements are there to form a background against which to unfold a plot about the triumph of Christian love. As Wayne Booth reminds us in *Rhetoric of Fiction*, an author is always subtly recommending some values over others. The recommendation is persuasive to the degree that readers accept as accurate to their experience the lives portrayed in the fiction. To readers more critical than my students, Keillor's novel is sometimes less than persuasive because he plays up harmony within the community while acknowledging but playing down sectarian differences. My students haven't read Hassler, but if they did, they would probably regard the sectarian rivalries as exaggerated. They strongly believe, or at least profess, that they and their communities are committed to egalitarian democracy and toleration, and that religious affiliation causes few or no conflicts with those values. For that very reason, though, their sympathy would lie with the characters in Hassler's novel who reject religious bigotry, just the reaction Hassler's fictional stance is designed to elicit. They would be moved by nostalgia at the close of *Lake Wobegon Days* when the narrator says: "Some luck lies in not getting what you thought you wanted but getting what you have, which once you have it you may be smart enough to see is what you would have wanted had you known." They would rejoice with Hassler in his triumphant ending. Young Brendan, Hank's son, who earlier felt guilt for a "sin of omission" in failing to go after Rufus, the town idiot, when he had wandered away, now saves him from falling into a grease pit, even though the touch of Rufus's hand disgusts and repels him. The selfishness and bigotry of sectarians of both persuasions stand in sharp contrast to this action of selfless love. And though even as he rescues Rufus, he "avoided looking into the idiot's repellent face," still "he felt virtuous and mature."

> "Thank you very kindly," said Mrs. Ottmann [Rufus's mother].
>
> "You're welcome," said Brendan, struggling to pry himself free of the idiot's grip.

It could not be clearer that in this case "the idiot" from whom Brendan struggles in vain to free himself is not merely Rufus, but also Christ (*GO* 326).

Note

1 A convenient source of information about Hassler is *Contemporary Authors*, New Revised Series, Volume 21.

Works Cited

Booth, Wayne. *The Rhetoric of Fiction*. Chicago: Chicago UP, 1961.

Dubas, Ellen. *Religious Affiliation and Social Interaction in a Small Town Community*. Dissertation in progress. Ann Arbor, MI: Michigan University Department of Anthropology, 1989.

Hassler, Jon. *Grand Opening*. New York: Ballentine, 1988.

Keillor, Garrison. *Lake Wobegon Days*. New York: Penguin, 1986.

Cornelia James Cannon and Walter Havighurst: Undermining the Immigrant Stereotype in Midwestern Fiction

Kenneth A. Robb

The impact of immigrant scientists on the development of American science has been incalculable, an impression that reading Laura Fermi's *Illustrious Immigrants: The Intellectual Migration from Europe, 1930-41* will confirm. The roster of major scientists who immigrated just during those eleven years is truly impressive—Einstein, Fermi, von Neumann, Godel, Gamow, Meyerhof, Luria, Delbruck, Neurath, and on and on. More recently, in an article on superconductivity, James Gleick described Ching-Wu Chu at the University of Houston, who was believed to have made a breakthrough in that field, as "speaking excitedly into the telephone, using one of the increasingly common languages of American physics—scientific Chinese, every fourth word an English technical term" and referred to Chu's teacher, "the grand old man of superconductivity," at the University of California at San Diego, German-born Bernd Matthias (30). But immigrant scientists have only rarely been represented in American literature.

The protagonists of two novels published before World War II are exceptions. Neither novel is widely known today, though I believe both deserve to be, and both may be of interest to students of midwestern literature. Cornelia James Cannon's *Red Rust* was published in 1928, a first novel; she went on to write another novel, *Heirs* (1930), and children's fiction. The author of the second novel, *The Winds of Spring* (1940), is Walter Havighurst, the well-known historian of the Great Lakes and Midwest. In fact, a forerunner of the protagonist of his novel is

Thure Kumlien, the subject of a sketch in his *Upper Mississippi: A Wilderness Saga*. Both works are historical novels, taking their place with Ole Rolvaag's *Giants in the Earth* (1927) and Johan Bojer's *The Emigrants* (1951-1959) after them, depicting the great nineteenth century Scandinavian immigration to and settlement in the Upper Midwest.

But the protagonists in the novels by Cannon and Havighurst are strikingly different from the protagonists in those other novels. The authors may be reacting against the Scandinavian immigrant pioneer stereotype and indicating that there were others who were *not* like Rolvaag's Per Hansa, "the buoyant, capable, pragmatic pioneer," as Roy W. Meyer has described him (59). An even better example of the stereotype is Peder Wold, the Norwegian immigrant in chapters five through fifteen in Havighurst's *Upper Mississippi* who, we learn as he fades out of the work, "is not an historical character; he is typical" (148)—that is, a carefully constructed stereotype. We first meet Peder, his wife Karen Mari, and their two children as they journey into Wisconsin, build a sod house and barn, break the sod, and plant Indian corn. Their first winter in the sod house, eating spare and repetitious meals, is described. In four or five years, the soil becomes depleted, the land is all taken up; friends stop by and describe "the great plain of Minnesota" (77), and soon Peder is restless to move on. In 1855 they settle briefly in Minnesota, then make the last move, to Dakota Territory. Again, Peder breaks the sod, this time helped by young Peder, and they plant the required ten acres and make a firebreak around their homestead in the sea of grass. The family and their neighbors labor on, surviving prairie fires, four years of plagues of Rocky Mountain locusts devouring everything, and the terrible winters of 1873 and 1881, while all the time newcomers arrive to fill the land. The church is finally built, a typical Norwegian Christmas celebration is described, and at the end of this section, Guri Wold happily marries a Kentuckian, Jeb Robbins, who trades with the Indians and then finally settles down to homesteading. In the end, Peder's image of a *gaard*, surrounded by "carefully tended gardens and fields" (68), which he had brought from Norway as his goal in the New World, has given way before the reality—the openness, the freedom, the immensity—of the Great Plains; he and his family have been transformed into Americans.

In contrast to Peder Wold and his peers in fiction and

nonfiction, the protagonists that Cannon and Havighurst create in their novels are terribly inept farmers and pioneers, but outstandingly successful scientists with considerable intelligence, imagination, and artistic sensibility.

The ineptitude of both protagonists as pioneers arises in part from their devotion to science. At the beginning of Cannon's *Red Rust,* Matts Swenson, who emigrated with his parents from Sweden to Minnesota when he was five, looks out in winter at "the familiar landscape, to the eye of youth so unchanging and unchangeable" (4), yet Matts is also depicted as aware of and fascinated by the teeming life beneath his feet as he walks with a friend: "Though human habitations were few, the world to his observant eye was full of life. He kept drawing August Lindblom's attention to the tracks of birds and rabbits, to the vanishing tail of a fox, or to the caw of a wintering crow" (8). Matts's interest in earthworms, bees, and ants is quickened by his reading of excerpts from Darwin's works which appear from time to time in the *American Farmer's Journal* (13, 26-28, 120 ff.). At last appear passages in which Darwin writes of "Variation and Selection" (26-28); Matts perceives that man may indeed "use this great gift of variability in nature to fill the earth with the best of things" (28), that his world is *not* so "unchanging and unchangeable" as he had thought.

Joined to his desire to be instrumental in bringing about change is Matt's altruism, so that as he reads Darwin's words late at night:

> The narrow walls of the little cabin seemed to part and let Matts's eye of imagination look out upon endless miles of prairie growing only such rich-bearing wheat, and upon grain elevators filled to over-flowing with golden kernels to feed a world of hungry men (28).

A passage from Darwin which he subsequently reads suggests to Matts the possibilities of cross-fertilization, and its closing words ignite his imagination: "Selection only improves; crossing changes the quality" (120). Matts determines to cross wheat grown from the seed of a big, heavy stalk which he had found and saved the previous summer with early-ripening wheat, the seed of which he will obtain from Sweden from an old neighbor of his father, whose hardy wheat his father has often spoken of. Painstakingly, off and on throughout the rest of the novel, Matts plants, cross-fertilizes, selects, and plants again, keeping the necessary records meticulously—until at the end he leaves as his legacy to humankind a hardy wheat that outproduces all other available wheat and is, to top it off, resistant to the scourge of red rust disease.[1]

In contrast to the geneticist of Cannon's *Red Rust* and most other literary Scandinavian immigrants, Jan Carl Sorensen in Havighurst's *The Winds of Spring* is a member of the gentry class in Sweden rather than a peasant and is a university-trained (Upsala) ornithologist, pupil of Elias Fries, who was, in turn, "pupil of the great Linnaeus" (4). On a hiking trip in northern Sweden to find "the roseate Arctic gull that Linnaeus had named and that had not since been found in Sweden, or in any country" (4), Jan falls and breaks his leg just at the point of success. He is rescued and nursed back to health by a peasant family and falls in love with their beautiful daughter, Margretta. When he determines to marry her, Jan is disowned by his father, and by chapter two, Jan and Margretta Sorensen are walking through the wilds of Wisconsin from Milwaukee toward Lake Koshkonong, where they plan to settle.

On the one hand, in *Red Rust* Cannon finds a central analogy for the effect of immigration in Matts's cross-fertilizing wheat from the Old World with wheat from the New to bring out the best traits of each through variation and selection, a symbolism that contemporary reviewers did not overlook.[2] Havighurst, on the other hand, emphasizes more the analogy that physical immigration to the New World opened up new intellectual worlds as well. When Jan Carl Sorensen hears the whippoorwill call at night:

> That strong, bold dusky call stirred him deeply. A voice out of the New World wilderness—the new and little-known world, a small part of which he had made it the object of his life to classify. It came to him with an intense and sudden joy that this was his purpose (63).

Rather than seeking to find and observe again Linnaeus's rare "roseate Arctic gull" in northern Europe, Jan is to contribute new specimens from the New World to the science of ornithology. He perfects his skill at collecting, preserving, and displaying specimens, and soon he is sending them off to Sweden, Germany, England, and Italy (145). His correspondence grows over the following years; as the postmaster reports some six years after Jan's settlement, "He's the best-known man around Cloud Prairie. If the truth was known I guess, he's famous—all those European fellows writing to him. Wax seals on their letters and raised gold crests" (206). The final accolade comes in 1871, when his pupil, a poor boy from a neighboring farm who has become a renowned botanist, returns to Cloud Prairie to report that at a dinner party in Cambridge, Massachusetts, Agassiz had said, referring to Jan, "The best field ornithologist in America lives at Cloud Prairie, Wisconsin" (319).

Both protagonists are sociable: children are especially fond of Matts (14, 39-40), and he is an accomplished, entertaining mimic (65); Jan is an organizer of holiday celebrations and a fascinating story-teller (100, 163, 192-195). But their neighbors and sometimes their wives look upon them as somewhat different, strange men, not cut out to be farmers.

Considering his relationship to others and connecting it with his growing knowledge of Darwin, the young Matts contemplates: "He knew his neighbors thought him queer. Was his queerness a variation in man, working for good or ill, of a kind with those that made for strength or weakness in the plant world?" (30) One neighbor says of him, "Got queer ideas, that fellow has, about spending his time" (100), and when he tries to tell his sister his plans for the wheat, "she thought his interest just a part of the strangeness that made him different from those about him" (123). His father finds him "like a crazy man" and wonders "why he had not been blessed with a nice, steady son like August Lindblom, who never wanted to read, but would hoe all day without saying a word or looking at anything except the weeds under his feet" (188). The Lindbloms, indeed, fit the stereotype of successful Scandinavian immigrants, and although August, Matts's friend from boyhood, admires him, "he could not help comparing the shabby unkemptness of Matts's farm with the neat barn and flourishing fields of the Lindbloms" (302). When Mr. Nelson, the prosperous miller from the big city, drives away after unsuccessfully offering Matts ten dollars for two heads of his improved wheat, he notes "the little farm behind [Matts] with its unmistakable signs of poverty and neglect" and thinks to himself: "*Pretty poor farmer* . . . but it looks to me as if he's got something there. Queer fellow! They says he's a little cracked, and I guess they're right, but there's something wonderful about those two ears of wheat" (272—my italics).

Jan Carl Sorensen, in Havighurst's novel, is initially set off from his neighbors by his higher social class, but soon his odd interest in birds and his inept farming distinguish him also. His new neighbors in Wisconsin "were entranced with this soft-handed newcomer, who was uppish and educated and a liar too. Looking for birds' eggs—more likely he was looking for simple people to listen to his loose tongue" (75). When a wolf raids their henhouse, Margretta sends him out to track it down, but Jan leaves the rifle at a neighbor's and brings back a warbler's nest from the hunt (142). He soon realizes how different he is from his neighbors:

> He worked faithfully, but when the season was over he had produced a scanty crop. The trouble was not in his intention but in something he could not control. *He simply did not have a farmer's instincts.* A row of corn, painfully cultivated, every weed buried under the broken crust of dirt, gave him no joy. It brought only the relief of a task completed (198—my italics).

He thinks of his neighbors (whom we are more accustomed to encountering in Scandinavian immigrant novels than him):

> All around him were farmers whose lives and ancestry had given them a deep personal relation to their work. A thousand years of hunger for land was in their farming. Their harvests were not merely matters of success or failure, but of piercing joy and pain. So their borders crept out (198).

In contrast, when Margretta urges Jan to claim the eighty acres adjoining theirs, he refuses, noting that "we haven't broken all our prairie yet" and hoping to himself that the land will go unclaimed, remain wild. Peter Lund, in this novel, is a close friend of Jan, but in contrast to him, Peter rises steadily from destruction to owning and farming hundreds of acres of land and to sitting on the Chicago Board of Trade (165, 222, 263); he lives the American Dream.

Margretta, having the farmer's instincts Jan lacks, is often baffled. Fortunately, unlike Rovaag's Beret, she is seldom homesick, is strong and healthy, and does more than her share of the farming, though she is discontent when Jan goes out to collect specimens while she works, and at one point she angrily pulls down the shelves on which he has arranged those specimens

(95, 103). It seems that the least exposure to cold and wet brings about the ague in Jan, and as a consequence, Margretta must take over the hard farm labor (127, 165); all too often "while Jan lay burning and quaking, sipping at a cup of coffee mixed with whisky and lying back while his head whirled like a tumbleweed, Margretta plodded over the furrows" (184). But Margretta never ceases to love Jan, and when he has won renown and the respect of his peers, "she realized that he had found another kind of fulfillment than the one she broke her heart for, and though it was beyond her understanding it was not beyond her joy" (319). In Jan's own wife, then, as well as in Peter Lund and Jan's neighbors, we find the aspirations and values usually found in the Scandinavians in immigrant novels, aspirations and values far different from the ones Jan Carl Sorensen holds and fulfills.

In Cannon's novel, Matts's wife, Lena, shares his work, helps him in his experiments, and after he dies, works to bring about the fulfillment of what he had aspired to accomplish. But in creating Lena, Cannon has departed as much from the stereotype of the Scandinavian immigrant's wife as she has departed from the stereotype in creating Matts. Matts first meets Lena as the wife of Olaf Jensen, who settles on land near the Swensons. Olaf beats Lena and abuses his children, and Matts attempts to protect them. Olaf dies in a farm accident about a year after the family's arrival; with his death, a great weight is lifted from Lena:

> There were moments when she seemed, in her thoughts, to have waked from a horrible nightmare. She had to check herself, as if from an indecency of happiness, when she saw by the sympathy of her neighbors how bereft they felt she was. But she could not think tragically of the future (148).

She soon conveys to Matts, who is twelve years her junior, her love for him, and he responds, "I love you, too . . . and I love the children. Would you like to have me come and take care of you and of them?" (195) Their marriage confirms the community in its judgement of both:

> News of Matts's approaching marriage met with universal disapproval. "Just like such a crazy fool," said Burghardt, "loading himself down with a big family and a woman old enough to be his mother. Didn't need to marry her either, as I can see" (201).

But Lena is confident that "she could make him happier in some ways than a younger woman, for she would ask less for herself and she would love his enthusiasms more" (262). Although Matts and Lena do not have children, they find happiness in the children Lena already has; and although Matts eventually discovers that "there lay within him possibilities of feelings more intense, more exquisite, more poignant, than any love he could give to Lena" (265), their marriage is generally a happy one until, in the end, Matts dies from a gunshot wound inflicted by one of Lena's sons who has become insane.

In many passages, the authors of these novels depict their protagonists as responding to nature with a poetic intensity, demonstrating that "it is a mistaken belief that the immigrant has no soul," as Rolvaag put it in his epigraph to *The Boat of Longing*. At one point, for example, Jan is described observing nature:

> Before the mists had risen from Red Lake, he was peering through the milkweed stems at the flocks of wild swans and pelicans that had settled there for the night. As the sun struck through the mist, the swans trumpeted and the pelicans stretched their grotesque wings. Rapidly, like a man in the midst of sudden and fleeting riches, he filled his sketching pad with figures—the pure grace of the swans, the pelicans' heavy flight, the sand-hill cranes stretching their long necks to feed in the sloughs of wild rice (129).

Here is Matts in a similar scene when he has taken some city men out to shoot ducks:

> After a time his bag was full and he put his gun down, watching with a never-sated interest the beautiful creatures swimming back and forth, their webbed feet opening and closing as they pushed ahead, or trailing behind them as they glided through the water. They fed rapidly, lifting their clumsy bodies into the air with a few quick strokes of their wings, brushing the tufted heads of the grasses with their feathered breasts as they passed (223).

Here, it seems to me, are sensibilities that are keener, sharper, more responsive to their surroundings than those of the stereotypical sodbusters.

Cornelia James Cannon went on to write another novel

about immigrants, *Heirs* (1930)—this time about Polish-immigrant farmers and millworkers in New Hampshire. Because the portrayal of immigrants in both novels is very sympathetic and because the symbolism of the wheat in *Red Rust* so clearly points toward the great virtues to be gained from the hybridization of strains from the Old World and the New, it seems quite possible that the author is opposing the general anti-immigrant aspect of the surge of American nativism in the 1920s and 1930s.[3] But the emphasis on Matts's ineptness as a farmer, his unconventional marriage to a widow twelve years his senior, and his distinctive contribution to the development of a rust-resistant strain of wheat may also signify Cannon's dissent from the stereotype of the Swedish-immigrant farmer.

When he wrote *The Winds of Spring,* Walter Havighurst knew Cannon's *Red Rust* and may have been "distantly influenced" by it, but he has "never felt indebted to [her] writing" (personal communication). The democratic inclinations of his novel's protagonist, Jan Carl Sorensen, manifested in his falling in love with the peasant girl, Margretta Heden, are further expressed in his defiance of his father and his emigration to America, but his physical delicacy and his intellectualism continue here to mark him off from the common herd. Nevertheless, although Jan Carl Sorensen might have been "illustrious" by birth in Sweden, in the United States he earns his illustriousness through his scientific achievements. Ironically enough, his perspective on science is that of the taxonomist of the early nineteenth century—establishing classes and orders, finding places in which to fit things, finding things to fit in places, and this is in contrast to the Darwinian and genetic concerns of Matts and his times later in the century. It is interesting that, though it may draw on the historical figure of Thure Kumlien, who is briefly described in *The Upper Mississippi,* for its primary inspiration, Havighurst's *The Winds of Spring* was written and published when the scientists, the "illustrious immigrants" Laura Fermi writes about, were fleeing Europe for the United States.

The choice of science as the alternative to farming for the protagonist's vocation may reflect the prestige of that field at the time the novels were written. The setting of the novels in the Midwest, however, seems inevitable, given the nature of the protagonists and the background and the interests of the novelists. Today, among other things, the novels can serve to remind us of our history and our immigrant heritage—remind us of the diversity of the settlers and admonish us against slothful stereotyping. Above all, I believe that *Red Rust* and *The Winds of Spring* are enterprising, questioning novels that do not deserve to be neglected.

Notes

[1] A few months after *Red Rust* was published, Paul De Kruif, in his *Hunger Fighters* (New York: Harcourt, Brace and Company, 1928), described the work of Mark Alfred Carleton in hybridizing wheat for rust resistance, using Russian strains he had collected (pp. 3-30); this may indicate special interest in the problem at that time.

[2] Rev. of *Red Rust*, by Cornelia James Cannon. *New York Times Book Review* (26 February 1928), 14. The anonymous reviewer goes on to suggest that the "ancient myth" of a "dark agricultural god . . . reincarnated as the dying savior of another alien race" is retold in the novel.

[3] On nativist movements, see, for example, Seymour Martin and Earl Raab, *The Politics of Unreason: Right-Wing Extremism in America, 1790-1970* (New York: Harper and Row, 1970). Or Morris Janowitz, "Black Legions on the March," in *America in Crisis: Fourteen Crucial Episodes in American History*, ed. Daniel Aaron (New York: Alfred A. Knopf, 1952), 304-325.

Works Cited

Bojer, Johan. *The Emigrants*, trans. A. G. Jayne. 1925. Lincoln: U of Nebraska P, 1978.

Cannon, Cornelia James. *Heirs*. Boston: Little, Brown, & Co., 1930.

—. *Red Rust*. Boston: Little, Brown, & Co., 1930.

DeKruif, Paul. *Hunger Fighters*. New York: Harcourt, Brace and Company, 1928.

Fermi, Laura. *Illustrious Immigrants: The Intellectual Migration from Europe, 1930-41*. Chicago: U of Chicago P, 1968.

Gleick, James. "In the Trenches of Science." *New York Times Magazine* 16 August 1987: 30+.

Havighurst, Walter. Personal letter to the author. 19 July 1988.

—. *Upper Midwest: A Wilderness Saga*. New York: Farrar and Rinehart, 1937.

—. *The Winds of Spring*. New York: Macmillan, 1940.

Janowitz, Morris. "Black Legions on the March." *America in Crisis: Fourteen Crucial Episodes in American History*. Ed. Daniel Aaron. New York: Alfred A. Knopf, 1952. 304-325.

Lipset, Seymour Martin and Earl Raab. *The Politics of Unreason*. New York: Harper & Row, 1970.

Meyer, Roy W. *The Middle Western Farm Novel in the Twentieth Century*. Lincoln: U of Nebraska P, 1965.

Moberg, Vilhelm. *The Emigrants. I: The Emigrants.* 1951. *II: Unto a Good Land.* 1954. *III: The Settlers.* 1956. *IV: Last Letter Home.* 1959. Trans. Gustaf Lannestock. New York: Popular Library, n.d.

Rev. of *Red Rust* by Cornelia James Cannon. *New York Times Book Review* 26 February 1928: 14-15.

Rolvaag, Ole. *Giants in the Earth.* 1925. New York: Harper and Brothers, 1929.

—. *The Boat of Longing.* 1921. Trans. Norma Solum. New York: Harper and Brothers, 1933.

Afterword

Midwestern Muckrakers

James Seaton

Muckraking is an old midwestern tradition. Not all of the writers whom President Theodore Roosevelt compared to "the Man with the Muckrake" in John Bunyan's *Pilgrim's Progress* (3) were from the Midwest, but a good many of the muckraking journalists had midwestern roots, such as Ray Stannard Baker, Charles Edward Russell, and David Graham Phillips, from Michigan, Iowa and Indiana respectively, while midwestern novelists like Hamlin Garland, Frank Norris, Theodore Dreiser and Sinclair Lewis (and Phillips as well) extended the muckraking spirit into fiction. Whether the affinity between the Middle West and muckraking arose from the contrast between the native goodness of the plains and the corruption of the East or because the Midwest itself so evidently needed reform is unclear. Lewis Mumford's comment that the best writing of the muckraking era "came from men who were caught in the maw of the Middle West. . . . " (121) points in the latter direction, while V. L. Parrington's suggestion that muckraking arose as the response of "an America still only half urbanized, still clinging to ideals and ways of an older simpler America. . . . " (404) to industrialism suggests the former.

Perhaps both Mumford and Parrington were right. The muckrakers found much to expose in the Midwest itself, but the standards by which the muckrakers judged political chicanery and corporate greed remained the "ideals and ways of an older simpler America." Not that the muckrakers were backward-looking, however. To their great credit they attempted to translate ideals of republican citizenship once meant only for an elite into responsibilities applicable to all those who could afford the new, cheap muckraking magazines like *McClure's, Hampton's* and *Everybody's Magazine.* Ida Tarbell's challenge concluding *The History of the Standard Oil Company* is typical: "And what are we going to do about it? for it is *our* business. We, the people of the United States, and nobody else, must cure whatever is wrong . . . " (292). The great era of muckraking ended with World War I, but the muckraking impulse has not died. Recently two books, both written by midwesterners, have appeared which critique a field ignored by the original muckrakers, perhaps because in pre-World War I America it was itself still governed by the "ideals and ways of an older and simpler America." Today, however, higher education is a growth industry. The college has been replaced by the "multiversity" and the ivory tower by the research institute. Charles J. Sykes's *ProfScam: Professors and the Demise of Higher Education* and Allan Bloom's *The Closing of the American Mind: How Higher Education Has Failed Democracy and Impoverished the Souls of Today's Students* have functioned like typical muckraking works: they have incurred the enmity of the most prominent people in the industry while arousing the public at large. One appeals to common sense and facts, the other to the great books—sources valued by the public, if not by contemporary theorists.

Though neither *Closing* nor *ProfScam* appeals to regional prejudices, the midwestern origin of their authors betrays itself in their muckraking. Bloom is the more explicit. The "fake Gothic buildings" of the University of Chicago fired his imagination by their contrast with the rest of a Middle West "not known for the splendor of its houses of worship or its monuments of political glory." With his first glimpse, the fifteen-year-old Allan Bloom "somehow sensed that I had discovered my life." In declaring his allegiance to values which seem utterly foreign to his region, Bloom re-enacts an old midwestern tradition, dramatized most vividly perhaps in *The Great Gatsby.* As the buildings at the University of Chicago represented to Bloom "the longing for I knew not what" (243), so Dan Cody's yacht anchored off Lake Superior represented to the young James Gatz "all the beauty and glamour in the world" (100-101). Gatsby's intoxication with the glamour of wealth seduces him into terrible moral lapses, errors of taste, and impossible aspirations. An easterner would have been less likely to invest mere money with such misplaced spiritual significance, but an easterner would likewise, in Fitzgerald's telling, have been less likely to possess the "heightened sensitivity to the promises of life," the "romantic readiness" (2) which Nick Carraway admires in Gatsby even after the worse has happened. *Closing* reveals that Bloom has never gotten over his initial intoxication with the university and learning, even though he learned that the buildings he admired were only "pseudo-Gothic" and "that Gothic is not really my taste" (243) anyway. He name-drops great thinkers the way a new midwestern millionaire might reel off his new jet set acquaintances. Bloom remains intoxicated by philosophy, still marked by a midwestern naivete and capacity for wonder. "For me," he says, "the promise of these buildings was fully kept" (244).

Charles Sykes's *ProfScam* is based, as he proudly notes, on an article written by his father, Jay Sykes, for *Milwaukee Magazine*, where Charles Sykes was editor. Sykes himself has taught at the University of Wisconsin at Milwaukee and at Marquette University in Milwaukee. *ProfScam* is a work of journalism, not an intellectual autobiography like *Closing*, and Sykes refrains from playing one region off against another. What he does criticize is the slavish imitation of the most prestigious universities, such as Harvard and Yale, by those wishing to join the charmed circle—such as the University of Illinois or even the University of Wisconsin at Milwaukee. Throughout he cites specifics:

> The upward pressure of small schools struggling toward the light of academic prestige meant that even in schools like the University of Wisconsin's poor relation, the University of Wisconsin-Milwaukee, one professor in the business school taught only four hours a week in a recent semester—all on Monday. (39)

If Bloom's intoxication with philosophy is marked by a midwestern naivete, Sykes's refusal to be awed by titles and degrees is equally midwestern. Because Harvard is "the nation's most prestige-encrusted university" (52), Sykes takes a special interest in noting evidence of its indifference to teaching. With muckraking zeal he employs Harvard's own catalog to calculate the flight of the senior faculty from undergraduate teaching:

> For the 1986-87 academic year, the [history] department listed 69 courses in modern European history, but 31 of them were bracketed [meaning they would not be offered that year]. Of the remaining 38 courses, only 20 were offered in the fall semester; of these only 12 were taught by tenured professors and three of those 12 were courses intended for graduate students. So out of 69 possible courses, only nine courses with full professors were designed solely for undergraduates in the department. (52-53)

Both Sykes and Bloom wish to recall the academy to an era when professors of the liberal arts recognized teaching as their primary responsibility and stood for a set of values different from those of commercial success. Sykes objects that today's professors

> are politicians and entrepreneurs who fiercely protect their turf and shrewdly hustle research cash while they peddle their talents to rival universities, businesses, foundations, or government. (7)

Sykes finds that today's university, like its professors, is "insatiable, opportunistic, and implacably anti-intellectual" (7); he laments "the tendency of American higher education to judge success on the basis of contracts, cash and clout" (234). In other words, he criticizes academics for accepting the standards of the society around them.

It is likewise Bloom's biggest objection to contemporary universities that their professors can discover no other standards than those of the society around them. Missed in the usual categorization of *The Closing of the American Mind* as a right-wing diatribe is Bloom's point that the "openness" promoted by academia makes criticism of the status quo impossible: "Openness, as currently conceived, is a way of making surrender to whatever is most powerful, or worship of vulgar success, look principled" (41). He can think of no stronger criticism of popular music than to say: "The rock business is perfect capitalism, supplying to demand and helping to create it. It has all the moral dignity of drug trafficking . . . " (76). Like Sykes, Bloom looks to the university for dedication to higher principles than those found in society at large. The university, argues Bloom, surrenders with equal swiftness to commercial ethics or to shouting students because it no longer believes in any code of ethics of its own. "The university," insists Bloom, "has to stand for something" (337).

Both Bloom and Sykes hold professors and universities to standards that go beyond the "contracts, cash and clout" which define success in the marketplace. In 1914 Walter Lippmann observed that the muckrakers had convinced the public that politicians should abide by standards of conduct beyond those of ordinary business. Lippmann nevertheless refrained from attacking the muckrakers for lack of realism or the public for hypocrisy. Instead, he argued that the insistence of the muckrakers on a higher standard of judgment for public officials "is one of the hopeful signs of the age. For it means that unconsciously men regard some of the interests of life as too important for the intrusion of commercial ethics" (30). Whatever else Sykes and Bloom are saying, they are arguing that the life of the mind as institutionalized in colleges and universities is among "the interests of life" to which Lippmann refers.

Politics, the muckrakers believed, was too important to be left to the politicians alone. To those numerous academics who resent the scrutiny of higher education by non-professionals incited by Bloom and Sykes, non-academics readers might reply, in the words of Ida Tarbell, "it is *our* business." And, every once in a while, one comes across an actual professor whose career reveals that the ideal of Sykes and Bloom is not entirely a fantasy.

David Anderson has never been particularly interested in "contracts, cash and clout," despite a bibliography that would guarantee all three in abundance. The contrast with current trends may be captured by Charles Sykes's quotation from Stanley Fish, chair at Duke, as Fish explains his willingness and ability to snare hot theoreticians—most of whom consider themselves ultraradical—by offering them six-figure salaries: "It's analogous to what's happening in the NBA. You no longer have the firm assumption that a star will play his whole career with one team" (192).

David Anderson has been playing in a different league. He has remained at Michigan State University throughout his teaching career, despite a record that by anybody's standards would make him a prize catch in the most prestigious programs. Even more amazing, he has spent his entire career teaching freshman composition, a task that, as Sykes documents, is almost universally foisted on graduate students or academic part-timers. The Society for the Study of Midwestern Literature, which he founded, has not been a vehicle for empire building but rather a means to encourage and assist younger scholars, including myself. David Anderson's books do not announce a radical theoretical transformation, nor do they otherwise draw attention to their author; they do convey the scope of the cultural heritage of the Midwest in clear, economic prose.

If Charles Sykes and Allan Bloom were to meet David Anderson, no doubt arguments would ensue. David Anderson would not agree with many of Charles Sykes's recommendations for minimizing professorial "scams," and he would have much to debate with Allan Bloom. But he might recognize in their work a rebirth of midwestern muckraking, and they might recognize in him evidence that the principles they reaffirm have not entirely vanished from American universities.

Works Cited

Bloom, Allan. *The Closing of the American Mind: How Higher Education Has Failed Democracy and Impoverished the Souls of Today's Students.* Forward by Saul Bellow. New York: Simon and Schuster, 1987.

Fitzgerald, F. Scott. *The Great Gatsby.* 1925. New York: Scribner's, 1953.

Lippmann, Walter. *Drift and Mastery: An Attempt to Diagnose the Current Unrest.* 1914. Ed. William E. Leuchtenburg. Madison: U of Wisconsin P, 1985.

Mumford, Lewis. *The Golden Day: A Study in American Literature and Culture.* 1926. Boston: Beacon, 1957.

Parrington, Vernon Louis. *The Beginnings of Critical Realism in America.* 1930. Ed. E. H. Eby. Vol. III of *Main Currents in American Thought.* New York: Harcourt, 1958.

Roosevelt, Theodore. "Speech, April 14, 1906." *The Muckrakers and American Society.* Ed. Herbert Shapiro. Boston: Heath, 1968. 3-8.

Sykes, Charles J. *ProfScam: Professors and the Demise of Higher Education.* Washington, D.C.: Regnery, 1988.

Tarbell, Ida M. *The History of the Standard Oil Company.* 1904. Vol. 2. Gloucester, MA: Smith, 1963. 2 vols., 1.

Chronological Bibliography of the Published Writings of David D. Anderson

Ronald M. Grosh

Books and Editorships

Critical Studies in American Literature. Karachi, Pakistan: The University of Karachi, 1964.

Louis Bromfield. New York: Twayne, 1964.

Sherwood Anderson. New York: Holt, Rinehart and Winston, 1967.

Sherwood Anderson's Winesburg, Ohio. New York: Barron Publishers, 1967.

Brand Whitlock. New York: Twayne, 1968.

Editor-in-chief: *The Black Experience.* East Lansing: Michigan State UP, 1969.

Abraham Lincoln. New York: Twayne, 1970.

Editor: *The Literary Works of Abraham Lincoln.* Columbus, Ohio: Charles E. Merrill, 1970.

Co-editor: *The Dark and Tangled Path.* Boston: Houghton-Mifflin, 1971.

Editor: *SSML Newsletter,* Vols. I-IX. East Lansing: Society for the Study of Midwestern Literature, 1971 to date.

Suggestions for the Instructor. Philadelphia: J. B. Lippincott, 1971.

Editor: *Sunshine and Smoke: American Writers and the American Environment.* Philadelphia: J. B. Lippincott, 1971.

Robert Ingersoll. New York: Twayne, 1972.

Editor: *MidAmerica,* (Yearbook for the Society for the Study of Midwestern Literature), Vols. I-XVII. East Lansing: The Midwestern Press, 1974 to date.

Editor: *Midwestern Miscellany,* Vols. I-II, IV-IX, and XI-XVII. East Lansing: The Midwestern Press, 1974 to date.

Editor: Sherwood Anderson's *Home Town.* Mamaroneck, NY: Paul P. Appel, 1975.

Editor: *Sherwood Anderson: Dimensions of his Literary Art.* East Lansing: Michigan State UP, 1976.

Regional Editor: *American Literary Manuscripts: A Checklist.* Athens: U of Georgia P, 1977.

Woodrow Wilson. Boston: Twayne, 1978.

Editor: *Sherwood Anderson: The Writer at his Craft.* Mamaroneck, NY: Paul P. Appel, 1979.

Ignatius Donnelly. Boston: Twayne, 1980.

Editor: *Critical Studies on Sherwood Anderson.* Boston: G. K. Hall, 1981.

Williams Jennings Bryan. Boston: Twayne, 1981.

Editor: *Michigan: A State Anthology.* Detroit: Gayle Research, 1983.

Editor: Sherwood Anderson Special Issue of *The Old Northwest* XV (1992).

Essays Collected in Books and Annuals

"Brand Whitlock." *Literary Ohio.* Cleveland: World Publishing, 1966.

"The Grotesques and George Willard." *Sherwood Anderson, Winesburg Ohio.* New York: Viking, 1966.

"Louis Bromfield." *Literary Ohio.* Cleveland: World Publishing, 1966.

"Sherwood Anderson After Twenty Years." *The Achievement of Sherwood Anderson.* Chapel Hill: U of North Carolina P, 1966.

"Pakistan's Search for National Identity." *Course of Study.* Washington, DC: National War College, 1967.

"Mohammed Iqbal." *Encyclopedia of World Literature of the Twentieth Century,* Vol. II. New York: Frederick Ungar, 1969.

"Pakistani Literature." *Encyclopedia of World Literature of the Twentieth Century,* Vol. III. New York: Frederick Ungar, 1971.

"Sherwood Anderson and the Coming of the New Deal." *Criti-*

cism and Culture (Papers of the Midwest Modern Language Association, 1969), 1972.

"Linguism, National Unity, and National Identity in Pakistan." *Resumes des Communications* XXIX. Congres Internationale des Orientalistes: Paris, 1973.

"The Boy's World of Booth Tarkington." *Midwestern Miscellany* I (1974).

"The Dimensions of the Midwest." *MidAmerica I,* (1974).

"Minnesota's Seven-Storied Mountaineer." *Midwestern Miscellany* II, 1975.

"The Uncritical Critics: American Realists and the Lincoln Myth." *MidAmerica* II (1975).

"Anderson and Myth." *Sherwood Anderson: Dimensions of his Literary Art.* East Lansing: Michigan State UP, 1976.

"The Art of the Midwestern Campaign Biography." *Midwestern Miscellany* IV (1976).

"Contemporary Pakistani Poetry: A Confluence of Traditions." *Resumenes: Asia del Sur.* Mexico City: 30 Congresso de Crencias Humans, 1976.

"Life, Not Death, Is the Great Adventure." *Sherwood Anderson: Dimensions of his Literary Art.* East Lansing: Michigan State UP, 1976.

"Linguism, National Unity, and National Identity in Pakistan." *Inde Moderne.* Paris: L'Asiatheque, 1976.

"Notes Toward a Definition of the Mind of the Midwest." *MidAmerica* III (1976).

"The Search for a Living Past." *Sherwood Anderson: Centennial Studies.* Troy, NY: Whitston, 1976.

"The Sherwood Anderson Centenary." *The Sherwood Anderson Centenary Program.* East Lansing, 1976.

"Brand Whitlock's Popular Political Reality." *Midwestern Miscellany* V (1977).

"The Queen City and a New Literature." *MidAmerica* IV (1977).

"Culture, Conflict, and Isolation: Three Commonwealth Writers in the Twilight of Empire." *Individuality and Community in Commonwealth Literature.* Valletta, Malta: The University of Malta, 1978.

"Dispersion and Direction: Sherwood Anderson, the Chicago Renaissance, and the American Mainstream." *MidAmerica* V (1978).

"Ignatius Donnelly in Retrospect." *Midwestern Miscellany* VI (1978).

"The Midwestern Town in Midwestern Fiction." *MidAmerica* VI (1978).

"Directions and Dimensions of American Literacy Studies in the 1980's." *Directions and Dimensions of American Culture Studies in the 1980's.* Bowling Green, OH: Bowling Green Popular P, 1979.

"'From East-Side to South-Side with Love': The Friendship of Sherwood Anderson and Paul Rosenfeld." *Midwestern Miscellany* VII (1979).

"Louis Bromfield." *Major Writers in English.* London: St. Martin's Press, 1979.

"Christopher Morley." *Dictionary of American Biography.* Supplement Six. New York: Charles Scribner's Sons, 1980.

"Daniel Drake, M.D.: The Franklin of the West." *MidAmerica* VII (1980).

"Eliot Paul." *Dictionary of American Biography.* Supplement Six. New York: Charles Scribner's Sons, 1980.

"*The Little Review* and Sherwood Anderson." *Midwestern Miscellany* VIII (1980).

"Louis Bromfield." *Dictionary of American Biography.* Supplement Six. New York: Charles Scribner's Sons, 1980.

"Michigan Proletarian Writers and the Great Depression." *A Half Century Ago: Michigan in the Great Depression.* East Lansing: Michigan State University, 1980.

"Octavus Roy Cohen." *Dictionary of American Biography.* Supplement Six. New York: Charles Scribner's Sons, 1980.

"Mary Roberts Rinehart." *Dictionary of American Biography.* Supplement Six. New York: Charles Scribner's Sons, 1980.

"Sinclair Lewis and the Nobel Prize." *MidAmerica* VIII (1981).

"Anderson and Myth." *Critical Essays on Sherwood Anderson.* Boston: G. K. Hall, 1981.

"Brand Whitlock." *A Bibliographic Guide to Midwestern Literature.* Iowa City: University of Iowa Press, 1981.

"Flannery O'Connor." *Dictionary of American Biography.* Supplement Seven. New York: Charles Scribner's Sons, 1981.

"Louis Bromfield." *A Bibliographic Guide to Midwestern Literature.* Iowa City: U of Iowa P, 1981.

"Louis Bromfield." *Dictionary of Literary Biography* 9, Part I. Detroit: Gale Research, 1981.

"The Professor and the Community: Program Development in Continuing Education." *Continuing Education and Development.* Kuwait University, 1981.

"Robert Hillyer." *Dictionary of American Biography*. Supplement Seven. New York: Charles Scribner's Sons, 1981.
"Sherwood Anderson." *A Bibliographic Guide to Midwestern Literature*. Iowa City: U of Iowa P, 1981.
"Sherwood Anderson and the Critics." *Critical Essays on Sherwood Anderson*. Boston: G. K. Hall, 1981.
"Sherwood Anderson in Retrospect." *Critical Essays on Sherwood Anderson*. Boston: G. K. Hall, 1981.
"Sherwood Anderson's Moments of Insight." *Critical Essays on Sherwood Anderson*. Boston: G. K. Hall, 1981.
"Three Generations of Missouri Fiction." *Midwestern Miscellany* IX (1981).
"Michigan Proletarian Writers in the Great Depression." *Mid-America* IX (1982).
"The Old Northwest, the Midwest, and the Making of Three American Iconoclasts." *Collected Essays on Ambrose Bierce*. Boston: G. K. Hall, 1982.
"From Memory to Meaning: The Boy's Stories of William Dean Howells, Clarence Darrow, and Sherwood Anderson." *MidAmerica* X (1983).
"Linguism, National Unity, and National Identity in Pakistan." *English Across Cultures*. Dortmund, Germany: Verlag Lambert Lensing GMBH, 1983.
"Midwestern Writers and the Myth of the Search." *Modern American Literature*. New York Frederick Ungar, 1983.
"The Room, the City, and the War: Saul Bellow's *Dangling Man*." *Midwestern Miscellany* XI (1983).
"Sherwood Anderson, Chicago, and the Midwestern Myth." *MidAmerica* XI (1984).
"Sherwood Anderson's Grotesques and Modern American Fiction." *Midwestern Miscellany* XII (1984).
"Chicago Cityscapes by Theodore Dreiser, Sherwood Anderson, Saul Bellow." *Midwestern Miscellany* XIII (1985).
"The Dean's Chicago." *MidAmerica* XII (1985).
"Sinclair Lewis and the Midwestern Tradition." *Sinclair Lewis at 100: Papers Presented at a Centennial Conference*. St. Cloud, MN: St. Cloud State U, 1985.
"Mark Twain, Sherwood Anderson, Saul Bellow, and the Territories of the Spirit." *MidAmerica* XIII (1986).
"'That Somber City' Since MidCentury." *Midwestern Miscellany* XIV (1986).
"The Greeley Phenomenon, or Some Parish! Some Priest!"

Midwestern Miscellany XV (1987).
"Sherwood Anderson's *Poor White* and the Grotesques Become Myth." *MidAmerica* XIV (1987).
"Hemingway and Henderson in the High Savannas, or Two Midwestern Moderns and the Myth of Africa." *MidAmerica* XV (1988).
"Saul Bellow and the Midwestern Tradition: Beginnings." *Midwestern Miscellany* XVI (1988).
"Jack Conroy and Proletarian Fiction." *Midwestern Miscellany* XVII (1989).
"Louis Bromfield." *Dictionary of Literary Biography* 86: *American Short Story Writers, 1910-1945.* Detroit: Gale Research, Inc., 1989.
"Sherwood Anderson." *Dictionary of Literary Biography* 86: *American Short Story Writers, 1910-1945.* Detroit: Gale Research, Inc., 1989.
"Sherwood Anderson in Fiction." *MidAmerica* XVI (1989).
"John Herrmann, Midwestern Modern, Part I." *Midwestern Miscellany* XVIII (1990).
"Sherwood Anderson Remembered." *MidAmerica* XVII (1990).
"John Herrmann, Part II." *Midwestern Miscellany* XIX (1991).
"Sherwood Anderson After Fifty Years." *The Old Northwest* XV (1992).

Journal Articles and Essays

Benjamin Rush: Pioneer Educational Philosopher." *College of Education Quarterly* V (1959).
"Emerson and Lincoln." *The Lincoln Herald* LXIX (1958).
"The Man Who Nominated Lincoln." *Northwest Ohio Quarterly* XXVI (1959).
"Margaret Fuller's Great Lakes Tour." *Inland Seas* XV (1959).
"Nationalism in Early American Literature." *National Republic* XLVI (1959).
"A Comparison of the Poetic Theories of Emerson and Poe." *The Personalist* XII (1960).
"Robbery or Warfare." *Northwest Ohio Quarterly* XXXII (1960).
"Small Boys and French Explorers." *Ohioana* III (1960).
"Walt Whitman: Nineteenth Century Man." *Walt Whitman Birthplace Bulletin* IV (1960).

"Walt Whitman's Poetic Philosophy." *Walt Whitman Birthplace Bulletin* IV (1960).
"The Battle of Fort Stephenson." *Northwest Ohio Quarterly* XXXIII (1961).
"Charles Dickens on Lake Erie." *Inland Seas* XVII (1961).
"Emerging Awareness in Sherwood Anderson's *Tar*." *Ohioana* IV (1961).
"Horace Greeley on Michigan's Upper Peninsula." *Inland Seas* XVII (1961).
"Major Small and *The Red Badge of Courage*." *The Lincoln Herald* LXIII (1961).
"Melville and Mark Twain in Rebellion." *Mark Twain Journal* XI (1961).
"Melville Criticism, Past and Present." *Midwest Quarterly* II (1961).
"The Second Michigan Cavalry Under Philip H. Sheridan." *Michigan History* XL (1961).
"A Transcendental View of Niagara." *Niagara Frontier* VIII (1961).
"Abraham Lincoln at Niagara." *Niagara Frontier* VIII (1962).
"A Comparison of the Poetic Theories of Emerson and Poe." *Revista De Estetica* III (1962). (Trans. into Italian.)
"The Fiction of the Great Lakes." *Northwest Ohio Quarterly* XXXIV (1962).
"John Disturnell Introduces the Great Lakes to America." *Inland Seas* XVIII (1962).
"Melville's Major Themes in Minor Keys." *Artesian* VII (1962).
"Poe's 'Ligeia' and his Literary Theory." *Artesian* VII (1962).
"The Remarkable Piatt Brothers of Mac-O-Chee." *Ohioana* V (1962).
"Sherwood Anderson's Use of the Lincoln Theme." *The Lincoln Herald* LXIV (1962).
"Sherwood Anderson After Twenty Years." *The Midwest Quarterly* III (1962).
"Songs and Sayings of the Lakes." *Midwest Folklore* XII (1962).
"Sherwood Anderson's Idea of the Grotesque." *Ohioana* VI (1963).
"American Literature in its Cultural Complex." *University College Quarterly* IX (1964).
"Contemporary Pakistani Literature." *The Pakistan Quarterly* XII (1964).
"English Writing in Pakistan." *Scintilla* V (1964).

"Pakistani Poetry Today." *Panorama* XVI (1964).

"American Literature in its Cutural Complex." *The American Journal* V (1965).

"American Literature in its Cultural Complex." *Ceylon Daily News* October 12, 1965.

"American Literature in its Cultural Complex." *Contemporary Magazine* I August 16, 1965. (Trans. into Chinese.)

"English Travelers to Niagara, 1785-1830." *New York History* XLVI (1965).

"Film Making in Pakistan." *Films in Review* XVI (1965).

"Helping a New Nation Emerge: The University of Karachi." *University College Quarterly* X (1965).

"The Odyssey of Petroleum V. Nasby." *Ohio History* LXXIL (1965).

"On Re-Discovering Brand Whitlock." *Ohioana* VIII (1965).

"Abraham Lincoln, Man of Letters." *University College Quarterly* XII (1967). (Reprinted by USIA, 1967.) (Trans. into Japanese in *Nichibei Forum* XIII [1967].)

"Brand Whitlock's Search for the Jeffersonian Ideal." *Papers of the Michigan Academy of Science, Arts and Letters* LI (1966).

"Ernest Hemingway, Voice of an Era." *The Personalist* XXVII (1966).

"Pakistani Literature Today." *Literature East and West* X (1966).

"Pakistan's Search for National Identity." *The Yale Review* LV (1966). (Reprinted by USIA, 1967.)

"Abraham Lincoln, Man of Letters." *The American Journal* VII (1967).

"Along the Great Trunk Road." *The Asian Student* December 16, 1967. (Review article.)

"The Artist in America." *University College Quarterly* XIV (1968). (Reprinted by USIA, 1967.)

"Hinduism, Islam, and Buddhism." *The Asian Student* October 7, 1967. (Review article.)

"Kipling in India: His Apprenticeship Years." *The Asian Student* December 2, 1967. (Review article.)

"New Insight in the Pakistani Short Story." *University College Quarterly* XII (1967).

"Pakistan Short Story Writers Discover New Horizons." *The Leader* October 6, 1967.

"Modern Asian Writing." *The Asian Student* XVII November 2, 1968. (Review article.)

"The Knowing Critic." *University College Quarterly* XIV (1969).
"The World of Willa Cather." *SSML Newsletter* II (1972).
"American Studies and American Tradition." *The American Examiner* (1973).
"Can Ohio and the Midwest Claim Ambrose Bierce?" *Ohioana* XIV (1973).
"Childhood Memories." *The Asian Student* XXI (January 6, 1973).
"A Departure in Criticism." *Ohioana* XVI (1973).
"The Idea of a Univesity: An Editorial Perspective." *University College Quarterly* XVIII (1973).
"The International Dimensions of General Education: An Editorial Perspective." *University College Quarterly* XIX (1973).
"Literary Miscellanies and Literary Study." *SSML Newsletter* III (1973).
"The Pleasures of Reviewing." *SSML Newsletter* III (1973).
"The Recognition of Reality." *Ohioana* XVI (1973).
"Sherwood Anderson's Real World." *Ohioana Quarterly* XVI (1973).
"Was He or Wasn't He? Warren G. Harding and His Biographers." *SSML Newsletter* III (1973).
"Women in Higher Education: An Editorial Perspective." *University College Quarterly* XVIII (1973).
"The Academic Dialogue: An Editorial Perspective." *University College Quarterly* XIX (1974).
"A Checklist of Midwestern Publishers." *SSML Newsletter* IV (1974).
"Chicago as Metaphor." *Great Lakes Review* I (1974).
"Cincinnati Publishing and the McGuffey Readers." *SSML Newsletter* IV (1974).
"Jack Conroy's Return." *SSML Newsletter* IV (1974).
"A Major New Chicago Novel." *SSML Newsletter* IV (1974).
"The University College at Thirty: An Editorial Perspective." *University College Quarterly* XX (1974).
"University Presses, Reprinted Works, and the Study of Midwestern Literature." *SSML Newsletter* IV (1974).
"Ahmed Ali and the Growth of a Pakistani Literary Tradition in English." *World Literature Written in English* XIV (1975).
"The Boy Scout Books and America in Transition." *Journal of Popular Culture* VIII (1975).
"General Education and the Last Quarter of the Twentieth Century." *University College Quarterly* XX (1975).

"Linguism, National Unity, and National Identity." *The Centennial Review* XIX (1975).
"Nuts and Bolts: An Editorial Perspective." *University College Quarterly* XXI (1975).
"The Professor and the World: An Editorial Perspective." *University College Quarterly* XX (1975).
"Sherwood Anderson, Teacher of Writing and his 'Writer's Book.'" *SSML Newsletter* V (1975).
"Willa Cather's Second Century." *SSML Newsletter* V (1975).
"The American Bicentennial and General Education: An Editorial Perspective." *University College Quarterly* XXI (1976).
"Bittersweet Moments." *The Asian Student* September 1976.
"The Collected Works of Abraham Lincoln Supplement." *Resources for American Literary Study* VI (1976).
"Do We or Don't We? An Editorial Perspective." *University College Quarterly* XXII (1976).
"Frederick Manfred and Siouxland." *SSML Newsletter* VI (1976).
"Literary Accomplishment of Anderson Impressive." Smyth County (VA) *News* September 7, 1976.
"A Memorial to John T. Frederick (1893-1975)." *SSML Newsletter* VI (1976).
"Midwestern Writers and Visions of the Land." *SSML Newsletter* IV (1976).
"New Books." *The Winesburg Eagle* I (1976).
"Revitalizing General Education: An Editorial Perspective." *University College Quarterly* XXI (1976).
"Sherwood Anderson and the Editors of *Time*." *American Notes & Queries* XV (1976).
"The Sherwood Anderson Centenary." *Ohio Quarterly* XIX (1976).
"Sherwood Anderson's First Century." *SSML Newsletter* VI (1976).
"The Study of Midwestern Literature: The State of the Art." *SSML Newsletter* VI (1976).
"Whose Machines in How Many Gardens?" *American Examiner* IV (1976).
"Woodrow Wilson, Man of Letters." *University College Quarterly* XXI (1976).
"The Beginnings of Ohio Literature." *Great Lakes Review* III (1977).
"The Future of General Education? An Editorial Perspective." *University College Quarterly* XXII (1977).

"A Humanist Speaks." Michigan State University *News Bulletin* January 13, 1977.

"Louis Bromfield, France, and the Ohio Countryside." *Adena* II (1977).

"On Keeping the Fulbright Record Straight." *The Fulbrighter Newsletter* I (1977).

"On Being a Generalist: An Editorial Perspective." *University College Quarterly* XXIII (1977).

"On Talking With Authors." *SSML Newsletter* VII (1977).

"A Partial Checklist of Midwestern General Magazines." *SSML Newsletter* VII (1977).

"Regional Reality: An Approach to Fiction." *SSML Newsletter* VII (1977).

"The Resurgence of General Education: An Editorial Perspective." *University College Quarterly* XXII (1977). (Reprinted in Michigan State University's *News Bulletin* January 20, 1977.)

"Sherwood Anderson: A Photographic Gallery." *Twentieth Century Literature* XXIII (1977).

"The Academic Community: An Editorial Perspective." *University College Quarterly* XXIII (1978).

"Edward A. Carlin and General Education: An Editorial Perspective." *University College Quarterly* XXIII (1978).

"On Re-Discovering Brand Whitlock." *SSML Newsletter* VIII (1978).

"On Teaching Writing: An Editorial Perspective." *University College Quarterly* XXIII (1978).

"A Profession, An Obligation, or a Way of Life: An Editorial Perspective." *University College Quarterly* XXIII (1978).

"The Changing Nature of General Education: An Editorial Perspective." *University College Quarterly* XXIV (1979).

"The Durability of Sherwood Anderson." *SSML Newsletter* IX (1979).

"From Main Street to South Street." *Wintermur Portfolio* XIV (1979). (Review essay.)

"The Generalist and the Study of Man: An Editorial Perspective." *University College Quarterly* XXIV (1979).

"A Glimpse at the Past." *SSML Newsletter* IX (1979).

"The Humanist and General Education: An Editorial Perspective." *University College Quarterly* XXIV (1979).

"A Humanities Perspective on World Crisis." *University College Quarterly* XXIV (1979).

"James T. Farrell: Memoir." *SSML Newsletter* IX (1979).

"The Midwest and the American Mainstream." *SSML Newsletter* IX (1979).

"Sherwood Anderson and the Two Faces of America." *The Winesburg Eagle* V (1979).

"Where Are We Going? An Editorial Perspective." *University College Quarterly* XXIV (1979).

"The Humanities and Graduate Education: An Editorial Perspective." *University College Quarterly* XXV (1980).

"Illinois! Illinois!" *Resources for American Literary Study* X (1980).

"Louis Bromfield's Myth of the Ohio Frontier." *The Old Northwest* VI (1980).

"Melville E. Stone, Eugene Field, and the Beginning of Chicago Literary Journalism." *SSML Newsletter* X (1980).

"Midwestern Writers and the Myth of the Search." *Georgia Review* XXXIV (1980).

"The Ohio Authors Program." *The Old Northwest* VI (1980).

"A Perspective on the University." *University College Quarterly* XXV (1980).

"Politics, Policies, and Procedures: An Editorial Perspective." *University College Quarterly* XXV (1980).

"Sherwood Anderson and the Seven Arts." *SSML Newsletter* X (1980).

"The State of the Society: An Editorial." *SSML Newsletter* X (1980).

"With Neither a Bang nor a Whimper: An Editorial Perspective." *University College Quarterly* XXV (1980).

"Another Biography? For God's Sake, Why?" *The Georgia Review* XXXV (1981).

"Brand Whitlock and Illinois Grassroots Politics." *Western Illinois Regional Studies* IV (1981).

"The Midwestern City as Metaphor and Reality." *SSML Newsletter* XI (1981).

"The New Regionalism and the Study of Popular American Culture." *SSML Newsletter* XI (1981).

"Sherwood Anderson and Edmund Wilson." *SSML Newsletter* XI (1981).

"Christopher Gist, Benjamin Lincoln, and the Opening of the Midwest." *SSML Newsletter* XII (1982).

"A Portrait of Jim Tully: An Ohio Hobo in Hollywood." *SSML Newsletter* XII (1982).

"Sherwood Anderson's Technologically Displaced Persons." *SSML Newsletter* XII (1982).

"The Lost Dauphin and the Myth and Literature of the Midwestern Frontier." *SSML Newsletter* XIII (1983).

"The Way it Was: Jessamyn West's *The Witch-Diggers*." *SSML Newsletter* XIII (1983).

"Sherwood Anderson, Letter Writer." *SSML Newsletter* XIV (1984).

"American Regionalism, the Midwest, and the Study of Modern American Literature." *SSML Newsletter* XV (1985).

"Ohio and the Demon." *SSML Newsletter* XV (1985).

"Sherwood Anderson, Letter Writer II." *SSML Newsletter* XV (1985).

"The Carrie Phillips Letters and the Presidency of Warren D. Harding." *SSML Newsletter* XVI (1986).

"From Marion, Ohio, Schoolroom to White House Cloakroom." *SSML Newsletter* XVI (1986).

"The Novelist as Playwright: Saul Bellow on Broadway." *The Saul Bellow Journal* V (1986).

"Sherwood Anderson's Letters." *Resources for American Literary Study* XIII (1986).

"The Writer's True Self." *Northwestern Ohio Quarterly* LVII (1986).

"The Chicago Short Fiction of Sherwood Anderson and Saul Bellow." *SSML Newsletter* XVII (1987).

"The Northwest Ordinance and the Emergence of The American Midwest: Some Bicentennial Observations." *SSML Newsletter* XVII (1987).

"Sherwood Anderson, Diarist." *SSML Newsletter* XVII (1987).

"The Eighteenth Annual Conference." *SSML Newsletter* XVIII (1988).

"George Ade: An American Original." *SSML Newsletter* XVIII (1988).

"A Measured Passion." *SSML Newsletter* XVIII (1988).

"Saul Bellow, Sojourner in New York." *Saul Bellow Journal* VII (1988).

"Sherwood Anderson: 'For the End.'" *SSML Newsletter* XVIII (1988).

"Sherwood Anderson's Letters." *Studies in American Fiction* XV (1988).

"Sherwood Anderson's Letters from the West." *SSML Newsletter* XVIII (1988).

"Frederick Manfred's Mid-America." *SSML Newsletter* XIX (1989).

"Hemingway and Henderson on the High Savannas: Or, Two Midwestern Moderns and the Myth of Africa." *Saul Bellow Journal* VIII (1989).

"Life Not Death Is the Great Aventure." *Northwest Ohio Quarterly* LXI (1989).

"The Nineteenth Annual Conference." *SSML Newsletter* XIX (1989).

"Thomas Beer." *SSML Newsletter* XIX (1989).

"William Dean Howells, William Howard Taft, George Harvey, and the Continuity of American Prose Fiction." *SSML Newsletter* XIX (1989).

"Women Poets and the Midwestern Literary Tradition." *SSML Newsletter* XIX (1989).

"My Lake Erie." *SSML Newsletter* XX (1990).

"The Roads of Regional America." *SSML Newsletter* XX (1990).

"Songs and Sayings of the Lakes." *SSML Newsletter* XX (1990).

"Twenty Years of Midwestern Literary Study." *SSML Newsletter* XX (1990).

Short Fiction

"Perfect Crime." *Eyas* IV (1949).

"Displaced Person." *Eyas* IV (1949).

"No Life to Go On." *Eyas* V (1950).

"Thirty Years to Midnight." *Eyas* VI (1950).

"Marionette." *Eyas* VI (1951).

"Italian Interlude." *Eyas* VI (1951).

"The Shadowed Path." *Eyas* VII (1952).

"The Path in the Shadow." *The Stylus* VII (1956).

"The Long Clear View." *Artesian* V (1960).

"By Bread Alone." *Vision* XIII (1964).

"The God-Hungry Ones." *Vision* XIII (1964). (Serialized in four parts.)

Verse

Three poems collected in *In Other than Scholarly Ways*. East Lansing: Years Press, 1980.

Contributors

Roger J. Bresnahan is Professor of American Thought and Language at Michigan State University. He has published several books on Philippine literature and Philippine-American relations, most recently *Angles of Vision: Conversations on Philippine Writing* (New Day, 1992), as well as numerous articles and book reviews on midwestern authors and on Southeast Asian studies. He serves as corresponding secretary of the Society for the Study of Midwestern Literature.

Scott Donaldson is Louise G. T. Cooley Professor of English Emeritus at the College of William and Mary in Williamsburg, Virginia. He has been Fulbright senior lecturer in Finland and Italy and Bruern fellow at the University of Leeds. He is the author of five literary biographies, including *Fool for Love: F. Scott Fitzgerald* (1983), *John Cheever: A Biography* (1988), and *Archibald MacLeish: An American Life* (1992).

Bernard F. Engel is Professor of American Thought and Language Emeritus at Michigan State University. He has served as Fulbright lecturer in Argentina and serves on NCTE-ERIC's Research Evaluation Committee. He is the author of *Marianne Moore* (1963, Twayne; rev. ed. 1989, G. K. Hall) and other studies of midwestern and modern literature.

Philip L. Gerber is Professor of English at SUNY Brockport. In 1989 he served as president of the Robert Frost Society; he is now a contributing editor to *Dreiser Studies*. His most recent book is *Bachelor Bess: The Homesteading Letters of Elizabeth Corey* (University of Iowa, 1990).

Jill B. Gidmark is Professor of English at the University of Minnesota. Her *Melville Sea Dictionary: A Glossed Concordance and Analysis of the Language in Melville's Nautical Novels* was published by Greenwood Press in 1982. She is also the flutist on *In Dulci Jubilo* and *Our Heritage,* two recordings issued by Augsburg Publishing House.

Ronald M. Grosh has recently published a three-part series on early American realism in *MidAmerica.* President of Educational Associates, Inc. and head of Springfield (Ohio) Christian Schools, he has recently completed a fellowship at the Newberry Library doing research on Joseph Kirkland.

John E. Hallwas is Professor of English at Western Illinois University. He was the founding editor of *Western Illinois Regional Studies* and co-edits Prairie State Books, a series published by the University of Illinois Press. His most recent book is *Spoon River Anthology*: *An Annotated Edition* (University of Illinois Press, 1992).

Leland Krauth is Associate Professor of English at the University of Colorado at Boulder. He serves on the editorial boards of *English Language Notes* and *Studies in American Humor.* His essay "Mark Twain: The Victorian of Southwestern Humor," was published in *On Mark Twain: The Best from "American Literature"* (Duke University Press, 1987).

William V. Miller is Professor of English at Ball State University and author of a number of Anderson studies. He has twice served on the Executive Board of the Society for the Study of Midwestern Literature and is currently editing a collection of Sherwood Anderson's short stories.

Robert D. Narveson is Professor of English at the University of Nebraska at Lincoln, where he teaches American literature, composition, and fiction writing. The first of his articles to appear in *MidAmerica* was "*Spoon River Anthology*: An Introduction" (*MidAmerica* 7); his most recent is "Immediate Effects and Ultimate Tendencies: Uses of Lincoln-Caesar Analogies by American Writers" (*MidAmerica* 15).

Marcia Noe is Professor of English at The University of Tennessee at Chattanooga. She is the author of *Susan Glaspell: Voice from the Heartland* (Western Illinois Monograph Series, 1983) and the editor of *Celebrate the Midwest! Poems and Stories for David D. Anderson* (Lake Shore Publishing, 1991).

Ronald Primeau is Professor of English at Central Michigan University. He has served as editor of *The Great Lakes Review* and is the author of *Beyond Spoon River: The Legacy of Edgar Lee Masters* (University of Texas Press, 1981).

Kenneth A. Robb is Associate Professor of English Emeritus at Bowling Green State University and book review editor of the *Mid-American Review*. In 1989 he won the Society for the Study of Midwestern Literature's Midwest Heritage Prize for his essay "Mary Hartwell Catherwood's Two Beaver Island Stories," and he continues to do research on midwestern writers.

James Seaton is Professor of American Thought and Language at Michigan State University. The author of *A Reading of Vergil's "Georgics"* (Hackkert, 1983), he has written numerous articles on American cultural criticism. In 1991 he won the Society for the Study of Midwestern Literature's Midwest Heritage Prize for his essay "Irving Babbitt, Midwestern Intellectual."

The late **Frederick C. Stern** was Professor of English at the University of Illinois at Chicago. In 1987 he was a Fulbright Fellow at Wilhelm Pieck University in the German Democratic Republic. His is the author of *The Revolutionary Poet in the United States: The Poetry of Thomas McGrath* (University of Missouri Press, 1989).

Guy Szuberla is Professor of English at the University of Toledo. He serves as assistant editor of *The Old Northwest* and as a member of the Executive Board of the Society for the Study of Midwestern Literature. In 1990 his essay "Ladies, Gentlemen, Flirts, Mashers, Snoozers, and the Breaking of Etiquettes's Code" was published in volume 15 of *Prospects*.

Ellen Serlen Uffen is Associate Professor of American Thought and Language at Michigan State University. Her essay "The Ladies of Waynesboro (a.k.a. Xenia) Ohio" was published in *MidAmerica* 15; she recently completed *Strands of the Cable: The Place of the Past in Jewish America Women's Writing* (Peter Lang Publishing, 1992).

Douglas Wixson is Professor of English Emeritus at the University of Missouri at Rolla. He has edited a collection of Jack Conroy's stories and folktales, *The Weed King & Other Stories* (Lawrence Hill, 1985) and Conroy's novel, *The Disinherited* (University of Missouri Press, 1991). His critical study, *Worker-Writer: Jack Conroy and the Tradition of Midwest Literary Radicalism, 1898-1935*, will be published by the University of Illinois Press in 1993.